Children's Literature
Selections and Strategies
for Students With Reading Difficulties:
A Resource for Teachers

Children's Literature
Selections and Strategies
for Students With Reading Difficulties:
A Resource for Teachers

by
Nancy S. Williams

Christopher-Gordon Publishers, Inc.
Norwood, Massachusetts

Copyright Acknowledgments

Every effort has been made to contact copyright holders for permission to reproduce borrowed material where necessary. We apologize for any oversights and would be happy to rectify them in future printings.

Excerpts from *King Bidgood's In The Bathtub,* text copyright 1985 by Audrey Wood, reprinted by permission of the publisher, Harcourt, Inc.

Excerpts from *Encounter,* text copyright 1992 by Jan Yolen, reprinted by permission of Harcourt, Inc.

Excerpt from *Koala Lou*, text copyright 1988 by Mem Fox, reprinted by permission of Harcourt, Inc.

Excerpt from *Lou Gehrig: The Luckiest Man*, text copyright 1997 by David A. Adler, reprinted by permission of Harcourt, Inc.

Excerpts from *Abuela* by Arthur Dorros, copyright 1991 used by permission of Penguin Putnam, Inc.

Excerpts from *Pink and Say* by Patricia Polacco. Copyright 1992 by Babushka, Inc. Used by permission of Philomel Books, a division of Penguin Putnam, Inc.

Excerpt from *Go, Dog. Go!* Text copyright 1961 by P.D. Eastman, used by permission of Random House, Inc.

Excerpt from *Horton Hatches the Egg* by Dr. Seuss, copyright 1940/1968. Used by Dr. Seuss Enterprises, L. P. Used by permission of Random House, Inc.

Excerpt from *Fly Away Home* by Eve Bunting, copyright 1991. Used by permission of Houghton Mifflin.

Excerpt from *Poppleton and Friends* by Cynthia Rylant, copyright 1997. Used by permission of The Sky Blue Press.

Excerpt from *Cedric Ceballos* by Mark Stewart, copyright 1996. Used by permission of Grolier Publishing.

The Fry formula graph, *Journal of Reading,* April 1968, page 513. Used by permission of the International Reading Association.

Copyright © 2000 Christopher-Gordon Publishers, Inc.

Christopher-Gordon Publishers, Inc.
1502 Providence Highway, Suite 12
Norwood, MA 02062
800-934-8322

Printed in the United States of America

10 9 8 7 6 5 4 3 2 1   05 04 03 02 01 00

Library of Congress Catalog Card Number: 99076813
ISBN: 1-929024-07-X

Table of Contents

Part III

Part IV

Part V
Working With Parents

Appendix A
Related References for Teachers

Appendix B
Book Lists of Selected Subjects

Preface

This book is intended to help teachers find, evaluate, and use quality children's literature for students who have difficulty reading. It is also appropriate for teacher training programs in special education and reading and language arts that address individuals with diverse reading abilities and needs. The book includes how to match students with books (e.g., how to give a reading interest inventory, determine children's reading levels, estimate the reading level of a book), provides resources and criteria for selecting quality fiction and nonfiction children's literature, and describes research-based strategies that promote literacy. A major portion of the book provides a description and analysis of 180 children's literature selections for struggling readers that include picture books, short chapter books, novels, poetry, and nonfiction. In addition, each literature selection presents learning opportunities that include oral language, reading, and writing.

The book is divided into five parts. Part 1 describes certain factors that affect a child's ability to read, understand, and enjoy good books. Choice, cognitive abilities, oral language, and reading level of student and book are important to consider when working with students who experience reading difficulties. Parts II and III address how to find, evaluate, and use quality books that are appropriate for these students. Part IV, the major part of the book, describes a broad sampling of children's literature selections that includes genre, reading and interest levels, synopsis, and learning opportunities that develop literacy skills. Part V includes suggestions for working with parents and presents responses to frequently asked questions, reading tips, and resources that promote successful literacy experiences.

Dedication

Always to Randy

And to my daughter Elizabeth, with heartfelt thanks
for her meticulous reading, good suggestions,
and computer expertise
throughout the duration of this project

Acknowledgments

I am grateful for the time and energy that many people have devoted to helping me select quality children's literature for children who struggle with reading. Kate Liston, a diagnostician and teacher of LD students and an adjunct instructor at DePaul University, has enthusiastically shared her expertise and has provided valuable input over the duration of this project. Chicago Public School teachers Julie Tabin Coller and Irene Martinez Grady, and Daryl Nitz, a classroom teacher in the Glenview School System, graciously provided names of authors and books that were favorites of students who experienced difficulty with some aspect of reading. From the beginning of my association with Chrisopher-Gordon, Susanne Canavan has provided her sharp insight, offered good suggestions, and given support. Thank you Sue for your confidence and trust. I would also like to thank the many students, teachers, and children with whom I have worked and from whom I have learned throughout several decades of teaching. Finally, a special thanks goes to my husband and daughter for initiating and supporting "the book."

Introduction

Mike, nine years old, can take things apart and put them together again. When he was three years old, he could put together almost any puzzle by himself. At age five, he built intricate towers of Legos that amazed even his parents. And on this seventh birthday, Mike began to help his father, a mechanic, build and repair old cars. Although he struggles with second grade reading materials, he loves David MaCaulay's *The Way Things Work* (1988), a detailed pen and ink, 373 page picture book containing technical vocabulary which describes the working of machines. He easily identifies illustrations of a transmission shaft, clutch, engine, and gearbox and explains to his impressed tutor how the clutch works.

Although Mike had always felt good about his achievements and abilities, his self-concept plummeted during first grade when he had difficulty remembering and matching sounds to letters. Now in fourth grade, Mike can read only simple text. He cannot remember most short vowels (i,e,o), vowel combinations (au, ou), and confuses many sight words (where, what, who, though, through). Although he enjoys listening to books read aloud in class and can retell what happens in the story, he has difficulty remembering what he reads because his attention is focused on decoding words (i.e., identifying sound equivalents of printed words).

Many students like Mike are able to understand stories that their peers can read, yet they can not decode words. Although reading, like any skill, takes practice, these children do not spend time reading because it is difficult for them. Rather than meeting with frustration and failure, students with reading difficulties would rather spend their time on activities where they know they can achieve success. Ironically, research shows that the more time spent on reading, the better the reading achievement. However, children with *different* reading needs and abilities are often given the *same* low level reading materials and instruction, despite their various reading levels (Vaughn, Moody and Schamm, 1998). As a result, these children come away believing that reading is boring because books are boring.

Like all children, struggling readers have different interests, reading abilities, and reading levels. When selecting books it is important for teachers to know:

- Which books will encourage students to engage in a critical discussion yet be at a reading level that they can read independently (recognize 98% of words on a page) or with instructional support (recognize 95% of words on a page).

- Which picture books are appropriate for older readers. Many easy books are designed for the interest of younger children, posing a problem for struggling older readers (Roller, 1996, 44).

- Which novels have well-developed, believable characters and an intriguing plot, as well as vocabulary and sentence length that do not overwhelm struggling readers.

- Which nonfiction books are appropriate in terms of interest, writing style, readability, and format.

This book is designed to provide teachers with suggestions and strategies for selecting and using quality children's literature written by distinguished children's authors that students with reading difficulties can read, understand, and enjoy. While reading decoding and comprehension strategies are emphasized, talking about and writing about good books, integral parts of a literacy program, are also addressed.

All children should have the opportunity to enjoy good children's literature. It is especially critical for students with reading difficulties to listen to and read well-written language structures and rich vocabulary. Reading not only provides entertainment, but it is a model for oral language and writing. Unfortunately, many struggling readers have been turned off from the benefits of reading good literature due to negative reading experiences and frustration with their difficulties. However, there is quality literature that children with reading difficulties can read and will enjoy reading. It is just a matter of knowing where—and how—to look for these books.

References

Roller, C. M. (1996). *Variability not disability: struggling readers in a workshop classroom*. Newark, Delaware: International Reading Association.

Vaughn, S., Moody, S.W., and Schamm, J.S. (1998). Broken promises: reading instruction in the resource room. *Exceptional Children, 64,* 211-225.

Children's Book Titles

The Way Things Work by David Macaulay (1988). Dorling Kindersely (London). New York: Houghton Mifflin.

Part I
Understanding Differences: Celebrating Strengths

For many children with reading difficulties, poor word identification skills are the stumbling blocks to successful reading. One bright, 14-year old student, for example, told his reading tutor that he had difficulty reading long words, such as *disastrous* and *unnecessary,* yet shied away from literature that was littered with simplistic vocabulary and shorter sentence structures. He found a complex plot and intriguing characters in Robert Cormier's *Tunes For Bears To Dance To,* as well as rich, meaningful words to practice decoding skills and strengthen reading vocabulary.

For some students, reading is an easily acquired skill. These children have often had favorable experiences listening to stories, repeating words or rhyming phrases, experimenting with letters, or hearing their favorite books read aloud, over and over again. However for others, even *with* these experiences, it takes effort and practice and is neither fun nor easy. Children with reading difficulties may have problems in memory (e.g., difficulty remembering and/or sequencing instruction), attention (focusing on a particular task for a given period of time), perception (e.g., interpreting letter sounds or letter symbols), conceptualization (e.g., understanding concepts and seeing relationships), and language (e.g., understanding vocabulary and sentence structures). Others may have missed extended periods of school instruction due to illness. For some, reading instruction just takes longer. For whatever reason, it is critical to provide enjoyable reading experiences with good books at an appropriate reading level. By supporting struggling readers through well-written texts that are neither too difficult nor too easy, teachers can help students practice and reinforce literacy skills. With the opportunity to hear, read, and talk about quality literature, these students are more likely to grow into independent, life-long readers.

Reading is a complex activity and many factors impact a child's success in reading. Among these are choice and interest, cognitive factors, oral language, and reading ability and level. The challenge for teachers is to find a variety of well-written books on the appropriate reading level for students to practice needed skills, yet ones that they want to read that promote meaningful discussion and higher-level thinking. When students are exposed to meaningful text and read stories, they actually want to discuss what is being read (Knapp and Associates, 1995). Reading and listening to quality literature exposes struggling readers to good stories, descriptive vocabulary, and a language of comparisons rich in metaphors and similes.

Interest and Choice

All readers, regardless of age or ability, choose books based upon their interests and experiences. Everyone loves to find a good book—one that they can't put down and hate to see end. We are enlightened, entertained, and refreshed by good writing. But no two individual's definition of a good book is the same. For adults and children alike, reading is a personal experience that is rooted in each person's interests and background experiences. Discounting a child's interest and choice in selecting books is a mistake that can lead a child away from a lifetime love of reading.

Children's interests are the single most important influence upon their attitudes toward reading (Spache, 1966, p. 2). Furthermore, since students bring their own experiences to the printed page, they are better able to predict unknown words and construct meaning when books are relevant to their lives. Many struggling readers are not interested in the topics and content of the material they can read and want to choose books that their peers are reading (Roller and Fielding, 1996). *Want* is the key word to success for children with reading difficulties. If children read something that they want to read and find enjoyable, they will spend more time reading. And practice improves reading. One way that teachers can provide struggling readers with positive and meaningful reading experiences is by becoming familiar with their strengths and interests (Deeds, 1981). What fascinates them? Excites them? Challenges them? Do Peter's eyes light up when talking about baseball? Or does Melissa spend every free moment talking about her dancing lessons? Good picture book selections for these students might include *Lou Gehrig: The Luckiest Man* (David Adler, 1997) and *Dance* (Jones and Kuklin, 1998).

The challenge for teachers is to provide readers with diverse abilities, backgrounds, and interests with a variety of quality books on different subjects and reading levels. "Choice is only as wide as the alternatives available" (Roller and Fielding, 1996, p. 45). But how can teachers choose appropriate alternatives? Reading inventories and checklists, interviews with students about their likes and dislikes, teacher observation, and input from parents are all ways of finding out about the interest of students.

Reading Inventories

Reading inventories are questions designed to reflect a student's interest and uncover information about their favorite books, authors, and hobbies. They may be checklists, fill in the blank statements, or open-ended questions. *The Reading Teacher's Book of Lists* (Fry, Kress, Fountoukidis, 1993) provides a primary interest inventory of 16 questions and an intermediate interest inventory of 23 questions for students. The questions cover everything from hobbies, favorite books, and TV shows to sports and school subjects. For example the Intermediate Inventory (p. 268) includes questions such as:

- My main hobbies or leisure time activity is (are) _____
- For pleasure I read _____
- The best book I have ever read was (title) _____
- The book I am reading now is (title) _____
- I would like to learn more about _____

Studies have shown that teachers often know very little about children's interests or children's literature, thus making it difficult to make good reading selections for students (Harris and Sipay, 1990).

Observation

The simplest and most effective way to determine children's reading interests is to watch their daily behavior and listen to their conversations (Harris and Sipay, 1990). When Matt told his reading tutor that he liked to perform magic tricks, she found a book of magic tricks to include in her materials. Matt followed the directions, strengthening sequencing skills, and performed a series of card tricks that enthralled his audience. His self-esteem blossomed as he taught others his magic tricks. Whether it is basketball, baseball, ballet, cars, insects, magic, or mystery stories, teachers must actively explore students' interests to ensure meaningful reading experiences.

Cognitive Factors

Children's thinking processes impact reading. Three models that have influenced the way educators look at thinking and learning are Piaget's cognitive-developmental theory, Vygotsky's sociocultural theory, and Gardner's theory of multiple intelligences. Jean Piaget, a Swiss biologist and psychologist, emphasizes discovery learning and describes mental stages through which children progress (Piaget and Inheldeer, 1969); L.S. Vygotsky (1962), a Russian psychologist, addresses the social aspect of learning; and Howard Gardner (1997), an American psychologist, maintains that each child has his or her own profile of intelligence. Each theory has implications for teaching children, including those with reading difficulties. Piaget helps raise awareness of the changes in children's thinking processes as they construct meaning through interacting with their world. Vygotsky, on the other hand, emphasizes the role of the adult in guiding learning. Finally, Gardner reminds us that children have a number of abilities they use when solving problems, and that teachers must be sensitive to the different ways in which children learn and provide more than one way of instruction.

Piaget's Four Stages

> *So we need pupils who are active, who learn early to find out by themselves, partly by themselves, partly by their own spontaneous activity and partly through material we set up for them. . . .*
>
> (Ginsburg and Opper, 1979, p. 238)

According to Piaget, cognitive development is an adoptive process in which children actively construct knowledge as they manipulate and explore their worlds. As they progress through the sensorimotor, preoperational, concrete operational, and formal operational stages, they view their world from unique perspectives (see table 1-1). Although each stage is represented by a specific age group, these ages are only estimates that generally reflect when children demonstrate these characteristics. Every child is different. Further, recent studies show that the cognitive competencies of children are affected by experiences and the child's familiarity with the task. Some researchers suggest that rather than a fixed stage, there are related competencies which children develop over time, depending on their maturity and background experiences.

Stage	*Age Level*	*Characteristics*
Sensorimotor	Birth to 2 Years	Learns through sensory (eyes, ears, and hands) and motor activity
Preoperational	2 to 7 Years	Uses symbols (language, play, drawing) to represent earlier sensorimotor activities
Concrete Operational	7 to 11 Years	Reasons logically about concrete objects
Formal Operational	11 Years and Above	Reasons abstractly; thinks about possible outcomes

(Berk, 1996)

Table 1–1: Piaget's Four Stages

- Sensorimotor: Children in the sensorimotor stage learn though sensory and motor activity. They like to touch, feel, and taste everything in sight. They take apart things, drop things, and discover that movement has predictable effects on objects (Berk, 1996). They enjoy actions and games, tactile books (books that children can touch, pull, manipulate) and the "Pat-a-cake, Pat-a-cake" rhythm of Mother Goose rhymes (Huck, Hepler, Hickman, and Kiefer, 1997).

- Preoperational: Children develop their ability to use language, play, and drawing to represent their experiences. They play dress-up, chatter among themselves, and draw pictures to represent familiar events. Their thinking is based on direct experiences and the way things look. For example, young children tend to believe that there is more liquid in a tall glass than in a wide one when the liquid content is actually the same. They enjoy cumulative stories which have repetitious language and events, such as the *Gingerbread Boy* folktale, where the sequence of action is repeated and builds from page-to-page (Huck, Hepler, Hickman, and Kiefeer, 1997). As the gingerbread boy runs away from the little old man and little old women, then the cow, the horse, and thresher, he cries out after each escape, *"Run! Run! As fast as you can! You can't catch me, I'm the Gingerbread Man!"*

- Concrete Operational: Children in the concrete operational stage are more flexible, logical thinkers. For example, they understand that when they pour equal amounts of soda pop into different size glasses, the content is the same although one appears to be more full than the other. Children in the middle elementary grades like to solve puzzles and mysteries, like finding their way out of mazes in *Anno's Math Games III* (1991, 1997) and solving the mystery of a missing body in *Disappearing Acts: A Herculeah Jones Mystery* by Betsy Byars (1998), an exciting story that is appropriate for students with word identification problems since it has short sentences, frequent dialogue, and a low reading level (mid-second to low-third grade).

- Formal Operational: In this last stage students in middle school develop abstract reasoning. They reason with symbols that do not refer to objects in the real world, such as advanced mathematics. They think of various sides and outcomes and enjoy complex novels and science fiction (Huck, Hepler, Hickman, and Kiefer, 1997). For example, Lois Lowry's Newbery Award book, *The Giver* (1993), invites the reader to experience a futuristic society in an ideal community of sameness and control. Lowry requires that her readers determine their own resolution from an exciting and ambiguous ending. (The estimated reading level is fourth grade.) Older children with reading difficulties often have problems decoding words, yet get caught up in a fast moving plot and believable, complex characters, like Lowry's protagonist Jonas, who faces conflicts within himself as well as with his parents and community.

Vygotsky's Social Learning

> *What a child can do in cooperation today he can do*
> *alone tomorrow.*
>
> (Vygotsky, 1962, p. 104)

Vygotsky's model adds another dimension to developmental theory by concluding that cognitive development begins on the social level and is then internalized. According to Vygotsky, cognitive development is a so-cially-mediated process which is dependent on the verbal guidance of adults and collaboration of peers as the child tries challenging tasks within the zone of proximal development (Berk, 1996). Several concepts of this model include:

- The Zone of Proximal Development (ZPD): This zone encompasses the range between the child's mental age and the level he reaches in solving problems with assistance (Vygotsy, 1962, p. 103). In order for children to be operating within their ZPD, they must be involved in an instructional activity that is too difficult for them to perform independently, yet one in which they can be successful with the support of an adult or capable peer (Dixon-Krauss, 1996). Vygotsy (1962) writes, ". . . the only good kind of instruction is that which marches ahead of development and leads it; it must be aimed not so much at the ripe as at the ripening functions" (p. 104). Often, children with reading difficulties are given instruction that is too easy (fill-in the blank questions and materials that they have already mastered) or too difficult (books that are too difficult to read and concepts that they do not understand). When instruction is directed at the appropriate level (ZPD), children have the opportunity to acquire new skills and feel successful about their learning.

- Mediated Learning: Using this instructional format, the teacher m*ediates* or augments learning by verbally interacting with the student to build comprehension and understanding. For example, if a student has difficulty sequencing events in a story, the teacher supplies prompts such as asking the student what happened first in the story, suggesting that he/she look back in the book to locate events and record and sequence them on a graphic organizer. The teacher does not provide the solution but provides guidance and a scaffold from which students can construct meaning. Support is gradually withdrawn as students become more proficient in solving a particular problem. For children with reading difficulties, this is an important step that is often neglected. For example, Kim knew if she waited long enough for a word she could not decode, her tutor would read it for her. Her tutor had modeled word identification strategies and had provided explicit instruction and guided practice in decoding words, yet did not provide opportunities for independent practice and problem solving.

- Inner Speech: According to Vygotsky, higher-level thinking derives from external social language that becomes internalized. Comparing inner speech to external speech, Vygotsky (1962) writes, "But while in external speech thought is embodied in words, in inner speech words die as they bring forth thought. Inner speech is to a large extent thinking in pure meaning" (p. 149). To apply this concept to the classroom, when children discuss literature in a collective form, exchange ideas, reflect and refine their thoughts, external social language helps to develop thinking skills. Through discussion and hearing other perspectives, students clarify their own thinking. This is an important activity for children with reading difficulties. Struggling readers can listen, learn, and be involved in story discussion with their peers, yet not have to read aloud. Reading is done elsewhere, at home, in a paired-reading situation, working with support staff, or following along in the book while listening to it on tape.

Gardner's Theory of Multiple Intelligences

We must account for the skills of a shaman and a psychoanalyst as well as of a yogi and saint.

(Gardner, 1983, p. 62)

Howard Gardner (1983), a professor of education at the Harvard Graduate School of Education, believes that we have a number of intelligences which enable us to solve problems. He emphasizes that children's minds are different from each other and that teachers must allow students to show their understanding in a variety of ways. Accordingly, teachers must provide instruction in a variety of ways: lecture and discussion (auditory input), films, overheads (visual input), or with hands-on, interactive activities. In a recent interview (Checkley, 1997), Gardner defines eight intelligences:

- Linguistic—to use language to express what's on your mind and to understand other people, such as writers, orators, speakers, and lawyers.
- Logical-mathematical—to understand the underlying principles of some kind of a causal system, like a scientist or logician, or the

ability to manipulate numbers, quantities, and operations like a mathematician.

- Spatial—to represent the spatial world internally in your mind, like a sailor or airplane pilot when they navigate their large spatial world, or like a chess player, sculptor, and architect when they represent a smaller spatial world.

- Bodily kinesthetic—to use your whole body or parts of your body to solve a problem, make something, or put on some kind of production, such as individuals who participate in athletics or in the performing arts, particularly dance or acting.

- Musical—to think in music, hear patterns, and recognize, remember, and manipulate them.

- Interpersonal—to understand other people, important skills for teachers, sales people, or politicians.

- Intrapersonal—to understand yourself.

- Naturalist—to discriminate among living things (plants and animals) and to be sensitive to other features of the natural world. It is central in roles as botanist or chef (Checkley, 1997).

Gardner's theory has implications for children who have difficulty reading, a skill which falls primarily in the linguistic area. He emphasizes the importance of nourishing children's special gifts, such as the artist, musician, dancer, or athlete. Children with reading difficulties often have poor self-concepts because they fail at reading, yet they may be extremely talented in other areas. In the autobiographical picture storybook, *Thank you, Mr. Falker,* author/illustrator Patricia Polacco (1998) describes a special fifth grade teacher who recognizes and celebrates her exceptional artistic ability and teaches her to read.

Like Patricia Polacco, children with reading difficulties demonstrate intelligence in many areas while struggling with some aspect of reading. For example, Karl, a fifth grader who read on the first grade level, was a black belt in Karate. Maria performed in ballet recitals, yet had severe spelling problems. Both excelled in what Gardner would describe as bodily kinesthetic areas and were excited to read books about their areas of expertise. Children who have difficulty reading often feel that they are dumb and cannot succeed. For these students it is especially important to celebrate their strengths as well as to address weaknesses in reading.

Reading Difficulties and Oral Language

A strong oral language base facilitates reading, and reading experiences in turn influence oral language (Teale and Sulzby, 1989). Oral language grows at an especially fast rate during the preschool years. By age four, children have acquired most of the elements of adult language and by five have mastered most grammatical rules (Glazer, 1989). However, not all children follow this sequence of development. Some children have difficulty understanding and/or recalling words to express themselves, using words in complete sentences, or remembering what they hear. They may have difficulty remembering a sequence of sounds within words or a sequence of words within a sentence (Johnson and Myklebust, 1967). These difficulties effect reading, decoding, spelling, reading comprehension, and oral and written expression such as retelling a story, writing a story summary, or writing a personal response to a book they have read. In addition, children with language difficulties may have problems reading and understanding homophones, words that sound the same but have different meanings and different spellings (e.g., *their, there, they're*), and homographs, words that are spelled the same but have different meanings. For example *bat* may refer to a baseball bat, a flying mammal, or a sharp blow.

There are a number of clever books that help students understand words and phrases that have multiple meanings. For example, the *Amelia Bedelia* books by Peggy and Henry Parish comically show students that words can be interpreted in various ways. Fred Gwynne's *A Chocolate Moose for Dinner, The King Who Rained,* and *The Sixteen Hand Horse* have hilarious drawings that literally represent sentences containing homonyms and idioms.

Reading stories with predictable text and well-illustrated drawings that are tied closely to the story help children with language problems acquire language, figure out grammar, and learn the structure of stories (Lerner, 1997). For example, Alex, a second grader with receptive language and decoding problems, listened intently as his tutor read Maurice Sendak's engaging picture book fantasy, *Where The Wild Things Are.* He was especially interested in the lively illustrations of monsters, their expressive faces and big teeth! After discussing the story and what the author meant by "gnashing" teeth, Alex wrote and illustrated his own story about a monster that loved to *gnash his teeth!* This descriptive word also presented opportunities to discuss the silent /g/ sound in other words beginning with *gn.* Easy to read chapter books with simple language structures, clever illustrations that closely depict story events, and meaningful stories include *Ant Plays Bear* (Betsy Byars, 1997), *Frog and Toad are Friends* (1971) and *Owl at Home* (1975) (Arnold Lobel), *Nate the Great* mysteries (Marjorie Weinman Sharmat and Craig Sharmat), and the *Poppleton and Friends* and *Henry and Mudge* series books (Cynthia Rylant). Picture books with simple sentences and illustrations that closely depict story information include *Are You My Mother* (P.D. Eastman, 1961), *Clifford: The Big Red Dog* (Norman Bridwell, 1963), *The Very Hungry Caterpillar* (Eric Carle, 1969), and *This is Baseball* (Margaret Blackstone, 1993, nonfiction).

Children who are not proficient in English may also have difficulty understanding English vocabulary and syntax and decoding words with sounds that are not prevalent or do not exist in their first language. Picture books that illustrate familiar vocabulary in first and second languages help readers make connections between concepts and printed words, and predictable picture storybooks with repetitive words and rhyming patterns provide language clues and develop phonics skills. For example, the picture book *My House Mi Casa* (Rebecca Emberley, 1990) contains colorful pictures that illustrate single words and short sentences in English and Spanish. *Green Eggs and Ham* (Dr. Seuss, 1969) introduces at least six phonics patterns that are repeated in familiar rhyming words: am (ham, Sam); ox (box, fox); ay (may, say); ai (train, rain); ar (car, are): and ou (house, mouse). *Go, Dog. Go!* (P. D. Eastman, 1961) contains simple sight vocabulary that is repeated throughout the story, such as *A red dog on a blue tree. A blue dog on a red tree* (p. 12), and illustrations that clearly depict the text. Eastman's story helped Raul, a second grader whose first language was Spanish, understand and use spatial words (up, down, around, in, out, on), color words (blue, red, yellow, green) and nouns (dog, tree, hat). After echo reading and discussing the story and illustrations, Raul cut out green, blue, and red dogs and yellow and red trees from colored construction paper and moved the cut-outs to represent various sentences in the story. Then he wrote and illustrated his own *Go, Dog. Go!*, using the same vocabulary in simple sentences.

In addition, teachers can help children with language differences read unfamiliar words that they use in their speaking vocabulary by transcribing their experiences and stories to create a meaningful reading text. This method, called the Language Experience Approach (LEA), creates an instant bond between reader and text since the story includes the student's own words and experiences. For instance, after Toshi listened to *The Very Hungry Caterpillar* (Eric Carle, 1969) and examined the beautiful collage illustrations, the second grader told his tutor that he also knew how moths became butterflies because he had seen this in Taiwan when he was visiting his grandparents. The striking illustrations and meaningful story helped to facilitate a lengthy discussion that later became the basis for a language experience story. This instructional approach also helps older students and adults with decoding problems develop reading vocabulary that is based upon background experiences and oral language. Table 1–2 describes activities that teachers can use in conjunction with the Language Experience Approach to strengthen and reinforce literacy skills.

ACTIVITY	FUNCTION
Retells story or relates personal experience;teacher transcribes story on to chart paper	Provides material for reading consisting of student's own oral language vocabulary
Reads story with teacher	Guided reading practice
Reads story alone	Independent practice
Writes unfamiliar reading vocabulary on index cards, e.g., "might"; reads words	Reinforces reading, spelling
Matches vocabulary cards to vocabulary in story	Recognition practice
Finds sound patterns in vocabulary words and generates new rhyming words, e.g., *might/fight, sight/right*	Develops phonics skills
Reads vocabulary cards	Recall practice
Cuts up sentences in LEA story; reads strips then mixes-up strips	Kinesthetic activity, reading practice
Arranges sentences in sequence of story; reads story	Strengthens sequencing skills

Table 1-2: LEA Based Reading Activities

Reading Level

In order to enjoy and understand a story, children must be able to read a book without struggling over words that are too difficult to read or understand. If the book is too difficult to decode, energy will be directed to reading the words rather than in understanding the story. How can you tell when a book is too difficult? A good way to begin is by estimating the student's reading levels. Reading levels include:

- The Independent Reading Level—fluent reading without assistance. Books should be at this level when children curl up in a chair and read for enjoyment.
- The Instructional Reading Level—adequate decoding and comprehension with assistance. Content area reading materials should be at this level where teachers provide assistance in recognizing and understanding unfamiliar words and concepts.
- The Frustration Level—material is too difficult to decode or comprehend. Students should not be given material at this level since it will only cause anxiety and frustration.

- Listening Capacity—highest level students can understand material read to them.This is the level at which students should be able to read if they can decode text.

Reading levels can be estimated in several ways. According to Lucy Calkins, Professor of Education at Teachers College, Columbia, if children can read 90% of the words so that they make sense they will be able to figure out the remaining 10%. However, the text is too difficult if less than 90% of the text makes sense (1997, p. 156).To determine if a book is "just right" (not too easy or too difficult), ask students if they understand the book, if there are just a few words per page they don't know, and if some places are smooth and some choppy when they read (Roller and Fielding, 1996).To attain more diagnostic information about how children read, teachers can administer a published Informal Reading Inventory (IRI) or construct their own consisting of classroom reading materials. Informal Reading Inventories are given individually to students about whom the teacher needs more information to plan effective instruction.

Informal Reading Inventories

Informal Reading Inventories help teachers estimate a student's independent, instructional, and frustration reading level, as well as determine strengths and weakness in reading decoding and comprehension. When students read orally, teachers can observe children's word identification strategies when they meet unfamiliar words. For example, do students substitute a word that makes sense in the sentence (i.e., reading for meaning), or do they substitute a word that begins with the same letter sound but that means something entirely different than the word in the story (i.e., relying too heavily on phonics cues)? On the other hand, if students successfully read the words but have difficulty answering comprehension questions or cannot retell the story, comprehension areas may need to be investigated.

Independent, instruction, and frustration reading levels can be determined when students read orally. Depending on the number of words children read accurately and their understanding of what they read, percentage criteria determine at which level the student performs. Leslie and Caldwell suggest the following criteria when orally reading in context (Qualitative Reading Inventory–II, 1995, p. 50):

- Independent Reading Level—Students recognize 98% or more of the words they read and comprehend 90% of the material.
- Instructional Reading Level—Students recognize 90% to 97% of words and comprehend 70% of the material.
- The Frustration Level—Students recognize less than 90% of words and comprehend less than 70% of material.

Percentage criteria vary slightly according to the particular reference or IRI used. There are a number of published IRI's, such as the Flynt-Cooter Reading Inventory (Flynt and Cooter, 1995), the Qualitative Reading Inventory-II (Leslie and Caldwell, 1995), and the Classroom Reading Inventory (Silvaroli, 1997).

Informal Reading Inventories consist of a graded set of selections beginning at a preprimer or primer level (kindergarten or first grade) and extending up to junior high or high school. Students generally read two selections at the same grade level—one orally and the other silently—and answer comprehension questions about both passages. The teacher records oral reading miscues (i.e., deviations from print) from the oral reading sample and assesses oral and silent reading comprehension by asking questions or having the student retell the story. Reading levels are determined by calculating the percent of oral reading accuracy (number of words read correctly out of the total number of words read) and reading comprehension (percent of questions answered correctly).

By analyzing oral reading miscues, teachers can identify areas to strengthen. For example, if Max reads "string" as "sting" and "straight" as "state," he may have difficulty decoding words with the consonant blend "str." This would be a focus for instruction. It is also important to examine a student's comprehension when reading orally and silently. If Max comprehends better in a particular mode, e.g., oral reading, attention is focused on strengthening silent reading comprehension while allowing him to softly read aloud. Because younger children practice oral reading in the primary grades, they usually have stronger reading comprehension skills when they read aloud than when they read silently.

Individual Reading Inventories provide estimates of reading levels and are tools for helping teachers select books that struggling readers can read and understand. Reading levels are *estimates*. Children may be able to read more difficult material if they have interest and background in the subject. For example, fifth grade students reading on a third grade reading level eagerly plowed through *Maniac Magee*, Jerry Spinelli's exciting story about an orphaned, run-a-way boy. They were caught up in the characters and story, even though some words and sentences were difficult to read. Conversely, if students are not interested in a book or lack sufficient background, comprehension may falter even though the reading level seems appropriate.

Constructing a Personal IRI

Because reading series and materials vary in terms of vocabulary, story content, and difficulty, some educators feel that the IRI should be based on the material that the child is reading in the classroom (Harris and Sipay, 1990). When teachers construct their own IRI, they have a better idea of whether the classroom reading material is too easy for a particular student (independent level), appropriate with instruction (instructional level), or too difficult (frustration level).

To construct an IRI, select a passage from a book that the student is currently reading or about to read. Discuss the title, what the book is or will be about, and ask the student to orally read the passage. Record the student's miscues on a copy of the same passage. It is also helpful to tape record the student to validate his (or her) oral reading. Then ask the student to retell the passage or answer comprehension questions that you have developed about the selection. Record the miscues in the following manner:

- Circle words that are omitted.
- Write the student's pronunciation above words that are mispronounced or substituted.
- Use a caret for words that are inserted.
- Write a large P ("pronounced") above words that you must pronounce for the student.

To determine the word recognition level, simply divide the total number of words in the passage by the number of words that the student reads correctly and multiply this quotient by 100. Compare the percent (i.e., percent of oral accuracy) to the percentage criteria. (See preceding section for percentage criteria). For example, in figure 2–1, Sara reads a short 100 word passage and reads 72 correct words (i.e., 28 miscues). Her percent of oral accuracy is 72% (72 divided by 100 times 100). This percentage corresponds to a *frustration reading level* (word recognition score below 90%). Sara omits word endings (ed, ing), and has difficulty reading compound words (neighborhood, inside), and sight words (were, had, when, gone). When she tries to read an unfamiliar word she substitutes a word with the same beginning sound, reading *small* for *smidgen* and *lunch* for *laundry*. Sara puts so much energy into reading words that she cannot pay attention to what she reads. When asked to retell the short story, she quietly murmurs that she cannot remember anything.

Instruction based upon this short oral reading sample could include: multisensory strategies to help Sara identify sight words with which she has difficulty; a focus on understanding word endings and compound words; and an emphasis on using the context or semantic and syntactic clues to support word identification. For instance, when Sara comes to an unfamiliar word she is instructed to read to the end of the sentence to predict what word would make sense in the story and then to use phonic cues to support her prediction. Sara is given books that are on her instructional level to read and to apply word identification strategies and is presented with many opportunities to read easy, enjoyable books to develop reading fluency and self-confidence.

Bees and Water Guns

wants
Susie wanted to play with the big kids. Her older sister and

neighbor   *play*
neighborhood friends (were) playing with water guns in the neighbor's yard

in
across the street. She was left inside with her grandma. Susie's and

went
Barbara's parents were (gone) on a short trip and (their) grandma Lilly (was)

stays   *likes*   *wants*
staying with them. Susie liked her grandma but she still wanted to play with

grandma   *gives*   *straight*   *in   so*
her sister. Her grandmother (had) given her strict orders to stay inside since

P   *has   small   temper   Then*
she was recovering from the flu and had a smidgen (of) temperature. When

down   *lunch*   *it easy*
grandma Lilly went downstairs to do the laundry, Susie made her escape.

Figure 1–1: Oral Reading Sample

Whether using a published IRI or constructing one from classroom reading materials, teachers will obtain important information about a student's reading strategies and abilities that will help them place appropriate books in the hands of struggling readers and avoid frustrating or failing reading situations. For example, Julia's reading tutor gave her the moving story of *The Hundred Dresses* by Eleanor Estes to read. The tutor thought it appropriate since it was a short chapter book of 78 pages with illustrations. Julia was a fifth grader who was struggling with reading. Limited diagnostic information revealed that Julia demonstrated weaknesses in decoding and was reading "below level." Her first reading experience with Estes' sensitive story was one of failure and frustration. Had the tutor administered an IRI she would have discovered that Julia's independent reading level was first grade, and her instructional level second grade. *The Hundred Dresses*, although short in length, contains some long sentences and has an estimated reading level of fourth grade. Students like Julia approach reading with anxiety since they have experienced many reading failures. It is important to provide struggling readers with books that will provide successful reading experiences and ones that they will enjoy and remember.

Readability Formulas

While there are many interesting and well-written books for children and young adults, some books are too difficult for students who struggle with reading. Frequently, books include an age range on the back cover (e.g., 8-12) but do not suggest a reading level. When teachers have difficulty determining if a book is too difficult, readability formulas are useful tools for estimating the reading level of a book.

Readability formulas are tools for *estimating* the difficulty of a book by examining the level of word difficulty and sentence length. Selections containing short sentences and short or familiar words are considered to be easier than selections containing longer sentences and longer or unfamiliar vocabulary.

The Fry Readability Formula is frequently used to provide an estimate of reading level because it is easy to use. The Fry Formula is based on the average number of syllables and the average number of sentences in three, 100 word sample passages. The average number of syllables and the average number of sentences are plotted on a readability graph (See Figure 2.1). Passages with longer sentences and words (words with more syllables) are considered more difficult than passages with shorter sentences and words. The directions include:

- Randomly select three sample passages near the beginning, middle, and end of the story (text) and count out 100 words.
- Count the number of sentences in the 100 words, estimating to the nearest tenth of a sentence.
- Count the total number of syllables in the 100 word passage; a syllable consists of a vowel sound (e.g., *three* and *stopped* have one vowel sound; *table* and *wanted* have two vowel sounds).
- Determine the *average* sentence length and the *average* number of syllables (e.g., add the syllables in each 100 word passage and divide by 3, the number of passages; follow the same process with the number of sentences in each 100 word passage).
- Plot these two numbers (average syllable length, average sentence length) on the graph.

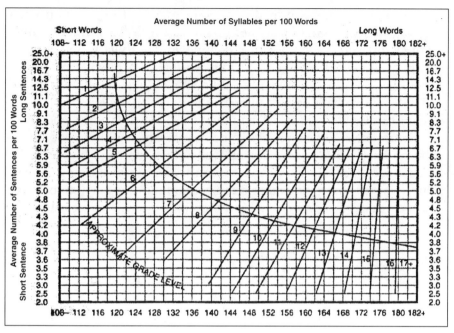

Figure 1–2: From Edward Fry, "A readability formula that saves time." *The Journal of Reading*, April 1968, p. 513. The Fry graph is in the public domain.

In the following example the Fry formula is used to estimate the reading level of a novel containing 125 pages. Three passage samples, each containing 100 words, are taken from pages 7, 57, and 101. Page 7 has 8.0 sentences and 123 syllables per 100 words, page 57 has 7.4 sentences and 127 syllables per 100 words, and page 101 has 7.4 sentences and 120 syllables per 100 words. The average number of syllables comes to 123.3 (123 +127+120 divided by 3) and the average number of sentences is 7.6 (8.0 + 7.4 + 7.4 divided by 3). These two numbers (123.3 and 7.6) when plotted on the Fry readability graph fall within the fourth grade reading level range. Fry suggests that if there is a great deal of variability in a syllable or sentence count, more sample passages should be added.

Page	Syllables	Sentences
7	123	8.0
57	127	7.4
101	120	7.4
Total	370	22.8
Average	123.3	7.6

Readability formulas provide only one source of information when matching students with books. They do not take into consideration a number of factors such as grammatical complexity, vocabulary, concept difficulty, the child's prior knowledge, and motivation (Harris and Sipay, 1990). Nor do they address the students' reading ability, whether the material is read independently or as part of instruction by the teacher, and the purpose for reading the text (Chall and Dale, 1995). Further, if the book is on the appropriate reading level but contains trite language and poor illustrations, the book is not a good choice. Well-written literature that relates to student's lives, contains descriptive vocabulary and image-building text, and includes quality illustrations that bring meaning to the story, support and enhance reading comprehension, and promote life-long reading habits.

References

Allen, V. (1989). Literature as a support to language acquisition. In Rigg and Allen (Eds.), *When they don't all speak English*. Urbana, IL: National Council of Teachers of English (55–64).

Berk, L.E. (1996). *Infants, children and adolescents* (2nd ed.). Needham Heights, MA: Allyn and Bacon.

Calkins, L. (1997). *Raising life long learners: A parent's guide*. Reading, MA: Perseus Books.

Chall, J. and Dale, E. (1995). *Readability revisited: The new Dale-Chall readability formula*. Cambridge, MA: Brookline Books.

Checkley, K. (1997). The first seven . . . and the eighth: A conversation with Howard Gardner. *Educational Leadership, 55,* 8–13.

Deeds, B. (1981). Motivating children to read through improved self-concept. In A. Ciani (Ed.), *Motivating reluctant readers*. Newark, DE: International Reading Association.

deVilliers, P. and deVilliers, J. (1979). *Early language*. Cambridge, MA: Harvard University Press.

Dixon-Krauss, L. (1996). *Vygotsky in the classroom: Mediated literacy instruction and assessment*. White Plains, NY: Longman.

Flynt, E.S. and Cooter, R. (1995). *Flynt-Cooter Reading Inventory*. Scottsdale, AZ: Gorsuch Scarisbrick.

Fry, E., Kress, J. and Fountoukidis, D.L. (1993). *The reading teacher's book of lists* (3rd ed.). Englewood Cliffs, NJ: Prentice Hall.

Gardner, H. (1983) *Frames of mind: The theory of multiple intelligences.* New York: Basic Books

Gardner, H. (1997). Multiple intelligences as a partner in school improvement. *Educational Leadership, 55,* 20–21.

Glazer, S. (1989). *Oral language and literacy development* (16–26). In Strickland and Morrow (Eds.), *Emerging literacy: Young children learn to read and write*. Newark, DE: International Reading Association.

Ginsburg, H. and Opper, S. (1979). *Piaget's theory of intellectual development* (2nd ed.). Englewood Cliffs, NY: Prentice Hall.

Harris, A. and Sipay, E. (1990). *How to increase reading ability: A guide to developmental and remedial methods* (9th ed.). New York: Longman.

Huck, C., Hepler, S. Hickman, J., and Kiefer, B. (1997). *Children's literature in the elementary school* (6th ed.). Madison, WI: Brown and Benchmark.

Johnson, D. and Myklebust, H. (1967). *Learning disabilities: Educational principles and practices.* New York: Grune and Stratton.

Leslie, L. and Caldwell J. (1995). *Qualitative Reading Inventory-II.* New York: HarperCollins.

Lerner, J. (1997). *Learning disabilities: Theories, diagnosis and teaching strategies* (7th ed.). New York: Houghton Mifflin

Knapp, M.S. and Associates (1995). *Teaching for meaning in high-poverty classrooms.* New York: Teachers College Press..

Piaget, J. and Inhelder, B. (1969). *The psychology of the child.* New York: Basic Books, Inc.

Roller, C. and Fielding, L. (1996). Choice makes reading instruction child centered. In C. Roller, *Variability not disability: Struggling readers in a workshop classroom* (pp. 43–54). Newark, DE: International Reading Association.

Silvaroli, N. (1997). *Classroom reading inventory.* Madison, WI: Brown & Benchmark.

Spache, G. (1966). *Good reading for poor readers.* Champaign, IL: Garrard Publishing Company.

Teale, W. and Sulzby, E. (1989). Emergent literacy: new perspectives. In D. Strickland and L. Mandel Murrow (Eds.) *Emerging literacy: Young children learn to read and write* (pp. 16–26). Newark, DE: International Reading Association.

Vygotsky, L. (1962). *Thought and language.* Ed. and translated by E. Hanfmann and G. Vakar. Cambridge, MA: M.I.T. Press.

Children's Book Titles

A Chocolate Moose for Dinner by Fred Gwynne (1976). New York: Prentice-Hall Books for Young Readers, a division of Simon and Schuster.

Amelia Bedelia by Peggy Parish (1963). New York: Harper Collins.

Dance *by Bill T. Jones and Susan Kuklin (1998). New York: Hyperion Books for Children.*

Disappearing Acts: A Herculeah Jones Mystery *by Betsy Byars (1998). New York: Penguin.*

Green Eggs and Ham by Dr. Seuss (1960). New York: Random House.

Go, Dogs. Go! by P.D. Eastman (1961). New York: Random House.

Lou Gehrig: The Luckiest Man by David Adler (1997). San Diego: Harcourt Brace & Company.

Maniac Magee by Jerry Spinelli (1990). Boston: Little, Brown and Company.

My House Mi Casa: A Book in Two Languages by Rebecca Emberley (1990). Boston: Little, Brown and Company.

Thank You, Mr. Falker by Patricia Polacco (1998). New York: Philomel Books.

The Gingerbread Boy illustrated by Scott Cook (1987). New York: Alfred Knopf.

The Giver by Lois Lowry (1993). Boston: Houghton Mifflin.

The Hundred Dresses by Eleanor Estes (1944). New York: Scholastic.

The Very Hungry Caterpillar by Eric Cole (1987). New York: Putnam.

This is Baseball by Margaret Blackstone (1993). New York: Henry Holt and Company.

Tunes for bears to dance to by Robert Cormier. New York: Dell.

Where the Wild Things Are by Maurice Sendak (1963). New York: Harper and Row.

Part II
Selecting Children's Literature

There is a plethora of children's literature in libraries and bookstores that present a wide range of choices for students and teachers. But with all of these available resources, how does one know which books to choose? First, book lists, recommendations, award winning books, and literature guidelines help teachers to consider the quality of children's books. In addition, there are many books written by distinguished writers that help struggling readers develop reading skills and enjoy reading. Good writers write good books, and many respected authors use familiar vocabulary, short sentences, and descriptive words and language patterns that benefit students with reading problems.

This section includes a brief discussion of children's book awards, resources for finding quality children's literature, and general guidelines for selecting quality fiction and nonfiction literature. Examples of children's books written and/or illustrated by respected authors and illustrators whose themes speak to a diverse group of students and whose writing supports the development of literacy are provided. Story themes about individuals with reading problems are also included and classroom literacy practices are addressed.

Awards for Children's Literature

Two prominent awards that are given annually are the Caldecott and the Newbery Awards sponsored by the Association for Library Services to Children, a division of the American Library Association. These books have a large gold Newbery or Caldecott Medal on the cover. There are also Honor Books (runner up selections) in each of these award categories.

The Caldecott Award is named in honor of Randolph Caldecott, a distinguished English illustrator of children's books in the nineteenth century, and is awarded to the most distinguished picture book for children published in the United States during the preceding year. Caldecott books described in this book include: *The Snowy Day* (Ezra Jack Keats, 1963); *Where the Wild Things Are* (Maurice Sendak, 1964); *The Girl Who Loved Wild Horses* (Paul Goble, 1979); *Jumanji* (Chris Van Allsburg, 1982); *King Bidgood's in the Bathtub* (Audrey and Don Wood, Caldecott Honor, 1985); *Free Fall* (David Wiesner, Caladecott Honor, 1989); *Tuesday* (David Wiesner, 1992); *Grandfather's Journey* (Allen Say, 1994); Yo! *Yes?* (Chris Raschka, 1994, Caldecott Honor); and *Smoky Night* (Eve Bunting and David Diaz, 1995).

The Newbery Award is named in honor of John Newbery, an English publisher of books specifically for children in the eighteenth century. This award is given to the author of the most distinguished contribution to children's literature. Newbery Award and Newbery Honor books discussed in this text include: *Roll of Thunder, Hear My Cry* (Mildred Taylor, 1977); *Bridge to Terabithia* (Katherine Patterson, 1978); *Dear Mr. Henshaw* (Beverly Cleary, 1984); *Sarah, Plain and Tall* (Patricia MacLachlan, 1986); *A Fine White Dust* (Cynthia Rylant, 1987); *Hatchet* (Gary Paulsen, 1988); *Scorpions* (Walter Dean Myers, 1989); *Maniac Magee* (Jerry Spinelli, 1991); *The Giver* (Lois Lowry, 1994); *Wringer* (Jerry Spinelli, 1998); and *Holes* (Louis Sachar, 1998).

Other major awards include the Coretta Scott King Award that recognizes African American authors and artists, the International Reading Association (IRA) Children's Book Award given to new authors of promise, and the National Council of Teachers of English Award (NCTE Award) given to a living American poet of juvenile poetry.

Resources

There are many reputable sources that help teachers select children's literature. These include general recommendations and reviews of children's literature as well as specific resources for struggling readers.

General Recommendations and Reviews

Recommendations and reviews written by authorities in reading and children's literature are found in numerous magazines, journals, and books. Specific magazine and journal recommendations are found in the following table. See Appendix A for additional, related resources for teachers.

Title/ Publisher	Age range	Frequency	Comments
The Horn Book Guide Horn Book, Inc., Boston, MA	Preschool through young adult	Two times a year	Provides critical annotations of current children's literature published in the United States within a six month period. The reference includes selections for preschool, picture books, easy readers, younger fiction, intermediate fiction, older fiction, biographies, history, science, the arts, sports, social sciences and others.
The Horn Book Magazine Horn Book Inc., Boston, MA	Preschool through young adult	Six times a year	Includes book reviews and features about award winning authors and illustrators, such as the March/April 1998 feature by Paul Zelinsky (winner of the 1997 Caldecott Medal for his picture book *Rapunzel*), "Why I Use Oil Paints So Much." The book reviews cover a number of areas (e.g., picture books, fiction, folklore, poetry and song, nonfiction, of interest to adults) and include a short description of the book and the intended audience. A star review (*) indicates that the majority of the reviewers believe the book to be outstanding.
The Reading Teacher IRA, Newark, DE	Ages one to twelve	Eight times a year	Contains articles written by reading professionals in the area of reading and reading instruction. The journal lists favorite books selected by children ("Children's Choices") in the October Issue and favorite children's books selected by teachers ("Teacher's Choices") in the November issue.
The Journal of Adolescent & Adult Literacy IRA, Newark, DE	Adolescent through adult	Eight times a year	Serves those interested in teaching reading to adolescents and adults; reflects current theory, research, and practice for reading professionals and encourages effective instruction. The journal lists favorite books selected by young adults ("Young Adult's Choices").
Book Links: Connecting Books, Libraries and Classrooms ALA, Chicago, IL	Preschool through young adult	Bimonthly	Provides book reviews, strategies, and classroom connections for using children's literature. A particular focus is linking books on a similar theme.
The New Advocate Christopher-Gordon Pub. Norwood, MA	Children's - Adolescent Literature	Four times a year	Includes scholarly articles that are of interest to practitioners and practical articles grounded in theory and research regarding the publication, writing, and teaching of children's literature. Articles come from classroom teachers, teacher educators, researchers, librarians, and children's authors and illustrators.

Table 2–1: Resources for selecting children's literature

Recommendations for Struggling and Reluctant Readers

There are also books and handbooks that provide literature recommendations and teaching strategies for struggling readers. A few of these include:

- *Variability, Not Disability* (Roller, 1996) describes the benefits of using children's literature with struggling readers in a reading and writing workshop. Paula Brandt provides resources for identifying children's books for struggling readers (pp. 144–145) and lists of book titles and authors for beginning-to-read series, chapter books series, chapter books, and easy-to-read informational books (pp. 150–151).

- *Teaching Struggling Readers: Articles from The Reading Teacher* (Allington, 1998) includes articles that address reading fluency, motivation, classroom organization, and family and community collaboration.

- *Easy Reading: Book Series and Periodicals for Less Able Readers* (Ryder, Graves, and Graves, 1989) provides recommended periodicals and a bibliography of 44 high interest/low vocabulary book series that includes publisher, authors, reading and interest level, description, supplementary material, and critical evaluation. The authors note that high interest/low vocabulary books are "far from great literature" (p. 12) and should be augmented by trade books.

- *The High/Low Handbook: Encouraging Literacy in the 1990s* (Libretto, 1990) describes how to select and evaluate high/low materials and provides annotated bibliographies of high/low books for disabled and reluctant readers.

- *Reluctant Readers* (Jobe and Dayton-Sakari, 1999) is full of good suggestions for books, websites, audiotapes, and tips for engaging reluctant readers in reading.

- *The Reading Teacher's Book of Lists* (Fry, Kress, and Fountoukidis, 1993), a resource for primary through senior high school teachers, includes lists of practically everything teachers would want to know (e.g., antonyms, synonyms, common word families, spelling patterns, punctuation rules). Chapter Ten is devoted solely to books and includes lists of Caldecott and Newbery Award books, picture books, predictable books, books most frequently read aloud in grades K–6, and selected book lists by children, parents, and educators (pp. 297–311).

Selecting Good Fiction

There are a number of factors to consider when selecting quality children's literature. For instance, illustrations, story plot, character development, and theme are all important. More specifically, children's fiction should include (Huck, Hepler, Hickman, and Kiefer, 1997):

- A well-constructed, moving plot that is credible, original and fresh.
- A significant theme that students can relate to, based on integrity and justice (e.g., friendship, love, life, death, bravery, growing up, overcoming fear or prejudice, peer relations).
- An authentic setting that supports plot, characters, and theme.
- A credible point of view that supports the story (e.g., written in first person—I or in third person—he, she).
- Convincing characterization in which the character develops and grows as the story unfolds.
- An appropriate writing style that supports the plot, theme, and characters and that creates and reflects the mood of the story.
- High quality illustrations that are integral to the story.

Moreover, students with reading difficulties need words they can read, vocabulary they can understand, and characters to whom they can relate. If sentences are too long or complex struggling readers may have difficulty understanding and remembering information. Short novels are preferred over longer ones because they do not overwhelm readers. Yet, in order to strengthen reading comprehension, the language must be rich, filled with image-building passages, and the story must have well-developed characters and a theme worth reading. For instance: Jeremy was a bright, soft-spoken high school student with reading difficulties stemming from a mild hearing loss. Reading assessments reflected poor scores in vocabulary and inference skills. Discussing the complex characters in Robert Cormier's chilling short story *Tunes For Bears To Dance To* (1992) became the vehicle for developing vocabulary and inference skills. Jeremy predicted the meaning of unfamiliar words that the author used to describe his multifaceted characters, looked them up in the dictionary to check his predictions, discussed when and where they could be used, and included the words in his writing. He made inferences as he predicted outcomes of characters' actions and discussed their motivations such as prejudice, guilt, and hate, always going back to the story to validate his responses.

Picture Books

Picture storybooks that have predictable stories with rhyming words and repetitious phrases reinforce phonics patterns and help students predict unfamiliar words. Phonics patterns must be applied to meaningful text or else they will be easily forgotten (Adams, 1990, p. 286). For instance, *Green Eggs and Ham, The Cat in the Hat,* and *Horton Hatches the Egg* are a few of the many books by Dr. Seuss that have rhyming words, repetitive phrases, creative stories and illustrations. *Green Eggs and Ham* (1960) was the first book that Marvin read, enjoyed, and proudly completed. He was a sixth grader reading on a first grade reading level. Other examples include *The Very Quiet Cricket* by Eric Carle (1990) and *King Bidgood's in the Bathtub* (1985, Caldecott Honor Book) and *The Napping House* (1984), both written by Audrey Wood and illustrated by Don Wood.

Some picture storybooks with exquisite illustrations, descriptive language, and intriguing stories are too difficult for struggling readers to read independently yet they provide good opportunities for predicting and developing listening comprehension. Students develop receptive language skills when they listen for specific events, predict what might happen next in the story, and discuss the meaning of descriptive vocabulary and figurative language. For example, *Grandfather's Journey* (Allen Say, 1993) and *The Girl Who Loved Wild Horses* (Paul Goble, 1978) have estimated reading levels of low fourth to low fifth grade, respectively. Both books, however, are written and illustrated by Caldecott Award winners, contain descriptive language, beautiful illustrations, and tell good stories.

Picture Books for Older Students

Recently, there has been an increase in picture storybooks that are geared to children in the middle grades and older (Huck, Hipler, Hickman, Kiefer, 1997). Older students with decoding problems will find humor, mature themes, and lower reading levels in a number of picture storybooks. For example, Jon Scieszka's funny fantasies *The True Story of the Three Little Pigs* (1989) and *The Frog Prince—Continued* (1991) are modern versions of the familiar folktales (*The Three Little Pigs* and *The Frog Prince)* that have hilarious plot lines and a second grade reading level.

Eve Bunting's books, *Smoky Night* (1994), *The Wall* (1990), and *Fly Away Home* (1991) have more serious, social themes yet all have lower reading levels between the first and second grade. Patricia Polacco's *Pink and Say* (1994) is a biographical picture storybook of friendship and separation during the Civil War between two fifteen-year-old Union soldiers— Say (Sheldon Russell Curtis, the author's great, great grandfather) who is Caucasian and Pink (Pinkus Aylee) who is African American. The *Encounter* by Jan Yolen (1992), a historical fiction picture storybook about Columbus' voyages to the New World, contains rich figurative language and is told from the point of view of a young Tainto Indian who, along with his village, suffer dire consequences from the "Encounter."

Easy Reading Books and Short Chapter Books

Many distinguished writers and illustrators of picture storybooks and award winning authors of longer works of fiction also write and illustrate easy reading books and short chapter books. These short books have familiar vocabulary, short sentences, and good stories with believable characters that promote discussion, strengthen comprehension, and develop reading fluency. In addition, chapter book mysteries promote sequencing skills since readers must locate and sequence clues to solve mysteries. A few examples of easy reading books written by respected authors that are described in Part IV include:

- *Summer Wheels* (1992) by Eve Bunting (Caldecott Award author)
- *Amelia Bedelia* books by Peggy and Henry Parish
- *The Golly Sisters Go West; Hooray for the Golly Sisters! The Golly Sisters Ride Again* by Betsy Byars (Newbery Award author)
- *Poppleton and Friends, Mr. Putter and Tabby,* and *Henry and Mudge* by Cynthia Rylant (Newbery Award author)
- *Frog and Toad Are Friends* by Arnold Lobel (Newbery Honor book)
- *Marvin Redpost: Is He a Girl?* Louis Sachar (Newbery Award author)
- *The King's Equal* by Katherine Paterson (1992) (Newbery Award author)
- *Time War Trio* chapter books by Jon Scieszka (*Tut Tut; The Good, The Bad, And The Goofy; The Not-So-Jolly Roger; Knights of the Kitchen Table; Your Mother Was A Neanderthal*)
- *Nate the Great* by Marjorie Weinman Sharmat and Craig Sharmat
- *A to Z Mysteries* by Ron Roy
- *Cam Johnsen Mysteries* by David Adler

Fantasy Novels

Fantasy provides opportunities for struggling readers to develop imagination, and to discuss and experience imaginary worlds or familiar worlds that have gone awry or include a bit of a twist! There are many respected fiction writers who write intriguing fantasies, yet who use familiar vocabulary and sentence structures rich in descriptive words and language that develop reading comprehension. A few examples include:

- *James and the Giant Peach* by Roald Dahl (1961)
- *Bunnicula* by Deborah and James Howe (1979)
- *The Puppy Sister* by S.E. Hinton (1995)
- *Keep Your Eye on Amanda* by Avi (1996, 1997)
- *What Do Fish Have To Do With Anything And Other Stories* by Avi (1997)
- *Holes* by Louis Sachar (1998) (Newbery Award, National Book Award)
- *Maniac Magee* by Jerry Spinelli (1990) (Newbery Award)

Realistic Fiction Novels

When students read good realistic fiction they experience situations that could happen, events that did happen (historical fiction), and believable characters and stories to which they can identify. Struggling readers have opportunities to develop higher-level comprehension skills when they make inferences, discuss descriptive vocabulary and figurative language, talk about plot and conflict, what motivates and changes characters, and describe the effect of time and place (setting) on the story. Like chapter book mysteries, mystery novels such as *The Herculeah Jones Mysteries* (Betsy Byars) and *The Felicity Snell Mysteries* (E.W. Hildick) are full of opportunities for prediction, sequencing events, and tracing clues. A few examples of convincing characters in stories filled with humor, adventure, and gripping plots include:

- *How to Eat Fried Worms* by Thomas Rockwell (1973) (humorous)
- *Ramona Quimbley, Age 8* by Beverly Cleary (1981) (humorous) (Newbery Award author)
- *A Fine White Dust* (1986) by Cynthia Rylant (Newbery Honor book)
- *Crash* (1996) and *Wringer* (1998) (Newbery Honor book) by Jerry Spinelli
- *Hatchet* (1987) (Newbery Honor book), *Brian's Winter* (1996), *Brian's Return* (1999), and *Nightjohn* (1993) (historical fiction) by Gary Paulsen
- *That Was Then, This Is Now* by S.E. Hinton (1971) (ALA Notable Book) (for older readers)
- *Tunes For Bears To Dance To* by Robert Cormier (1992) (for older readers)
- *Don't you dare read this, Mrs. Dumphrey* by Margaret Peterson Hadix (1996) (International Reading Association Award) (for older readers)

Selecting Good Nonfiction

Nonfiction is often overlooked when selecting books for students with reading difficulties. This is an important area since struggling readers have interests, background experiences, and talents that can be explored and celebrated through nonfiction. For example, Janelle was a graceful dancer and had taken ballet lessons since she was a small child. She excelled in dance but struggled with reading. Janelle wanted to read about ballet and dance and was excited to find the nonfiction picture books *Isadora Dances* (1998), a biography of Isadora Duncan, by Rachel Isadora (Caldecott Medal artist), and *Dance* (1998) by modern dancer and choreographer Bill T. Jones and photographer Susan Kuklin.

Nonfiction books also introduce students to text organizations that they will meet in classroom, content-area reading such as comparison/contrast, cause/effect, and time/order relations. In addition, students learn to relate visual information (e.g., illustrations, photographs, charts, graphs) to text, predict from captions and subheadings, look up unfamiliar words in a glossary, locate information in a table of contents, and summarize and review information. Most importantly, struggling readers learn new information in fascinating ways and find valuable resources to support their personal interests and content-area learning. When selecting nonfiction books, look for (Goforth, 1998)

- Information that is accurate and current.
- A qualified and interesting writer.
- A logical organization.
- An appealing format with photographs, illustrations, or archival documents.

Informational Books

There are a number of fascinating informational books that address a variety of areas and interests. Many books contain little text and are filled with quality photographs taken by professional photographers. In *The NBA Game Day* (Layden and Preller, 1997), 26 sport photographers take the reader behind the scenes in the NBA. Susan Kuklin's color photographs of dancer Bill Jones in *Dance* (1998) inform the reader about the grace, line, and movement of the human body. *The Eyewitness Readers* (Dorling Kindersley Publishing) are short paperback books that are written on four progressive reading levels (Levels 1–4, preschool though grade 4) and contain colorful, fascinating, and informative photographs and illustrations about various subjects. (See *Dinosaur Dinners* (1992) by Lee Davis in Part IV.) Detailed illustrations describe the intricate workings of hundreds of machines in David Macaulay's *The Way Things* Work (1988). *Ed Emberley's Drawing Book of Animals* (reissue, 1994) is a step by step book of easy drawing instructions for making animals. The *Magic School Bus* picture books, written by Joanna Cole and Illustrated by Bruce Degen, are popular picture storybooks that combine fiction and factual science information. *Anno's Math Games III* (1982) by Mitsumasa Anno develops abstract thinking through intriguing games and puzzles and Stuart J. Murphy's easy to read, colorful picture books *A Fair Bear Share* (1998) and *Get Up and Go!* (1996) introduce readers to regrouping and time lines, respectively.

In addition, alphabet books present a range of information in creative ways while strengthening letter sound relationships and reading comprehension. Books that interest older readers include: *NBA Action from A to Z* (James Preller, 1997), containing action sport photographs and baseball information; *Antics! An Alphabetical Anthology,* by Cathi Hepworth (1992) with eccentric ants illustrating single words (listed alphabetically) that contain the word ant; and *The Z Was Zapped* by Chris Van Allsburg (1987), requiring readers to predict what happens to alphabet letters that are engaged in harrowing episodes depicted by Van Allsburg's surrealistic chalk drawings.

Autobiographies and Biographies

Reading about actual people and how they face challenges and over-come hardships to accomplish dreams is important for children who struggle with their own learning problems. For instance, in the short pho-tographic biography of *Cedric Ceballos* by sportswriter Mark Stewart (Grolier All-PRO Biographies), the basketball star relates his difficulty with reading: *I knew that the letters on the page made a word, but sometimes I had to look for a long time before that word popped into my head. I knew I wasn't stupid. I just saw things differently than other kids* (p. 8). Other motivating and inspiring books include: *I Can't Accept Not Trying* (1994) by Michael Jordan (a short chapter book); *Lou Gehrig:The Luckiest Man* by David Adler (1997) (picture book); *Home Run (1998)* by Robert Burleigh, about the legendary hitter Babe Ruth (picture book); and *The Story of Martin Luther King* by Margaret Davidson (1986).

In addition, biographies provide opportunities for struggling readers to understand and illustrate text relationships since good writers describe the complex make-up of individuals, emphasize important events that im-pact subsequent events (cause/effect relations), and often organize infor-mation in chronological order (i.e., time/order relations). For example, *Sadako and the Thousand Paper Cranes* by Eleanor Coerr (1977) is a short, 56 page biography that tells the moving story about a twelve-year-old Japanese girl from Hiroshima who was infected with the "atom-bomb disease" (leukemia) when she was two years old. A description map and cause/effect map of the main story events are represented in Part III, Text Structures. For basketball fans, *Reach Higher* (1996) by Scottie Pippen and Greg Brown contains numerous photographs and illustrations that depict important events in the athlete's life. A time-line map of these events is also included in Part III.

Poetry

Poetry speaks to emotions and allows struggling readers to experience the thoughts and feelings of others and to express their own in creative ways. For example, in *Reach for the Moon* (1994, Pfeifer-Hamilton Publish-ers), poet Samantha Abeel, a junior high school student with learning dis-abilities, writes eloquently about herself, the sunrise, her grandmother's quilt, and fall leaves. In the preface, Samantha reminds readers to never let a disability stop them from what they are good at or what they want to do.

In addition, poetry helps students with reading difficulties strengthen word identification and develop reading fluency. Poetry verses are short and easy to read and poems with rhyme, repetition, and alliteration rein-force letter sounds and phonics patterns and help readers predict unfamil-iar words. For example, in "Friendly Fredrick Fuddlestone" (*For Laughing Out Loud: Poems To Tickle Your Funnybone,* Jack Prelutsky, 1991), Arnold

Lobel uses words that begin with the letter *F* twenty wonderful times! How many times can students hear the /f/ sound? How many words can they think of that start with the same sound? Shel Silverstein's three poetry books, *Where the Sidewalk Ends* (1974), *A Light in the Attic* (1981), and *Falling Up* (1996) contain hilarious poems with various rhyming words and patterns. In *Lunch Money and Other Poems About School* (1995), Carol Diggory Shields describes clock-watching in which she repeats the *Click, jump* of the clock 14 times ("Clock-Watching," pp. 34–35)! In Maya Angelou's dramatic poem *Life Doesn't Frighten Me* (1978) with bold paintings by Jean-Michel Basquiat (1993), short, rhyming verses precede each repeated refrain.

Reading poetry also develops abstract thinking skills. Like reading novels that contain figurative language, reading and discussing poetry that contains similes and metaphors provide opportunities for students to experience familiar events and situations in new and extraordinary ways. For example, in *For the Love of the Game: Michael Jordan and Me* (1997), Eloise Greenfield compares Michael Jordan's smooth jump landing to a plane gliding to the ground. In "Riding on a Train" (from *Honey I Love*, 1972), the poet writes about raindrops that crawl backwards on the train window. The haiku poetry collection *Cool Melons—Turn To Frogs! The Life and Poems of Issa* (1998) invites readers to interpret the poet's feelings about nature and life.

Children's Literature and Diversity

There are many distinguished writers and artists whose stories and illustrations celebrate diversity and promote an understanding and respect for differences as well as support the development of literacy. A few of the authors and illustrators represented in Part IV include:

Authors and Illustrators of Picture Books

- Ezra Jack Keats, award winning African American author and artist, writes and illustrates easy to read picture books about the special, everyday experiences of Peter and his dog Willie as he plays in the snow (*The Snowy Day, 1962*, Caldecott Medal), finds a cat (*Hi, Cat!,* 1970) and learns to whistle (*Whistle for Willie*, 1964).

- Chris Raschka writes and illustrates *Yo! Yes!* (1993, Caldecott Honor Book), a short picture storybook with 29 easy words (e.g., yes, who, me, you, oh) about a sad looking Caucasian boy with no friends and a sympathetic African American boy who will be his friend.

- Patricia Polacco, an author and illustrator of Ukrainian heritage, tells an autobiographical story about herself and her two African American friends, Stewart and Winston, and their gramma, Miss Eula Mae Walker in *Chicken Sunday* (1992).

- Allen Say writes and illustrates elegant picture storybooks that stem from his Asian background and experiences. *Tree of Cranes* (1991) tells the autobiographical story about the author celebrating his first Christmas in Japan, *Tea and Milk* (1999) is about his mother's struggle to become Japanese after growing up American, and *Grandfather's Journey* (Caldecott Medal, 1993) describes the adventures of the author's grandfather who comes to America as a young man.

- Mem Fox, an Australian writer, includes repetitive words and phrases in *Koala Lou* (1988), a charming story about a little Koala bear that enters the Bush Olympics to get her mother's attention.

- Leo and Diane Dillon, Caldecott Award wining artists, celebrate cultures from around the world in their elegantly illustrated picture book *To Every Thing There Is A Season* (1998). The familiar, simple text from the Book of Ecclesiastes is depicted in large capital letters. A single phrase appears on each page and is illustrated by unique styles of art that include Ireland, Egypt, Japan, Mexico, Greece, India, Europe (the middle ages), North American (Pueblo art), Ethiopia, and China.

- Arthur Dorros (1991) writes about a little girl and her grandmother who fly over New York City in the whimsical picture book *Abuela*, illustrated in colorful, collage paintings by Elisa Kleven.

Poets and Writers of Longer Fiction

- Sheila Hamanaka's free verse poetry book *All the Colors of the Earth* (1994) contains colorful, expressive pictures of children from diverse races, tumbling across pages and accompanied by simple descriptive phrases and sentences.

- Langston Hughes (1934, 1994), a celebrated writer of African American experiences, writes short, powerful, and moving poems that evoke images and feelings in *The Dream Keeper and other poems*.

- Gary Soto writes about growing up Mexican American. In *The Skirt* (1992), a short 74 page novel, nine year old Miata frantically tries to recover her mother's *folklorico* skirt that she left on the school bus.

- Eleanor Estes writes about differences and the consequences of making fun of others in *One Hundred Dresses* (1944).

- Walter Dean Myers, winner of two Newbery Honor books and a five-time winner of the Coretta Scott King Award, writes fiction, nonfiction, and poetry. Both *Scorpions* (1998, Newbery Honor) and *Slam* (1996), a novel for young adults, include complex characters, urban landscapes, and descriptive language such as when Slam notes, *The streets in the South Bronx can look ragged, but a day of classes when everybody knows what's going on but you can make them look good* (p. 19).

- Judith Ortiz Cofer writes a moving collection of short stories about teenagers growing up in a Puerto Rican barrio in Paterson, New Jersey, in *An Island Like You stories of the Barrio* (1995) (ALA Best Book for Young Adults).

- Jacqueline Woodson's powerful short novels about differences, prejudice, and caring include *I Hadn't Meant to Tell You This* (1994) (Coretta Scott King Honor Book) and *From the Notebooks Of Melanin Sun* (1995) (Coretta Scott King Honor Book).

Story Themes and Reading Problems

Several recent books describe individuals that excel in some areas while struggling with reading. For example, in the picture book biography *Cedric Ceballos* by sportswriter Mark Stewart (1996), the NBA star remarks that the only thing he found difficult was reading (p. 8). In the autobiographical picture storybook *Thank You, Mr. Falker* (1998), writer/ illustrator Patricia Polacco tells how she shines in art but struggles in reading, ridiculed by peers as she stumbles over words. *Emma's Magic Winter* by Jean Little (1998) is a short I-Can-Read chapter book about a little girl who is too shy to read aloud in front of the class (she only reads in a whisper) yet who has a marvelous imagination. Barbara Barrie's novel, *Adam Zigzag* (1994), describes a bright, popular teenager who has severe reading problems. In Jacqueline Turner Banks' novel, *Egg-Drop Blues* (1995), Judge, who has difficulty decoding words and remembering what he reads, successfully competes in a science fare competition. In *Holes* (Louis Sachar, 1998), Stanley teaches Zero to read in exchange for digging his quota of holes at Camp Green Lake. And Max (*Freak the Mighty,* Rodman Philbrick, 1993), who thinks he is dumb because he has problems learning, gives his friend Kevin legs as he hoists him up on his strong shoulders. In return, Kevin (who is stunted in size and wears a leg brace) shares his quick wit and his imagination. All of these individuals have special stories to share with readers.

Using Children's Literature in the Classroom

Students with reading difficulties benefit from hearing, reading, and discussing books with classmates yet often need individual attention to address learning needs. When these students participate in whole group activities, small heterogeneous literature groups, homogeneous guided reading groups, or partner reading, they have opportunities to interact with classmates and strengthen literacy skills. For example, listening to a story read aloud in class allows students to develop listening skills, and discuss and enjoy a story that may be too difficult for them to read independently. Further, when teachers read aloud they have opportunities to model and discuss effective strategies, as well as facilitate discussion of the story (or poem), figurative language, and vocabulary. Participating in literature groups with strong readers, children with reading difficulties hear different perspectives and share their own. Small guided reading groups where students of similar ability read the same book allows teachers to direct instruction to specific needs. Providing time for individual reading when everyone reads, enables teachers to model the pleasure of reading and helps to develop life-long reading habits.

The learning strategies described in Part III promote literacy skills in whole class, small group, or individual reading situations. For example, struggling readers are involved in whole class activities when they choral read, participate in readers theater, play charades based on story characters, or share favorite books. Graphic organizers that represent story structures, compare characters, or sequence events help readers clarify, organize, and remember information and can be developed individually, or as a whole class, small group, or peer activity. Likewise, students can make inferences, discuss figurative language, character motivations, and story themes in various group settings or when working individually with support staff or student or parent volunteers. Children practice word identification strategies when they meet unfamiliar words in meaningful reading situations whether reading independently or with others.

Most importantly, for students and teachers, is to find the right book, fiction or nonfiction, that engages struggling readers, that peaks their interest and relates to background experiences—books that they choose to read and are successful in reading. Having a wide assortment of books on different reading levels (and multiple copies of books) and a variety of situations for interacting with peers in literacy activities allow children with reading difficulties to belong to a community of readers while growing and developing their literacy skills.

References

Adams, M.J. (1990). *Beginning to read: thinking and learning about print.* Cambridge, MA: MIT Press.

Allington, R.L., Ed. (1998). *Teaching struggling readers: articles from the reading teacher.* Newark, DE: International Reading Association.

Book Links: Connecting Books, Libraries, and Classrooms. Judy O'Malley, Ed. American Library Association.

Fry, E., Kress, J., and Fountoukidis, D.L. (1993). *The reading teacher's book of lists* (3rd ed.). Englewood Cliffs, NJ: Prentice Hall.

Goforth, F. (1998). *Literature and the learner.* Belmont, CA: Wadsworth Publishing.

Hillman, J. (1999). *Discovering children's literature* (2nd ed.). Upper Saddle River, NJ: Merrill Publishing.

Horn Book Guide, Horn Book Magazine. The Horn Book, Inc., 11 Beacon Street, Boston, MA.

Huck, C., Hepler, S, Hickman, J., and Kiefer, B. (1997). *Children's literature in the elementary school* (6th ed.). Madison, WI: Brown and Benchmark.

Jobe, R., and Dayton-Sakari, M. (1999). *Reluctant readers: connecting students and books for successful reading experiences.* York, Maine: Pembroke Publishers.

Journal of Adolescent & Adult Literacy. Newark, DE: International Reading Association.

Libretto, E.V. (1990). *High/low handbook encouraging literacy in the 1990s.* New York: R.R. Bowker.

Reading Teacher. Newark, DE: International Reading Association.

Roller, C. (1996). *Variability not disability: Struggling readers in a workshop classroom.* Newark, Delaware: International Reading Association.

Ryder, R., Graves, B., and Graves, M (1989). *Easy reading: book series and periodicals for less able readers* (2nd ed.). Newark, DE: International Reading Association.

The New Advocate. Norwood, MA: Christopher-Gordon.

Children's Book Titles

Chapter Books

A to Z Mysteries: The Absent Author by Ron Roy (1997). New York: Random House.

Amelia Bedelia by Peggy Parish (1963). New York: Harper Collins.

Cam Johnsen and the Scary Snake Mystery by David Adler (1997). New York: Viking, Penguin Group.

Emma's Magic Winter by Jean Little (1998). New York: HarperCollins Publisher.

Marvin Redpost: Is He a Girl? by Louis Sachar (1993). New York: Random House.

Nate the Great and the Tardy Tortoise by Marjorie W. Sharmat and Craig Sharmot (1995). New York: Bantam Doubleday Dell.

Poppleton and Friends by Cynthia Rylant (1997). New York: The Sky Blue Press, Scholastic.

Summer Wheels by Eve Bunting (1992). San Diego: Harcourt Brace Jovanovich.

The Golly Sisters Go West by Betsy Byars (1985). New York: Harper and Row.

The Time Warp Trio: The Not So Jolly Roger by Jon Scieszka (1991). New York: Penguin Group.

Novels

A Fine White Dust by Cynthia Rylant (1986). New York: Simon and Schuster.

Adam Zigzag by Barbara Barrie (1994). New York: Bantam Doubleday Books.

An Island Like You stories from the Barrio by Judith Ortez Cofer (1995). New York: Penguin Group.

Brian's Winter by Gary Paulsen (1996). New York: Bantam Doubleday Dell.

Brian's Return by Gary Paulsen (1999). New York: Delacorte Press.

Bunnicula by Deborah and James Howe (1979). New York: Atheneum.

Disappearing Acts: A Herculeah Jones Mystery by Betsy Byars (1998). New York: The Penguin Group.

Don't you dare read this, Mrs. Dunphrey by Margaret Peterson Haddix (1996). New York: Aladdin Paperbacks, imprint of Simon & Schuster.

Egg-Drop Blues by Jacqueline Turner Banks (1995). Boston: Houghton Mifflin Company.

Freak the Mighty by Rodman Philbrick (1993). New York: Sky Blue Press, an imprint of Scholastic.

From the Notebooks of Melanin Sun by Jacqueline Woodson (1995). New York: Scholastic.

Hatchet by Gary Paulsen (1987). New York: Penguin Group.

Holes by Louis Sachar (1998). New York: Frances Foster Books, Farrar, Strauss and Giroux.

How to Eat Fried Worms by Thomas Rockwell (1973). New York: Dell.

I Hadn't Meant to Tell You This by Jacqueline Woodson (1994). New York: Delacorte Press.

James and the Giant Peach by Roald Dahl (1961). New York: Puffin Books.

Nightjohn by Gary Paulsen (1993). New York: Bantam Doubleday Dell.

Scorpions by Walter Dean Myers (1988). New York: Harper Trophy, a Division of HarperCollins.

Slam by Walter Dean Myers (1997). New York: Scholastic Press.

That Was Then, This Is Now by S.E. Hinton (1971). New York: Puffin Books, the Penguin Group.

The Hundred Dresses by Eleanor Estes (1944). New York: Scholastic.

The Puppy Sister by S.E. Hinton (1995). New York: Bantam Doubleday Dell.

The Purloined Corn Popper: A Felicity Snell Mystery by E.W. Hildick (1997). Tarrytown, NY: Marshall Cavendish.

The Skirt by Gary Soto (1992). New York: Bantam Doubleday Dell.

Tunes For Bears To Dance To by Robert Cormier (1992) New York: Dell Publishing, a division of Bantam Doubleday Dell Publishing Group, Inc.

What Do Fish Have To Do With Anything? And Other Stories by Avi (1997). Cambridge, MA: Candlewick Press.

Picture Books

Abuela by Arthur Dorros (1991). New York: Dutton Children's Books.

Chicken Sunday by Patricia Polacco (1992). New York: Philomel Books.

Encounter by Jan Yolen (1992). New York: Harcourt Brace Jovanovich.

Fly Away Home by Eve Bunting (1991). New York: Clarion Books.

Grandfather's Journey by Allen Say (1993). New York: Houghton Mifflin.

King Bidgood's in the Bathtub by Audrey Wood (1985). San Diego: Harcourt Brace Jovanovich.

Koala Lou by Mem Fox (1988). San Diego: Gulliver Books, Harcourt Brace Jovanovich.

Pink and Say by Patricia Polacco (1994). New York: Philomel Books, a division of The Putnam & Grosset Group.

Smoky Night by Eve Bunting (1994). San Diego: Harcourt Brace & Company.

Thank You Mr. Falker by Patricia Polacco (1998). New York: Philomel Books.

The Girl Who Loved Wild Horses by Paul Goble (1978). New York: Aladdin Paperbacks, an imprint of Simon & Schuster.

The Magic School Bus in the Time of the Dinosaurs by Joanna Cole (1994). New York: Scholastic.

The Napping House by Audrey Wood (1984). New York: Harcourt Brace Jovanovich.

The Snowy Day by Ezra Jack Keats (1962). New York: Viking Press.

The True Story of the Three Little Pigs by Jon Scieszka (1989). New York: Penguin Books.

The Very Quiet Cricket by Eric Carle (1990). New York: Philomel Books, a division of The Putnam & Grosset Book Group.

Tree of Cranes by Allen Say (1991). New York: Houghton Mifflin.

Yo! Yes! by Chris Raschka (1993). New York: Orchard Books.

Nonfiction

Anno's Math Games III by Mitsumasa Anno (1982, 1991, 1997). New York: A PaperStar Book, The Putnam & Grosset Group.

Antics by Cathi Hepworth (1992). New York: Putham's Sons, a division of Putnam and Grosset Book Group.

Cedric Ceballso by Mark Stewart (1996). New York: Grolier All-PRO Biographies, Grolier Publishing.

Dance by Bill T. Jones and Susan Kuklin (1998). New York: Hyperion Books for Children.

Dinosaur Dinners by Lee Davis (1998). Dorling Kindersley (London). New York: DK Publishing, Inc.

Ed Emberley's Drawing Book of Animals by Ed Emberley (reissue 1994). Boston: Little, Brown and Company.

Home Run by Robert Burleigh (1998). San Deigo, CA: Harcourt Brace & Company.

I Can't Accept Not Trying by Michael Jordon (1994). New York: HarperCollins.

I Have a Dream: The Story of Martin Luther King by Margaret Davidson (1986). New York: Scholastic.

Isadora Dances by Rachel Isadora (1998). New York: Viking.

Lou Gehrig: The Luckiest Man by David Adler (1997). San Diego: Harcourt Brace and Company.

NBA Action from A to Z by James Preller (1997). New York: Scholastic.

Reach Higher by Scottie Pippen and Greg Brown (1996). Dallas, TX: Taylor Publishing.

Sadako and the Thousand Paper Cranes by Eleanor Coerr (1977). New York: Bantam Doubleday Dell.

The NBA Game Day: From Morning until Night, Behind the Scenes on the NBA by J. Layden and J. Preller (1997). New York: Scholastic.

The Z Was Zapped by Chris Van Allsburg (1987). New York: Houghton Mifflin.

Poetry

All the Colors of the Earth by Sheila Hamanaka (1994). New York: William and Morrow and Company.

Cool Melons Turn to Frogs!: The Life and Poems of Issa translated by Matthew Gollub (1998). New York: Lee & Low.

For Laughing Out Loud: Poems to Tickle Your Funnybone selected by Jack Prelutsky (1991). New York: Alfred A. Knopf.

For the Love of the Game: Michael Jordan and Me by Eloise Greenfield (1997). New York: HarperCollins.

Honey I Love and Other Love Poems by Eloise Greenfield (1978). New York: Harper and Row.

Life Doesn't Frighten Me by Maya Angelou (1978) with paintings by Jean Michel Basquiet (1993). New York: Stewart, Taboari & Changi.

Lunch Money and Other Poems About School by Carol Diggory Shields (1995). New York: Puffin Books, Penguin Group.

Reach for the Moon by Samantha Abeel (1994). Duluth, MN: Pfeifer-Hamilton.

The Dream Keeper and Other Poems by Langston Hughes (1932, 1960, 1987, 1994). New York: Alfred A. Knopf, Inc.

To Every Thing There Is A Season by Leo and Diane Dillon (1998). New York: The Blue Sky Press, an Imprint of Scholastic.

Where the Sidewalk Ends by Shel Silverstein (1974). New York: Harper and Row.

Part III
Learning Strategies

There are many research-based learning strategies that support literacy when students read, discuss, and write about children's literature. This section highlights a few of the many learning strategies and activities, including art and drama extensions to literature, that strengthen oral expression, word identification, reading comprehension, and writing for children with reading difficulties.

Word Identification

Word-level reading problems are of primary importance for most children with specific reading disabilities (Torgesen and Wagner, 1999). Word identification strategies that help struggling readers identify unfamiliar words include phonics (i.e., letter-sound correspondences), contextual clues (semantic and syntactic cues), syllabication strategies, and structural analysis (e.g., root, prefix, suffix). Fluent reading also requires the automatic recognition of sight words or high frequency words that occur frequently throughout reading (e.g., *there, was, the, for, are*). Multisensory instruction and games reinforce the learning of these troublesome words.

Phonics and Rimes

The goal of teaching phonics is to allow children to read connected text independently (Adams, 1990, p. 272). In order to successfully apply phonic cues, children must be able to segment spoken language into words, syllables, and phonemes (i.e., smallest units of speech sounds). They must be able to hear, identify, and manipulate sounds in words. This ability is called *phonological awareness,* an area that poses difficulty for many students with reading problems. These children frequently have difficulty hearing rhyming patterns, detecting the differences in beginning, medial, or ending sounds (*cat* differs from *pat* in the initial consonant), identifying individual sounds that make up words (*cat* has three sounds /k/ /a/ /t/), and blending sounds together (*k+a+t = cat*). Activities that support these skills include singing rhyming songs, listening to and reading poems and predictable books with rhymes and alliteration, playing word games (e.g., creating rhyming words, identifying the beginning sounds in words, counting sounds in words), and clapping or tapping to syllables.

Struggling readers have particular difficulty with vowel sounds. According to Mr. Grayson, a character from *Maniac Magee* (Jerry Spinelli, 1990) who never learned to read in school: *Vowels were something else. He didn't like them, and they didn't like him. There were only five of them but they seemed to be everywhere* (p. 101). This is where rimes, phonics patterns, and stories like Dr. Seuss come to the rescue.

Vowel sounds do not tend to vary in rimes, are relatively easy to remember and to blend back together, and introduce readers to a number of different words (Adams, 1990, pp. 320–324). A *rime* consists of a vowel sound plus the following consonant or consonants (e.g., *at, boat*). The beginning consonant is called an *insert* (e.g., *c* at). Phonics patterns consist of words that have the same rime such as *at, fat, sat*. Reading researchers Dombey and Moustafa (1998) suggest that children learn to read by building a repertoire of words that they can recognize at sight and from which they can analyze patterns or rimes. Then they are able to identify these familiar patterns in unfamiliar words, a whole-to-part phonics process. Other researchers suggest using both a whole-to-part and part-to-whole process. Brady and Moats (1997) write that children benefit from systematic instruction that emphasizes regular patterns in written English and from reading stories that enable them to practice their decoding knowledge (p. 10). The following activities help children to hear, identify, and use rimes and phonics patterns in word identification:

- Read poems and picture books that include alliteration and rhyme such as *Green Eggs and Ham* and *The Cat in the Hat* by Dr. Seuss and poetry books by Shel Silverstein, Douglas Florian, Jack Prelutsky, and Carol Diggory Shields. (See Poetry, Part IV, for descriptions.)

- Match and sort words with similar rhyming patterns (e.g., one syllable words with *at* pattern go in one pile, words with *in* pattern in another).

- Make new words. Add beginning consonants or *inserts* (e.g., *h, c, m, s*) to rhyming patterns or *rimes* (*at*) to make new words (*hat, cat, mat, sat*); manipulate cut-out letters, magnetic letters, and anagrams to make new words.

- Make analogies between known and new words. Identify a familiar pattern (*an*) in an unfamiliar word (St*an*); say pattern and blend preceding consonant or consonants(*St*) to identify the new word (analogy, or compare/contrast method).
- Write simple sentences or create short poems that contain a rhyming pattern or patterns.
- Reinforce phonics patterns by reading poems and stories that contain the same pattern.

Reading Long Words

Students with reading difficulties often have trouble sounding out long words. Rather than breaking down polysyllabic words into syllables or smaller meaningful units that they can sound out, students inefficiently try to sound out letter sound by letter sound. Frequently, struggling readers cannot hear syllable breaks in long words and need strategies that provide visual cues such as segmenting a word between two consonants (VC/CV) or identifying the word stem and applying the rules of 3's and 2's (Deshler, Ellis, Lenz, 1996). Strategies to help students read polysyllabic words include:

Syllable Generalizations: Separate words into syllables by applying syllable generalizations and then sound out individual syllables. Use the context to see if the word makes sense. A syllable is a word or word unit that contains one vowel sound such as *the, a, va/ca/tion*. Students can learn generalizations by discovering similar patterns in words (e.g, *let/ter* and *ap/ply* have two syllables that occur between two double consonants) and applying generalizations to unfamiliar words in isolation and in context. Some struggling readers need explicit instruction in recognizing syllable patterns, guided practice in applying a generalization with words that are examples and non-examples, and independent practice applying the generalization to polysyllabic words they read in context. The following generalizations are fairly consistent and help readers get in the "ballpark" to approximate the sound of an unfamiliar word.

- VC/CV: separate a word between two consonants that are not consonant blends or consonant digraphs (pic/ture; pat/tern; rab/bit). Consonant blends are two or three consonants in which each sound is blended (*st*eep, *str*eet, *tr*ee). Consonant digraphs are two consonants with one sound (*sh*ut, *ch*urch, *wh*at, *th*ough).
- V/CLE: words ending in a consonant followed by *le* usually form the final syllable (e.g., ta/ble, syl/la/ble).
- V/CV or VC/C: a single consonant between two single vowels may go with either syllable (ro/bot and rob/in). Use the context to determine the syllable and vowel sound.

- Divide between compound words (ball/game and fair/ground).
- Prefixes and suffixes usually form separate syllables (catch/ing, re/make, un/tie).

Structural Analysis: Identify and discuss the meaning in word structures such as the root stem, suffixes, prefixes, and compound words. Use multisyllabic words from reading and first emphasize inflectional suffixes such as *s, ed,* and *ing* since these inflections appear first in reading material (Durkin, 1981, p. 81). Inflectional suffixes affect grammar and not the inherent meaning of the root word. Discuss the meaning of the root stem and then compare the similarities and differences in word meaning and usage when suffixes are added. Collect words from reading that contain inflections such as *ing* words and write them on a wall chart. Create a word map that includes the root word in the center and words with the same stem plus inflectional suffixes extending from the circle (e.g., read—reader, reading, readable). Discuss how the suffix affects grammar and meaning and use the word in oral language activities and writing. Follow the same procedure for words with derivational suffixes (i.e., affect meaning such as less—homeless) and prefixes such as pre—preschool, re—reread and compound words.

Rules of 3's and 2's (Deshler, Ellis, Lenz, 1996): Examine the word stem and use the rules of 3's and 2's to break the word into more manageable units to read. Rule of 3's: If the first letter is a consonant, underline the first three letters (bro-ken). Rule of 2's: If the first letter is a vowel, underline the first two letters; continue applying the 3's and 2's rules for the remaining letters until all words in the stem have been broken into syllables (in come). Vowel digraphs, i.e., two vowels with one sound, are counted as one letter (e.g., augment). If you cannot make sense of the word, drop the first letter in the stem and then apply the 3's and 2's rules starting with the second letter.

Recognizable Clusters: Look for familiar spellings or vowel patterns to figure out big words, such as auto in automobile, and favor in favorite. First, build a store of big words (seven or eight letters) by collecting big words from reading. Write the words on a wall chart or chalkboard and emphasize the spelling pattern (e.g., tion—vacation, motion, commotion) (Cunningham, 1995, p. 125). Emphasize word roots, rather than little words in bigger words when the bigger word is an inflected word, a derivative, or root such as caring (care not car), restudy (study not rest) and waste (not was) (Durkin, 1981, p. 98).

Context Clues

Frequently students with reading difficulties fail to use context clues (vocabulary and sentence structure) to identify unfamiliar words. They often stop when they come to a word they do not know, guess, or substitute the word that first pops into their head that has the same beginning sound as the unfamiliar word. However, when struggling readers have constant practice in reading stories, they naturally learn to use context clues (Lerner, 1997, p. 413).

Use the following strategies to facilitate using context clues:

- Raise awareness of phonological, syntactic and semantic cues: What word makes sense in the sentence? What is the sentence about? What sound does the word start with? Can you think of a word that makes sense in the sentence that beings with this sound?

- Use cloze activities: Delete selected words in a language experience story or book passage and ask students to supply the missing words. For example, read a sentence aloud and delete a word for students to supply. Write a short passage or sentence on an overhead projector and leave blanks for selected words. Ask students to predict the missing word by thinking of a word that would make sense in the sentence (using context cues). For instance, write the following sentence from *Poppleton and Friends* (Cynthia Rylant) on an overhead and ask students to predict the missing word at the end of the sentence: *"Poppleton had a big beach chair, which he _____ (unfolded).* Read the sentence aloud and ask students to use their background experiences to help them think of a word that makes sense and that sounds right in the sentence. Have they taken a chair to the beach before or have they seen people with beach chairs? What do they have to do before sitting in the chair? Initially, delete words at the end of the sentence since students will have more meaning cues by reading the words at the beginning and middle of the sentence. To provide phonics cues, include the first letter sound of a deleted word.

Sight Words

Sight words are words that occur frequently throughout reading (e.g., was, as, have, were, with). Reading researchers have compiled lists of basic sight words that make up over half of all written material (Dolch Basic Sight Words, 1936; Fry, Kress, and Fountoukidis' 300 Instant Words, 1993). Although children's speaking vocabulary is full of such words, students must recognize them automatically to be fluent readers. High frequency sight words pose problems for struggling readers on two accounts: many are function words such as conjunctions (and) and prepositions (on, under) and hold little meaning; and many are difficult to sound out because of the irregular letter-sound patterns (e.g., their). It is important to read these words in a meaningful context so that readers have surrounding language clues to predict unfamiliar words. Multisensory instruction, activities using word walls, word sorts, and word games such as Bingo and Concentration reinforce the learning of sight words.

Multisensory Instruction (VAKT): Simultaneously use tactile (touch) and kinesthetic (movement) stimulation and auditory (hearing) and visual (seeing) modalities to enhance learning and memory. For example, look at a target word (visual cue), hear and pronounce the word (auditory cue), trace the word in sand, finger paint, or on letters made from a rough surface such as sandpaper or crayon (tactile and kinesthetic stimulation). Then write the word from memory and check the spelling with the target word. Repeat the process two or three times to ensure learning. Read the word in various meaningful contexts and include the word in simple written sentences or a short story.

Word Walls (Cunningham, 1995; Hall and Cunningham, 1999): Write high frequency sight words, new words, or troublesome vocabulary encountered during reading on a wall chart. Words can be grouped alphabetically (e.g., *w—w*hat, *w*hen, *w*ho) or made visually distinctive by using different colors (e.g., words starting with *w* are one color) or by cutting around the word configuration. In addition to high frequency words, write words that represent beginning sounds and letter combinations (e.g., digraphs—ch, wh, th; blends—tr, st, br), irregular spelled words (e.g., because, was), contractions, and rhymes. Write words on index cards or paper backed with magnetic tape so words can be moved around and sorted. Students read words, sort words, find them in reading, and use them in oral and written language activities.

Word Sorts: Word sort activities help students to focus on the various features of a word (Cunningham, 1993, 1995, [3rd ed.]; Hall and Cunningham, 1999). Select five to six words from a language experience story or trade book, words that students have difficulty reading but that are in their speaking vocabulary. Write the words on index cards. Read the words and discuss features in words such as beginning sounds, similar rhyming and spelling patterns (e.g., th*an*, f*an*, p*an*), or difficult homophones (their, there, they're). Ask students to sort words according to a specific category such as words having the same spelling patterns or beginning sounds. (See selection on Games for a description of Concept Word Sorts.)

Sight Word Games: Board games provide practice in recognizing and reading sight words and can be played in small groups. Write sight words on a game board with spaces that say "go back one space," "advance two spaces," etc. Laminate the board or cover it with clear contact paper. Words may also be written with a grease pencil and changed as needed (Mercer and Mercer, 1998, p. 351). Add interest to a game board by drawing movie or cartoon characters on certain spaces and beginning and ending squares. Students roll dice, move their marker (colored construction paper shapes or buttons), and read each word. If they cannot read a particular word, they must move back to their original space.

Reinforce sight word recognition and recall by playing Bingo. Make four or five Bingo cards for a small group containing four to six squares across and the same amount down. Write sight words in each square. As each word is read aloud, students locate the word on their card and cover it with a marker (button, colored shape). The winner is the first player to cover all of his or her squares in any direction and successfully read each word.

Strengthen memory and recall by playing Concentration. Write sight words in duplicate on index cards, shuffle the cards, and turn face down on a table. Students turn over two cards to find a correct match. They must correctly read each word as they turn over a card. If the two cards show the same word, the student keeps the cards. The winner is the one with the most cards. Play Concentration with peers, parent volunteers, or support staff.

Reading Fluency

Struggling readers often read slowly, word by word. Their energies are focused on reading words and not on understanding the story. To develop reading fluency, and thus comprehension, provide a selection of easy books for students to read and reread that are on a high instructional or independent reading level (95%–98% word recognition). The following activities provide opportunities for students to hear fluent reading and to practice oral reading in ways that ensure success and develop reading confidence.

- Paired Reading: Pair two students of different reading abilities. The more fluent reader acts as a model for the other student. Each student takes turns reading aloud from material that is suited to his/her reading level. When sitting side by side, the listener follows along in the reading text. After reading a passage, the reader retells what he/she has read. Through retelling, students focus on comprehending and communicating what they have just read in a non-threatening atmosphere (Tierney, Readence, and Dishner, 1990, p. 433).

- Buddy Reading: Two students of similar ability take turns reading the same book in a supportive atmosphere. Students may also read in unison, take turns reading the entire book, or read a different book to each other (Fountas, 1999, p. 17).

- Shared Reading: Write a short passage or poem on chart paper for students to read and reread that is on their instructional level. First read the passage, pointing to each word or phrase, and model fluent reading. Next, ask students to read the passage with you. Direct students' attention to useful visual information. For example, ask students to locate high frequency words. Cover selected words and ask children to predict the word using the surrounding text (Hundley and Powell, 1999, p. 159-160).

- Readers Theater: Students select, practice, and read aloud specific character parts or lines in a story or poem. For example, select parts of the King, Queen, Page, Duke, or Court in *King Bidgood's in the Bathtub* (Audrey and Don Wood). Each part repeats words and rhymes. Also use rhyming and repeated verse in cumulative stories such as *The Gingerbread Boy.*

- Choral Reading: Teachers model fluent reading and then students read selected lines aloud together. Choral reading requires repeated reading of a text, is low anxiety, no failure, and promotes language learning (McCauley and McCauley, 1992). Use poems and picture books that have repeated lines or refrains such as "Rat for Lunch" from Jack Prelutsky's humorous poetry book *a Pizza the size of the Sun* (1994, 1996).

- Sharing Poetry: Students read their favorite short poem to a peer, small group, or classroom. This can be a paired or buddy reading activity or shared with a larger audience. For example, *Sports! Sports! Sports! A Poetry Collection* by Lee Bennett Hopkins (1999) contains short, easy to read poems about a number of sports. "Any Excuse Will Do" (for not making a basket!) (Nikki Grimes, p. 28) has two short sentences and 14 words; "High Dive" by Lee Bennett Hopkins describes the thrill of diving off a high diving board in four short sentences and 16 words. This activity provides opportunities to practice and reread short lines and share great poems.

- Books on Tape: Students hear fluent reading and associate oral vocabulary to printed words by listening to stories and following along in the book. Many books and novels may be purchased with accompanying audio tapes. Ask parent and student volunteers to tape books and follow these guidelines (Mercer and Mercer, 1998): tape in a quiet place; read with expression; take a break every 15 minutes; identify the book title, author and chapters; ring a bell at the end of each page to help students follow along in the story.

Reading Comprehension

Vocabulary Concepts

Students with reading comprehension problems often have difficulty understanding vocabulary. They may know a narrow definition of a word without understanding that some words have multiple meanings (e.g., "board" may mean a piece of wood or to "board" a train), share similar characteristics (synonyms) and categories, or are word opposites (antonyms). Students who do not read often have limited vocabularies and receive low scores on vocabulary tasks.

General suggestions for teaching vocabulary include (Irwin and Baker, 1989, p. 126): teach words that are relevant to students; focus on the use of context clues and word parts (i.e., root words, affixes); limit the number of words you teach; use concrete examples and non examples whenever possible; and provide opportunities to use the words in discussion and in written assignments.

In addition, graphic organizers and matrixes such as Semantic Word Maps (webs), the Frayer Model (Frayer, Frederick, Klausmeir, 1969), and the Semantic Feature Analysis (Johnson and Pearson, 1978) generate discussion, provide examples and non-examples, and provide a visual framework that helps students understand and develop vocabulary concepts.

Semantic Word Maps: illustrate relationships among words. The target word is written in a circle (on chalkboard, chart paper, etc.) with descriptors such as definition, characteristics, and examples extending from the circle. Additional information, such as sentences from the story containing the word, personal definitions, and non-examples may be added, as well. Schwartz and Raphael (1985) suggest including categories (What is it?), characteristics (What is it like?), illustrations (What are some examples?) and comparisons (How are examples the same or different?). Students brainstorm ideas and receive feedback and information as needed. For example, Jason was confused about the meaning of the word "alien." Before reading the short chapter book *Aliens for Dinner* by Stephanie Spinner (1994), a word map generated a good discussion and clarified misconceptions about this word. (See Figure 3–1 on page 50.)

The Frayer Model (Frayer, Frederick, and Klausmeir, 1969): provides middle school and secondary students with different ways to think about the meaning of word concepts (Tierney, Readence, and Dishner, 1990) and develops understanding of content area reading vocabulary. Students form hierarchical word relationships by listing essentials, examples, non-essentials and non-examples of a particular word. For instance, after reading *The Magic School Bus in the Time of the Dinosaurs* (Joanna Cole), a sixth grader and his tutor used this strategy to clarify and classify information about dinosaurs. First, Mark found characteristics that were prevalent in all dinosaurs (essential characteristics) and listed dinosaur names (examples). Next, he discovered differences among the examples (some were plant eaters and others ate meat). Lastly, he included non-examples in his table, i.e., reptiles that were not dinosaurs. Mark referred back to the story to clarify information throughout this process. (See Figure 3–2 on page 50.)

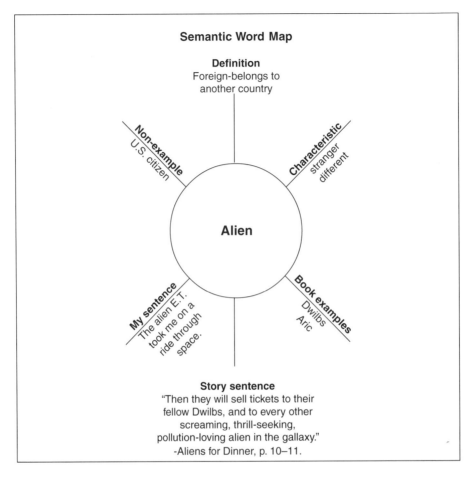

Figure 3–1: Semantic Word Map—*Aliens for Dinner*

DINOSAURS – PREHISTORIC REPTILES	
ESSENTIALS: prehistoric reptiles: backbone, lay eggs, straight legs, walk or run fast	NON-ESSENTIALS: cold-blooded (some may have been warm blooded); eat meat (some eat plants); chew food, hunt in packs
EXAMPLES: brontosaurus, allosaurus, stegosaurus, diplodocus	NON-EXAMPLES: snakes, crocodiles, turtles, lizards

Figure 3-2: Frayer Model—*The Magic School Bus in the Time of the Dinosaurs*

The Semantic Feature Analysis (SFA) (Johnson and Pearson, 1978): develops vocabulary concepts and categorization skills when students find similarities and differences in related words (Tierney, Readence, and Dishner, 1990). This strategy helps students form broader vocabulary concepts and review information by comparing and contrasting words in the same category. For example, in Figure 3-3, a category (dinosaurs) is written above a matrix. Next, words or examples in the category (e.g., names of dinosaurs) are listed vertically in the matrix. Then, features (traits, characteristics) are written horizontally on the matrix. Students study each feature and write (+) if the word contains the feature and (–) if the word does not contain that feature. Janet used this strategy to compare and contrast dinosaurs after reading the *Magic School Bus in the Time of the Dinosaurs* (Joanna Cole). Referring back to the story, the features she selected were size (small and large), eating habits (meat eaters, plant eaters), and time periods (Triassic, Jurassic, Cretaceous). Dinosaurs (vocabulary) included Tyrannosaur, Troodon, Brachiosaurus, Coelophysis, Duckbill, Prosauropod, and Allosaurus.

DINOSAURS							
	Triassic (220m)	Jurassic (213m)	Cretaceous (144m)	Meat Eaters	Plant Eaters	Large	Small
Tyrannosaur	–	–	+	+	–	+	–
Coelophysis	+	–	–	+	–	–	+
Brontosauris	–	+	–	–	+	+	–
Trodan	–	–	+	+	–	–	+
Duckbills	–	–	+	+	–	+	–
Prosauropods	+	–	–	–	+	+	–
Alosaurus	–	+	–	+	–	+	–

m=million years ago

Figure 3–3: Semantic Feature Analysis—
The Magic School Bus in the Time of the Dinosaurs

Text Relationships

Students with comprehension problems often have difficulty sorting out story characters, remembering the setting and understanding how time and place relate to the story, sequencing story events as the story unfolds, identifying the resolution or how the problem or conflict was resolved, and understanding the theme. In addition, students frequently have difficulty identifying relationships that authors use to convey main ideas in fiction and nonfiction writing such as cause/effect, comparison/contrast, and time/order relations.

Graphic organizers such as story maps (also referred to as webs), cause/ effect, description, problem/solution, comparison/contrast, and time line (chronological order) maps, provide a visual/spatial format to help students organize, understand, and remember information. Used before reading, maps provide opportunities for prediction. Used during and after reading, maps generate discussion and provide frameworks for organizing, clarifying, and remembering information. Maps also serve as a prewriting outline from which students organize information to write a paragraph (e.g., use a compare/contrast map to compare and contrast two characters), a summary (use a story map to summarize the story), or an original story (write a mystery story using a problem/solution map).

Story Maps/Chapter Maps: visually represent the elements or parts of a story such as characters, setting, plot, events, resolution, and help readers develop a sense of story (Tierney, Readence, and Dishner, 1990). Story maps are depicted in various ways such as web-like forms or linear displays that include a list of characters, followed by the problem, main events, and resolution. Use a story map before reading and ask students to predict characters and time and place after discussing the story title, book cover, and illustrations. Use maps during and after reading to generate discussion about specific story elements and to help students clarify and review story characters and events. Maps may also represent the action in one chapter. Chapter maps are especially useful when events skip back and forth in time or when a number of events occur in one chapter. For example, in chapter eight of *Hatchet* (Gary Paulsen), Brian battles with a porcupine in the middle of the night and finally discovers how to make a fire. At least five main events occur in this exciting chapter. In Figure 3–4, a chapter map lists characters, describes two settings, identifies the problem, and describes the five main events that occur in the chapter. The *Hatchet* illustration supports the story events and provides students with additional visual clues.

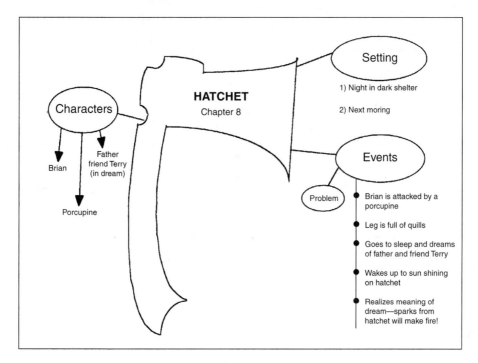

Figure 3–4: Chapter Map—*Hatchet*

Character Maps: describe attributes of story characters and help students identify, sort out, and remember character information that is pertinent to the story. List (or draw) the story title in a center box or circle. Write character's names and descriptions in circles or boxes that extend from the center title. Character maps are especially helpful when stories contain multiple characters, plots, and time lines. In *Holes* by Louis Sachar (1998), four generations of characters weave together to tell a fascinating story of mystery and missing information—created by *holes*—that the reader must fill. See Figure 3-5.

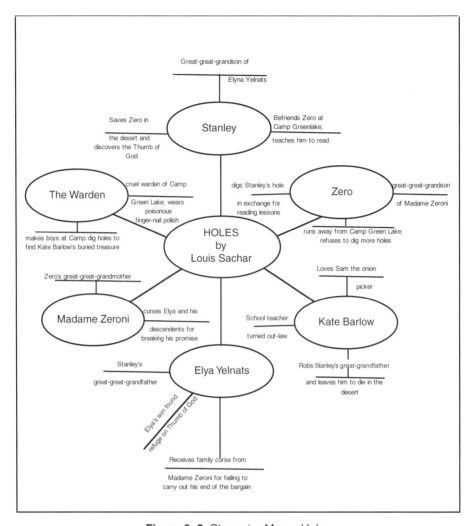

Figure 3–5: Character Map—*Holes*

Description Maps: describe a central character or event. Like a word map, a name or topic is enclosed in a circle with information (characteristics, hopes, fears, accomplishments, relationships, or the 5W's—who, what, when, where, why) extending from it. This map helps students identify and remember important descriptive information. It is especially useful with biographies when authors describe various aspects of an individual's character over the course of the book. In Figure 3-6, a descriptive map captures the characteristics of twelve-year-old Sadako in the biography *Sadako and the Thousand Paper Cranes* by Eleanor Coerr. Book pages are added to support certain information.

Description Map

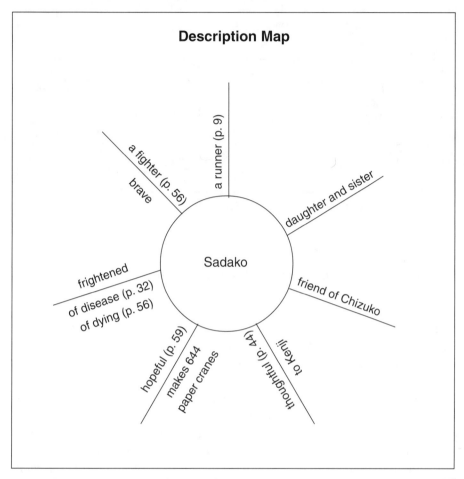

Figure 3–6: Description Map—*Sadako and the Thousand Paper Cranes*

Cause/Effect Maps: represent information that has a causal relationship and help struggling readers understand and follow a chain of events. Cause/effect maps clarify events in content areas such as social studies, history, and science. Authors emphasize cause/effect relationships in narrative text, as well. Words such as *because, while, since, resulting from, consequently* introduce these relationships. The cause/effect map in Figure 3–7 illustrates the chain-like effects of war, disease, illness, and finally, hope, described in *Sadako and the One Thousand Paper Cranes* by Eleanor Coerr.

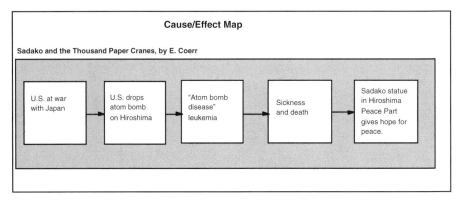

Figure 3–7: Cause/Effect Map—*Sadako and the Thousand Paper Cranes*

Comparison/Contrast Maps: illustrate similarities and differences. Students develop higher-level thinking skills when they compare and contrast information such as illustrations, books, authors, and story elements. When comparing illustrations, students analyze nonverbal information and become more sensitive to the ways in which illustrations support and extend a story and why illustrators use particular materials and styles. Further, students have opportunities to analyze what they see in pictures in addition to what they read. For example, in the Caldecott Award winning book *Smoky Night* (Eve Bunting, 1994) about a fire and riot that forces two neighbors to recognize and appreciate their differences, David Diaz paints in bright acrylics on watercolor paper. He outlines figures in heavy black lines that look like stained glass windows and uses photographs for background, emphasizing textures of materials (beans, burlap, tin, and wallpaper) to portray urban scenes described in the story. His bold, colorful illustrations provide information and insights about urban life in a high-rise.

On the other hand, in *Jumanji* (1981, a Caldecott Medal winning book), Chris Van Allsburg uses only black and white in his surrealistic chalk drawings to tell a suspenseful fantasy about two bored children and a board game that gets out of hand. In Figure 3–8, a Venn Diagram is used to compare the two artists and the ways in which they tell their stories. Van Allsburg's colors (black and white), media (chalk), and style (surrealistic) are listed on the left and Diaz's colors (bright colors), media (acrylics), and style (abstract, stylized) are recorded on the right. Similarities such as an illustrator's supporting theme, emotional appeal, use of shapes, and texture are listed in the middle.

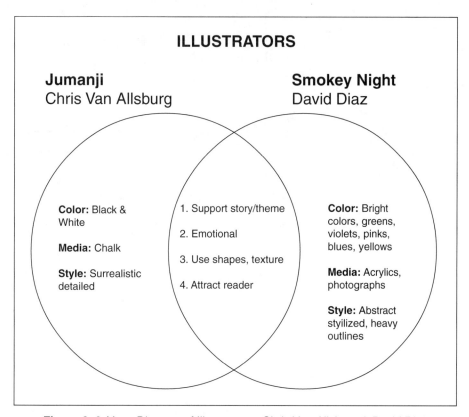

ILLUSTRATORS

Jumanji
Chris Van Allsburg

Smokey Night
David Diaz

Color: Black & White

Media: Chalk

Style: Surrealistic detailed

1. Support story/theme

2. Emotional

3. Use shapes, texture

4. Attract reader

Color: Bright colors, greens, violets, pinks, blues, yellows

Media: Acrylics, photographs

Style: Abstract styilized, heavy outlines

Figure 3–8: Venn Diagram of Illustrators—Chris Van Allsburg & David Diaz

Books with well-developed characters present rich opportunities for analyzing and comparing character traits and behaviors. For example, Figure 3-9 compares the faithful dog Harold to the suspicious cat Chester in the humorous fantasy *Bunnicula* (Deborah and James Howe, 1979). Since the story is told in first person from Harold's point of view, readers must interpret character traits and behaviors from Harold's perspective, as in the following example: *given the fact that Mr. Monroe is an English professor, Chester developed a taste for reading early in life. (I on the other hand, have developed a taste for books. I found "Jonathan Livingston Seagull" particularly delicious)* (p. 18-19). Words for students to look for that signal a comparison include *either, even, but, though, same, different from, however,* and *on the other hand* as used in the prior excerpt from *Bunnicula.*

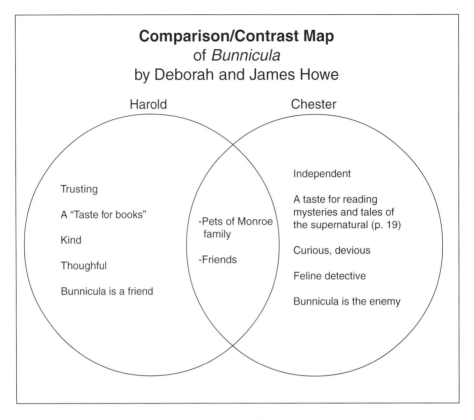

Figure 3–9: Venn Diagram of Characters—*Bunnicula*

Problem/Solution Maps: reflect a single problem or solution or multiple problems and solutions. Problem/solution maps help students identify, sequence, and remember problem/solution relations in narratives (especially mysteries) and informational text (e.g., history—1930 Depression). Like other maps, this graphic organizer can be drawn in various ways. For example, use two separate columns to represent a chain of problems and solutions with arrows extending from the original problem to the solution and back again to the next problem. This model is used to describe Poppleton's problem (dry skin) in this easy chapter book, *Poppleton and Friends* (Cynthia Rylant). As usual, Poppleton's friend, Cherry Sue, comes to the rescue with several solutions that create additional problems. (See Figure 3-10).

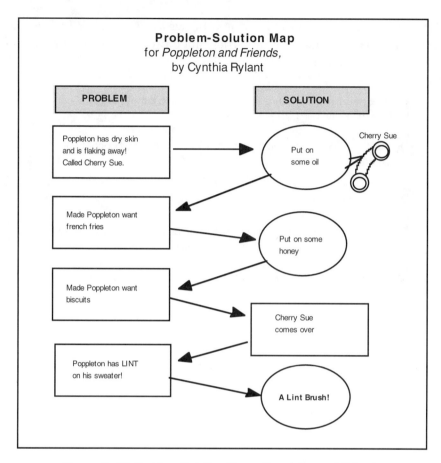

Figure 3–10: Problem/Solution Map—*Poppleton and Friends*

Time Line Maps: illustrate information that reflects a sequence of events or chronological order. Words that signal this organizational structure include *first, second, third, before, after, last, next, o'clock.* Time line maps are especially helpful when comprehension depends on selecting and sequencing important events in biographies, historical fiction books, or content area reading such as history or social studies. Figure 3–11 shows a time line map from the autobiography *Reach Higher* (Scottie Pippen with Greg Brown, 1996).

Inference Skills

Students with reading difficulties often have difficulty making inferences. They are reluctant to make their own interpretations for fear that they may be wrong (Lerner, 1997). Mark, a fourth grader with decoding and comprehension difficulties, would not predict what might happen in the story because he knew he would be wrong. Only after his tutor assured him that he could not be wrong since predictions may or may not come to pass, did Mark venture an opinion.

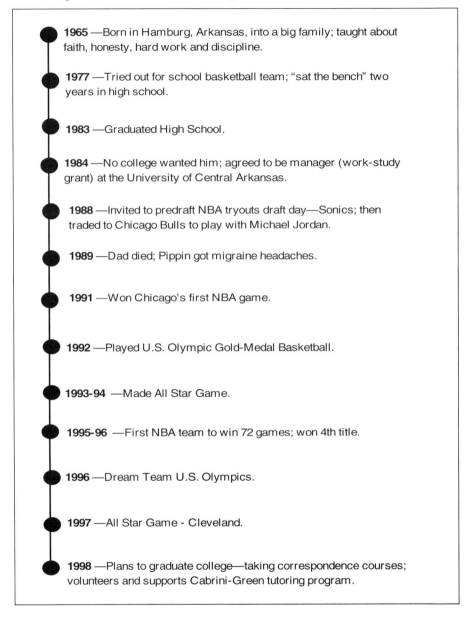

1965 —Born in Hamburg, Arkansas, into a big family; taught about faith, honesty, hard work and discipline.

1977 —Tried out for school basketball team; "sat the bench" two years in high school.

1983 —Graduated High School.

1984 —No college wanted him; agreed to be manager (work-study grant) at the University of Central Arkansas.

1988 —Invited to predraft NBA tryouts draft day—Sonics; then traded to Chicago Bulls to play with Michael Jordan.

1989 —Dad died; Pippin got migraine headaches.

1991 —Won Chicago's first NBA game.

1992 —Played U.S. Olympic Gold-Medal Basketball.

1993-94 —Made All Star Game.

1995-96 —First NBA team to win 72 games; won 4th title.

1996 —Dream Team U.S. Olympics.

1997 —All Star Game - Cleveland.

1998 —Plans to graduate college—taking correspondence courses; volunteers and supports Cabrini-Green tutoring program.

Figure 3-11: Timeline Map – *Reach Higher*

Use the Directed Reading—Thinking Activity (DR-TA) (Stauffer, 1969) to support making predictions. First discuss the story title and cover illustration and ask students to predict what they think the story will be about and why they think so. During appropriate stops in the story, ask students to verify or modify predictions and make new ones based on what has happened in the story. Questions that guide children in examining the evidence, evaluating previous predictions, and generating new ones include: Why did you make your prediction? What do you think now? What do you think will happen next? (Tierney, Readence, and Dishner, 1990, p. 14). Make and modify predictions along with your students and share your reasoning. Predictions cannot be *wrong*, however they can be modified based on discussion, further reading, and new information. Use the same format to encourage children to make predictions when they listen to a story.

Select illustrations that support inferential thinking. Illustrations are integral parts of picture storybooks, and often the artist provides information that is left unsaid, or that must be inferred in the story text. For example, in *Chicken Sunday* (1992), Patricia Pollaco's expressive, watercolor illustrations are filled with visual information that elaborates upon her autobiographical story. In the story two boys throw eggs at Mr. Kodinski's back door as the young author and her two young friends approach the hat shop. Why do neighborhood boys throw eggs at Mr. Kodinski? The text only states that big boys were yelling and pelting eggs at Mr. Kodinski's back door. In order to answer this question, students must connect information contained in illustrations to the story text, and use prior knowledge. Mr. Kodinski says, *all I want to do is live my life in peace* (unpaged). Miss Eula tells the three innocent children that Mr. Kodinski has suffered so much in his life that he deserves more than eggs thrown at him. A subsequent picture of the hat maker and the children having tea depicts the concentration camp identification tattoo on Mr. Kodinski's arm. The illustrations in John Burningham's *Granpa* (1984) support inferential thinking. In this gentle picture book about the loving relationship between a grandfather and granddaughter, a double-page illustration ends the poignant story. There is no text. The illustration on the left page shows the little girl sitting on a chair sadly gazing at her granpa's empty chair, pictured on the right. What happened to granpa? Why can't he come out to play?

Use personal experiences to interpret character behavior. Well-written books with three dimensional characters and good stories that are relevant to the reader provide opportunities for students to interpret character behavior and motivation when they make connections between story events and their own experiences. For example, why did a particular character act this way? Why do you think so? (Find evidence in the story to support your reasoning.) What would you have done? Have you had similar feelings or experiences that might explain a character's behavior? Do you know anyone like the character? Why do you think the author wrote the story? Discussions framed around these types of questions help readers refer back to the text to find evidence for their interpretations and to use and validate their own experiences as well.

Figurative Language

Quality children's literature, from picture storybooks, to novels, to poetry, contains figurative language that conveys meaning, heightens imagery, and provides opportunities for students with reading difficulties to develop abstract thinking skills and to obtain a richer meaning of story. A few examples from many selections described in Part IV that contain similes and metaphors include: *The Girl Who Loved Wild Horses*—Paul Goble (picture book); *James and the Giant Peach*—Roald Dahl (fantasy novel); *Disappearing Acts*—Betsy Byars (mystery novel); and *For the Love of the Game: Michael Jordan and Me*—Eloise Greenfield (poetry). *Amelia Bedelia* stories (Peggy and Henry Parish) and the picture books *A Chocolate Moose for Dinner, The King Who Rained,* and *The Sixteen Hand Horse* (Fred Gwynne) contain humorous examples of how idioms, homonyms, and homophones can be interpreted literally.

Students who have comprehension problems need explicit instruction in order to understand how idioms, similes, and metaphors bring humor and meaning to writing. For example, use concrete objects to represent abstract ideas to help students understand the nature of figurative language. In teaching metaphors, poetry teacher Judith Steinberg (1999) uses a Russian nesting doll that contains smaller dolls and asks fifth graders what else the doll might stand for (e.g., family, generations of women, layers of experience) (pp. 324-331).

Identify metaphors and similes in reading. Teach the vocabulary needed to comprehend the selected phrase and discuss how the comparison conveys meaning (Irwin and Baker, 1989, pp. 97-98). Urban sixth graders were enthusiastically reading *Bridge to Terabithia* (Katherine Paterson), but were confused when the author compares Jess's feelings toward his friend's father with having a canker sore: *Jess's feelings about Leslie's father poked up like a canker sore. You keep biting it, and it gets bigger and worse instead of better. You spend a lot of time trying to keep your teeth away from it. Then sure as Christmas you forget the silly thing and chomp right down on it. Lord, that man got in his way* (p. 78). Many students knew what0 canker sore felt like but did not know what they were called. After the teacher explained what a canker sore was, students energetically described them, what they felt like, and why the author used this descriptive comparison (Williams and Trotter, 1998, p. 8-13)!

Finally, generate enthusiasm for using figurative language. Use idioms and figurative language yourself and ask students to tell you what you really mean. Discuss why people use idioms. Illustrate idioms, create a dictionary of favorite idioms, act out idioms (playing Charades), and use idioms, similes, and metaphors in writing (Irwin and Baker, 1989, p. 98).

Mental Imagery

Making mental pictures facilitates memory (Deshler, Ellis, Lenz, 1996) and helps students comprehend what they have read (Gambrello and Jawitz, 1993). Ask children to picture in their minds how certain characters look, sound, and act. Use descriptive text as in the following passage from the Newbery Award winning novel *Holes* by Louis Sachar (1998): *The shovel felt heavy in Stanley's soft, fleshy hands. He tried to jam it into the earth, but the blade banged against the ground and bounced off without making a dent. The vibrations ran up the shaft of the shovel and into Stanley's wrists, making his bones rattle (p. 26).* Ask students to visualize how Stanley looked and how he felt. What words did the author use to convey visual images (e.g., *soft, fleshy*) and sound images (*banged, vibrations, bones rattle*). Share your own images and describe how seeing characters in your mind helps you remember the story.

Higher-Level Questions

Rich responses to literature involve asking the right questions, creating an environment where conversation is welcome, allowing students the time to articulate their thoughts out loud, and encouraging and accepting diverse responses (Lehr, 1994, p. 18). Students with reading difficulties need many opportunities to engage in meaningful conversations that develop higher-level thinking skills and to feel safe in doing so. Frequently, it is in these areas such as making inferences, forming comparisons, evaluating and extending what they read, that they have difficulty. Reading and listening to good stories present numerous opportunities for students to recall facts, make inferences, discuss figurative language, evaluate and compare characters, and extend story. Discuss a variety of questions that require students to use background experiences and story information to validate their response. Encourage students to ask questions themselves and to formulate questions for peers to answer. The following questions based on the fantasy *Bunnicula* (Deborah and James Howe) range from factual questions (texturally explicit) to those requiring inference and evaluation (textually implicit) and creative (or applied) thinking.

- What did the rabbit look like? Is there proof that he looked like a Vampire? Find it and read it. (detail)
- Why do you think Harold liked Bunnicula? Support your answer by finding references in the story. Why did Chester think Bunnicula was a vampire? (inference—making connections in text)

- What makes the story a fantasy? (differentiating between realistic fiction and fantasy)

- What does Chester mean when he says, *This is larger than the two of us* (p. 82). (figurative language)

- What happened to Harold's nose when it *"suddenly and involuntarily closed . . ."* (p. 65). (vocabulary meaning, root word, and prefix)

- Do you think that the authors made the characters believable? Why? (evaluative/background experience—has student had experiences with a cat or dog to help them evaluate the authenticity of the book characters?)

- What passage or part did you like? Why? (evaluative)

- Did anything bother you about the story? (evaluative)

- How would you write a sequel? For example, would Chester finally "get" Bunnicula? (extending story/creative thinking)

Modeling and Self-Monitoring

When teachers "think aloud," they verbally describe and model their own thinking processes as they construct meaning from text. This strategy provides explicit examples for readers to follow as they see teachers model different strategies used to attain meaning from what they read. Share a good story like Cynthia Rylant's Newbery Honor book, *A Fine White Dust*. Read aloud this gripping story and stop at appropriate places to discuss the story, share your thinking processes, and encourage students to do likewise. For example, make predictions, develop images, link story information to prior knowledge, and describe strategies that you use to read unfamiliar words.

- Make Predictions—I think Pete will leave home because Rufus said he would take care of Pete's parents. It doesn't seem like there is anybody left to stop Pete. What do you think he will do?

- Develop Images—If I try to see the character in my mind I will remember him better. I think the Preacher Man looks like a small, agile man that can work a crowd and that has blue eyes that change from warm and welcoming to hard and cold. He has a smile that can be soft and genuine or cruel and mean-looking. He is like a chameleon, he changes. What pictures do you have of the Preacher Man? What do you think he looks like?

- Link Story Information to Prior Knowledge—I wonder if Pete will leave home? I think that if Pete does leave home he will come back because he loves and cares about his parents. When you care about someone you want to see that they are all right. What do you think?

- Identify Unfamiliar Words—What is the word "revival?" The sentence does not give me enough information to predict what the word is. I'll try the V/CV syllable rule, when I see a single consonant (/v/) between two vowels (/e/, /i/) I'll first try to divide the word after the vowel and before the consonant (re/vi/val). Does that sound right and make sense in the context? Yes, it does. (See Word Identification.) Are there other strategies I could have used?

In addition to modeling comprehension strategies, it is important to provide opportunities for students to use and internalize them during meaningful reading situations. One way to do this is to develop a self-monitoring checklist that includes word identification and comprehension strategies that have been modeled and discussed in class. Language arts resource teacher Kathy Quick (1999) uses a "think along self-monitoring sheet" (adapted from Glazer's self-monitoring strategies, 1992) for 4th grade reluctant readers to use during literature study groups. After students read aloud portions of a chapter, they check and discuss strategies on the self-monitoring sheet (strategies that have been modeled and discussed in class) that have helped them to understand the story. Strategies listed on the sheet include predicting (before and during reading), asking oneself questions, visualizing, making analogies (e.g., this reminds me of), rereading, reviewing the 5 W's (who, what, when, where, why), and summarizing after reading. Word identification strategies include rereading (before clues, reading ahead (after clues), sounding out letters, looking for word parts, substituting a word, using a dictionary, and asking someone for assistance. By using the self-monitoring sheet, students share and compare comprehension strategies they use while discussing and enjoying good stories (p. 81-84).

A Process for Writing

Students with reading difficulties often have problems expressing themselves in writing. Most dislike writing. Some students have difficulty forming legible letters. Many have difficulty spelling and only write words that they can spell—their effort is directed toward avoiding spelling errors rather than in expressing what they want to say. When spelling mechanics dominate and words are not allowed to flow freely, content suffers (Graves, 1983, p. 194).

When students have opportunities to brainstorm and organize ideas, write a draft, and then revise and edit their writing, they concentrate first on meaning and then on spelling, grammar, and punctuation. Further, researchers find that teacher modeling and collaborative editing facilitate the independent writing skills of students with difficulties in written expression (Hallenbeck, 1996; Gover and Englert, 1998). Teacher modeling and peer editing are part of a writing process framework that includes planning (brainstorming and organizing ideas), drafting, revising, and editing. Using correct spelling, grammar, and punctuation, all important skills and stumbling blocks for many writers, are addressed *after* students have opportunities to transfer their thoughts to paper. This framework includes:

- Planning—sketching, brainstorming ideas, outlining, using graphic organizers to organize main ideas and details.
- Drafting—putting thoughts down on paper.
- Revising—focusing on meaning (e.g., rereading, getting input from others, adding, deleting, rearranging material).
- Editing—correcting spelling and punctuation.
- Publishing—presenting final work (e.g., making a book, displaying story on wall).

The process writing framework is especially beneficial for students that have written language problems since it helps students focus first on planning and transferring thoughts to paper, and then on spelling, punctuation, and grammar. For example, this approach enabled Joel to successfully write his own story based on the wordless picture book *Tuesday* by David Wiesner. Joel, a third grader, was receiving reading support to strengthen areas in reading decoding, spelling, and written formulation. Together, he and his tutor wrote their own story based on the picture book theme—the invasion of animals on Tuesday. First they drew a map that included their story titles in a middle circle and wrote specific times (e.g., 8:00 p.m., 11:21 p.m., 4:38 a.m.) on lines extending from the circle that were noted in Wiesner's story. Then they brainstormed and jotted down events that occurred at each specific time, such as, at 8:00 p.m. ten fat, happy pigs floated through the air and landed in downtown Chicago and at 11:21 they invaded the Sears Tower. Next they wrote drafts and exchanged their stories for each other to read and comment on. By writing and sharing her draft, the tutor modeled how receiving and incorporating feedback were integral parts of her writing as well. Finally, each concentrated on proofreading and editing. Proofreading is an important step that many students omit. Joel circled spelling and punctuation errors that he could identify and correct. The tutor helped Joel correct the remaining errors. Reoccurring errors in spelling and grammar, such as *there* and *their,* and run-on sentences were addressed in subsequent instruction. Joel typed his revised story on the computer, illustrated it, and proudly displayed it in the reading lab. Success, success, success! No red marks and a story to be proud of.

Writing Activities

Writing activities such as creating ABC books and stories to wordless picture books and picture storybooks encourage creativity, a personal response, and provide authentic writing experiences. Using rhyming patterns to write humorous poetry reinforces phonics and supports written expression. Describing story characters in bio-poems, acrostic poems, and cinquain poetry provides students with a structure for writing and strengthens reading comprehension. For example, write and illustrate an ABC book. Model your book after *NBA Action from A to Z* (James Preller) or write a National League ABC book using baseball information (players, plays, teams, clothes). Read *Eating the Alphabet: Fruits & Vegetables From A to Z* (Lois Ehlert) and use ice cream flavors. Read *Antics! An Alphabetical Anthology* (Cathi Hepworth) and create and illustrate words from A to Z that contain the word pattern *ant* or some other word pattern. Create your own personal ABC book and illustrate each letter and picture association.

Select wordless story picture books like *Tuesday* and *Free Fall* by David Wiesner or *The Mysteries of Harris Burdick* by Chris Van Allsburg and write a story to accompany the illustrations. Select a picture storybook illustrated by a favorite artist and write a story to accompany the drawings. Then compare your story to the original text. Marie, a fifth grader who needed reading support, was mesmerized by David Delamare's detailed paintings in the Hans Christian Andersen fantasy, *The Steadfast Tin Soldier* (retold by Katie Campbell). She studied the moving, realistic paintings of the paper ballet dancer and the one-legged soldier and wrote her own story, using the illustrations as prompts. Then she listened to the story on tape while following along in the text and compared her version to Andersen's fantasy.

Write a humorous poem using phonic patterns in rhyming picture books and poetry selections. For example, read Shel Silverstein's *Sick* (p. 58, *Where The Sidewalk Ends)* and use the short vowel pattern *ump* (mumps, bumps, lumps) and long vowel patterns *ay* (today, say, nay, play), *ue* (blue, flue, Sue), and *oke* (choke, broke, wrote, note) to write about "Sue's Sick School Day."

Write poetry that adheres to certain guidelines. Bio-poems, acrostic poems, and cinquain poems provide a framework from which students can organize their thoughts and produce a poem of their own. The bio-poem describes a person's life (or book character) by noting characteristics, feelings, experiences, and accomplishments. This poem follows this format:

Line 1)   First name
Line 2)   Three or four adjectives that describe the person
Line 3)   Important relationship (daughter, father)
Line 4)   Two or three things, people, or ideas that the person loves
Line 5)   Three feelings the person experiences
Line 6)   Three fears the person experiences
Line 7)   Accomplishment

Line 8)   Two or three things the person wants to see happen or wants to experience

Line 9)   His or her residence

Line 10) Last name

Writing bio-poems about specific characters enhances reading comprehension. When students write about a book character they identify feelings and significant events that the character experiences. Mark, a junior high school student receiving reading support, wrote a bio-poem about Brian Robeson, the main character in *Hatchet*. Mark referred back to the story to review and select information that he wanted to include in his poem. For his final copy, he used different computer fonts to highlight Brian's fears and desires. (See Figure 3–12.)

BIO-POEM ON BRIAN ROBESON

Brian
Motivated, brave, and smart
Friend of Terry
BIKING, HAMBURGERS, THANKSGIVING DINNER
He felt lonely, depressed, and frightened
HE FEARED CRASHING, SEEING THE BEAR, AND SEEING HIS MOM IN THE CAR WITH ANOTHER GUY
His accomplishments were landing the plane and not dying
He wanted to see his parents back together again, wanted to find food, and wanted people to rescue him
Hampton, New York
Robeson

Figure 3–12: Bio-Poem—*Hatchet*

The acrostic poem uses the letters of one's name or the name of another person, place, or thing as the initial letters of a word for each line.
Each line tells something significant about the person, place or thing. A
variation is to put the name vertically into the middle of the poem. Christine, a student receiving reading support, used both forms to describe her
feelings about music:

> **M** alarchy
> **U** seless
> **S** tupid
> **I** cky
> **C** razy

> Music is a bunch of **M**alarchy,
> It is so **U**seless
> And very **S**tupid.
> Plus, the teacher is **I**cky
> And very **C**razy.

The cinquain poem is a five-line poem that uses descriptive words to
portray a person, place, or thing. This format includes:

Line 1)   One word for the title

Line 2)   Two words that describe the title

Line 3)   Three words that express action related to the title

Line 4)   Four words that express a feeling about the title

Line 5)   One word that either repeats the title or expresses a word
          closely related to the title

Keith, a fifth grader receiving reading and spelling support, used this
form to describe his best friend Luis. He centered his poem on the computer and used the bold type to emphasize his feelings.

Luis

Nice, Playful

Laughing, Massaging, Helping

Luis Took Me Out.

Commanding, Annoying, Pestering

Not Mean.

Using form poetry encouraged writing and boosted the self-confidence
of all three students. It provided a framework for organizing thoughts and

expressing feelings about story characters (Mark's bio-poem), friends (Keith's best friend), and a school subject (Christine's music poem). Most importantly, students were successful and felt good about their writing and themselves.

Art and Drama

Many students who have difficulty reading enjoy and excel in art and drama. Further, art and drama extensions to literature bring meaning and enjoyment to reading. The following activities provide opportunities for individual expression, creativity, and support reading comprehension.

Art Extensions

- Study the media used by a favorite illustrator and use the same materials to illustrate a scene or design a book cover. For example, arrange and glue cut-out pieces of tissue paper in a collage design. Add paint if you like. (See picture books by Eric Carle and Ezra Jack Keats.)

- Use your own media and style to illustrate a favorite part. Include information that is not found in the text.

- Sketch to Sketch Strategy (Harste, Short, Burke, 1988). Get in small groups. After reading a selection, draw a sketch of what the selection meant to them. Each artist shares their drawing with the group. After group members share their interpretation of the drawing, the artist shares his interpretation. This strategy helps students realize that meaning can be created in many communication systems (p. 353).

- Illustrate clues in a mystery book. Use pictures to indicate a person, place, or thing and arrows to show a progression of events. (See *Felicity Snell Mysteries* by E.W. Hildick. The book is full of picture clues that support sequencing information.)

- Make simple puppets (staple cardboard figures to sticks/tongue depressors or make paper bag puppets) to represent characters in rhyming, cumulative stories and act out the stories. (Use folktales like *The Gingerbread Man* and *The Three Billy Goats Gruff,* and other cumulative stories such as *The Napping House* by Audrey and Don Wood.)

- Design character masks to wear for Readers Theatre.

- Illustrate stories in a can. Cut a strip of paper 1/2 inch narrower than the diameter of the lid and at least 12 inches long. Use a coffee can and plastic lid. Divide the story strip into several sections to depict the title page and to illustrate major events from the story. Leave a 3 inch blank at each end of the strip. Insert the story strip into the can with the conclusion on the bottom. Cut a straight vertical slit slightly wider than the story strip in the plastic lid. Carefully pull the strip through the slit and share your story. (Good for strengthening sequencing skills.)

Drama Extensions

• Participate in Readers Theater Practice, read, and perform short story parts from a script. Use picture storybooks, short chapter books, and novels that contain dialogue. The narrator's role reads non-dialogue lines. For instance, the easy chapter book *Poppleton and Friends,* by Cynthia Rylant, contains three short stories with simple and clever dialogue by Poppleton (the pig), Sherry Sue (the llama), and Hudson (the mouse). Chapter 12 of *How to Eat Fried Worms,* a short novel by Thomas Rockwell, contains hilarious dialogue by Billy, Allen, and Joe, as the two boys watch Billy choke down his fifth worm.

• Act out a favorite part from a story. Select a favorite event or chapter and take the role of a particular character. Peers guess the book, event, or character.

• Play Charades and act out literal interpretations of idioms. Teams score points when they correctly identify the actual meaning of the idiom. Use concrete objects when possible, such as a button to act out "Button your lip." (Irwin and Baker, 1989, p. 98).

• Improvise new situations. Create a new situation based on a story and use your imagination to play it out (Huck, Hepler, Hickman, and Kiefer, 1997, p. 691). Explore different points of view, expand secondary characters, or extend and create new situations for primary characters.

Games

Literacy skills develop through practice. Games provide opportunities for struggling readers to practice skills in an enjoyable way. Most skills can be reinforced in a game format. For example, reinforce sight words and reading vocabulary by playing Word Board Games, Bingo, and Concentration, described earlier in this section. Also use commercial games like Boggle and Scrabble.

Crossword Puzzles reinforce vocabulary words, reading comprehension, and spelling. Select seven or eight words that you want to emphasize or that have significance to the story. Write single words or short phrases below the puzzle that describe each word and that corresponds to word squares. To provide additional clues add beginning letter sounds (also blends and digraphs) to the crossword puzzle. Use graph paper and let students develop their own crossword puzzles. In Figure 3–13, the crossword puzzle from the fantasy *Bunnicula* includes adjectives and nouns such as *tranquil, quiver, imagination, garlic, rabbit, fangs,* and *shot* (as in vaccination). The crossword puzzle in Figure 3–14 includes the following vocabulary from *Stone Fox* (John Reynolds Gardiner): *treacherous, thumping, potatoes, taxes, amateur, property.*

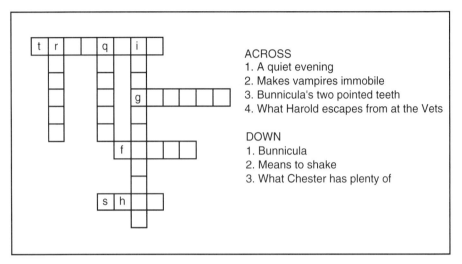

ACROSS
1. A quiet evening
2. Makes vampires immobile
3. Bunnicula's two pointed teeth
4. What Harold escapes from at the Vets

DOWN
1. Bunnicula
2. Means to shake
3. What Chester has plenty of

Figure 3–13: Crossword Puzzle with Clues—*Bunnicula*

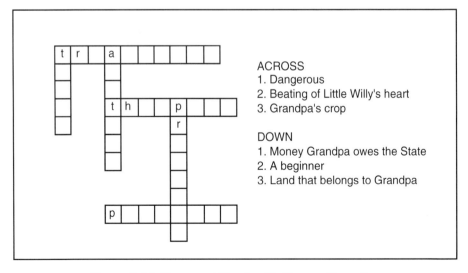

ACROSS
1. Dangerous
2. Beating of Little Willy's heart
3. Grandpa's crop

DOWN
1. Money Grandpa owes the State
2. A beginner
3. Land that belongs to Grandpa

Figure 3–14: Crossword Puzzle with Clues—*Stone Fox*

Concept Word Sorts help students develop comprehension and critical thinking in content area instruction (Zutell, 1999). Write 10 to 15 words on separate index cards. Ask students to sort the words into different piles, depending on some feature the words share. For example, after reading *The Magic School Bus in the Time of the Dinosaurs* (Joanna Cole) use names of dinosaurs, time periods (Jurassic), adjectives (small and light, eats meat, eats plants), and reptiles of today. Instruct children to sort the words into groups and describe their rationale for placing a word in a specific group. Teachers can choose the categories for sorting words (i.e., closed sort) or students can choose their own categories for sorting (i.e., open sort). When students form their own categories, fellow classmates try to guess why words are grouped in certain ways. Zutell (1999) notes that when students form their own categories they have a greater sense of control over their own learning and teachers gain valuable insights by observing how children think and categorize words (p. 108).

Synonym/Antonym Word Games provide practice in expanding vocabulary concepts. Select words from books that students are reading and write the words on index cards. Students select a card, read the word, and supply an antonym (or synonym). Use as a board game or card game. Add homonyms, idioms (e.g., *Amelia Bedelia* books) and similes and metaphors, depending on the particular book, style of author, and classroom instruction.

The Comprehension Game (Mercer and Mercer, 1998, p. 552) reinforces skills relating to vocabulary, story comprehension, and synonyms. Make a game board with red, blue, or white squares and cut out cards of red, blue, and white construction paper. On the set of red cards write story questions pertaining to *who, what, when, why, where, how* questions; on the blue set write vocabulary words; on the white cards (synonym cards) write a sentence with a word underlined. Players roll the dice (or spinner), go to the numbered square, and select a card that represents that color. If it is red students answer a story question, blue a vocabulary question, and white, provide a synonym to the underlined word. If students are correct they stay on the square. If they are incorrect they go back to the Start. Other players decide whether each task is answered correctly, referring back to the story if necessary.

Story Jumble provides practice in sequencing a story. Cut a short story that is at a student's independent reading level into parts (setting, events, endings), paragraphs, or sentences. Write segments on an index card. Students read each card and arrange them to make the story make sense (Bos and Vaughn, 1994). Modify this activity by using picture storybooks, short chapter books, and novels. After reading a story, write five or six major events that occurred on sentence strips. Ask students to arrange the strips in the correct sequence and then read the sentences. Students can also brainstorm important events and write them on index cards for other peers to sequence.

Who Am I? Select a favorite book character to represent and provide classmates with a description of your character. For example, represent Stanley Yelnats (*Holes* by Louis Sachar) and say, "My family has been cursed for four generations and I dig holes in the desert." Only questions that can be answered by a Yes or No are allowed.

References

Adams, M.J. (1990). *Beginning to read: Thinking and learning about print.* Cambridge, MA: MIT Press.

Bos, C. and Vaughn, S. (1994). *Strategies for teaching students with learning and behavior problems.* Needham Heights, MA: Allyn and Bacon.

Brady, S. and Moats, L. (1997). *Informed instruction for reading success: Foundations for teacher preparation.* A position paper of the International Dyslexia Association. Baltimore: The International Dyslexia Association.

Cunningham, P. (1995, 1999). *Phonics they use: Words for reading and writing* (2ⁿᵈ ed.). New York: HarperCollins College Publishers.

Deshler, D., Ellis, E., and Lenz, B. (1996). *Teaching adolescents with learning disabilities.* Denver: Love Publishing Company.

Dombey, H. and Moustafa, M. (1998). *Whole to part phonics.* Portsmouth, NH: Heinemann.

Dolch, E. (1936). A basic sight vocabulary. *Elementary School Journal, 36,* 456-460.

Durkin, D. (1981, 1976). *Strategies for identifying words* (2nd ed.). Boston: Allyn and Bacon.

Fountas, I. (1999). Word matters: a curriculum for helping children become word solvers. In I. Fountas and G.S. Pinnel (Eds.) *Voices on word matters* (p. 17). Portsmouth, NH: Heinemann.

Frayer, D., Frederick, W., and Klausmeier, H. (1969). A schema for testing the level of concept mastery. (Technical report No. 16). Madison, WI: University of Wisconsin Research Development Center for Cognitive Learning.

Fry, E.B., Kress, J.E., and Fountoukidis, D.L. (1993). *The reading teacher's book of lists* (3rd ed.). Englewood Cliffs, NJ: Prentice Hall.

Gambrell, L., and Jawitz, P. (1993). Mental imagery, text illustrations, and children's story comprehension and recall. *Reading Research Quarterly, 28,* 264-273.

Glazer, S.M. (1992). *Reading comprehension: Self-monitoring strategies to develop independent readers.* New York: Scholastic Professional Books.

Graves, D. (1983). *Writing: Teachers and children* at *work.* Portsmouth, NH: Heinemann Educational Books.

Grover, M. and Englert, C. (1998). Orchestrating the thought and learning of struggling writers. *Center for the Improvement of Early Reading Achievement.* Ann Arbor: University of Michigan.

Hall, D. and Cunningham, P. (1999). Multilevel word study: word charts, word walls, and word sorts. In I. Fountas and G.S. Pinnell (Eds.) *Voices on word matters* (pp. 114–130). Portsmouth, NH: Heinemann.

Hallenbeck, M. (1996). The cognitive strategy in writing: Welcome relief for adolescents with learning disabilities. *Learning Disabilities Research & Practice, 11,* 107–119.

Harste, J., Short, K, and Burke, C. (1988). *Creating classrooms for authors: The reading-writing connection.* Portsmouth, NH: Heinemann.

Hundley, S. and Powell, D. (1999). Investigating letters and words through shared reading. In I. Fountas and G.S. Pinnel (Eds.) *Voices on word matters* (pp. 159–160). Portsmouth, NH: Heinemann.

Huck, C., Hepler, S., Hickman, J., and Kiefer, B. (1997). Children's literature in the elementary school (6th ed.). Madison, WI: Brown and Benchmarks Publishers.

Irwin, J. and Baker, I. (1989). *Promoting active reading comprehension strategies: A resource book for teachers.* Englewood Cliffs, NJ: Prentice Hall.

Johnson, D. and Pearson, P. (1978). *Teaching reading vocabulary.* New York: Holt, Rinehart and Winston.

Lehr, S. (1994). Conversations with children: Extending oral and written response to literature. In J. Hickman, B.E. Cullinan, and S. Hepler (Eds.). *Children's literature in the classroom: Extending Charlotte's Web* (pp. 17-34). Norwood, MA: Christopher-Gordon.

Lerner, J. (1997). *Learning disabilities: Theories, diagnosis and teaching strategies* (7th ed.). New York: Houghton Mifflin.

MaCauley, J. and McCauley, D. (1992). Using choral reading to promote language learning for ESL students. *The Reading Teacher, 45,* 526-533.

Mercer, C. and Mercer, A. (1998). *Teaching students with learning problems.* Upper Saddle River, NJ: Merrill, an imprint of Prentice Hall.

Quick, K. (1999). "I see my father's face . . .": Teaching comprehension strategies through literature study. *The New Advocate, 12,* 81-84.

Schwartz, R. and Raphael, T. (1985). Concept of definition: A key to improving students' vocabulary. *The Reading Teacher, 39,* 198-205.

Stauffer, R. (1969). *Directing reading maturity as a cognitive process.* New York: Harper and Row.

Steinbergh, J. (1999). Mastering metaphor through poetry. *Language Arts, 76,* 324-331.

Torgesen, J., and Wagner, R. (1999). Alternative diagnostic approaches for specific developmental reading disabilities. *Learning Disabilities Research & Practice, 13 (4),* 220-232.

Tierney, R., Readence, J., and Dishner, E. (1990). *Reading strategies and practices: A compendium*. Needham Heights, MA: Allyn and Bacon.

Williams, N. and Trotter, G. (1998). Urban sixth graders build bridges to Terabithia. *Illinois Reading Council Journal, 26,* 8–13.

Zutell, J. (1999). Sorting it out through word sorts. In I. Fountas and G.S. Pinnell (Eds.) *Voices on word matters* (pp. 103–113). Portsmouth, NH: Heinemann.

Children's Book Titles

A Fine White Dust by Cynthia Rylant (1986). New York: Simon and Schuster Children's Books.

A Pizza the Size of the Sun poems by Jack Prelutsky (1994, 1996). New York: Greenwillow Books.

Aliens for Dinner by Stephanie Sprinner (1994). New York: Random House.

Antics by Cathi Hepworth (1992). New York: G.P. Putnam's Sons, a division of Putnam and Grosset Book Group.

Bunnicula by Deborah and James Howe (1979). New York: Atheneum.

Chicken Sunday by Patricia Polacco (1992). New York: Putnam & Grosset Group.

Eating the Alphabet: Fruits and Vegetables from A to Z by Lois Ehlert (1989). New York: Harcourt Brace & Company.

Granpa by John Burningham (1984). New York: Dragonfly Books, Crown Publishers, Inc.

Green Eggs and Ham by Dr. Seuss (1960). New York: Random House.

Hatchet by Gary Paulsen (1987). New York: Penguin Group.

Holes by Louis Sachar (1998). New York: Frances Foster Books, Farrar, Straus and Giroux.

How to Eat Fried Worms by Thomas Rockwell (1973). New York: Dell Publishing.

Jumanji by Chris Van Allsburg (1981). Boston: Houghton Mifflin.

King Bidgood's in the Bathtub by Audrey and Don Wood (1985). Orlando: Harcourt Brace Jovanovich.

Maniac Magee by Jerry Spinelli (1990). Boston: Little Brown and Company.

NBA Action from A to Z by James Preller (1997). New York: Scholastic.

Poppleton and Friends by Cynthia Rylant (1997). New York: Sky Blue Press, an imprint of Scholastic.

Sadako and the One Thousand Paper Cranes by Eleanor Coerr (1977). New York: Bantam Doubleday Dell.

Sports! Sports! Sports! A Poetry Collection by Lee Bennett Hopkins (1999). New York: HarperCollins.

Smoky Night by Eve Bunting (1994). San Diego: Harcourt Brace & Company.

Stone Fox by John Reynolds Gardiner (1980). New York: Harper Trophy, a division of HarperCollins.

The Magic School Bus in the Time of the Dinosaurs by Joanna Cole (1994). New York: Scholastic.

The Mysteries of Harris Burdick by Chris Van Allsburg (1984). Boston: Houghton Mifflin.

The Snowy Day by Ezra Jack Keats (1962). New York: Viking Press.

The Steadfast Tin Soldier by Hans Christian Andersen, retold by Katie Campbell (1990). Morris Plains, NJ: The Unicorn Publishing Company.

Tuesday by David Wiesner (1991). Boston: Houghton Mifflin.

Where the Sidewalk Ends by Shel Silverstein (1974). New York: Harper and Row.

Part IV
Book Listings
and Analysis

This section describes a representative sampling of quality children's literature. Each selection includes a brief synopsis, an estimated reading grade level (where appropriate) and interest grade level, lists of books by the same author, and learning opportunities specific to each selection. Reading levels are not indicated (NA) for poetry, wordless picture books, or for picture books containing few words or sentences. Categories include picture books, easy reading books and short chapter books, novels, poetry, and nonfiction (biography and information books). Book titles appear alphabetically according to genre (e.g., picture books). Math picture books are included under nonfiction because of the informational content. For an easy reference to this section, a complete list of book titles by genre is presented in Appendix C. A subject list of literature selections (e.g., math/science) can be found in Appendix B. This is not an inclusive list by any means, but rather, selections of children's literature that are written and illustrated by respected writers and artists and that provide enjoyment and learning opportunities for students with reading difficulties.

Picture Books
Books with Rhyming Words, Repeated Phrases, and Cumulative Stories

Title: *Alexander and the Terrible, Horrible, No Good, Very Bad Day* by Judith Viorst, illustrated by R. Cruz (1972). New York: Atheneum, Macmillan Publishing.

Genre: fiction

Reading Level: 2

Interest Level: primary

Synopsis: Alexander's day reminds all readers of how bad a day can go! From gum in his hair, singing too loud in school and making a mistake during counting time, to having a cavity and making a mess in his dad's office, Alexander's troubles multiply as the sun goes down. The catchy phrase in the title is repeated seven times in the book. The clever, black and white pictures are tied closely to the text, illustrating Alexander's bad luck from morning until night.

Learning Opportunities: Read the story and have students chime in when they hear the familiar phrase that describes Alexander's day. Write the main events of Alexander's day on sentence strips for students to arrange in the correct order and reread (e.g., breakfast, car pool, singing time, the trip to the dentist, dinner time, and bed time). Students write about their own terrible day, beginning with breakfast, preceding to school, after school, and finally evening, ending each episode with the repeated refrain. For students that feel more comfortable with writing prompts, write the repetitive phrase after a specific event (e.g., eating breakfast, during recess, after school) and ask students to complete each sentence.

By the Same Author: *Alexander, Who Used to be Rich Last Sunday; Absolutely Positively Alexander: The Complete Stories; Alexander Who's Not (Do You Hear Me? I Mean It!) Going to Move; The Tenth Good Thing about Barney.*

Title: *Are You My Mother?* by P. D. Eastman (1960, 1988). New York: Random House.

Genre: fantasy

Reading Level: low 1

Interest Level: kindergarten–primary

Synopsis: Short sentences and comical illustrations tell the story about a little bird who falls out of his nest and searches for his mother. Sight vocabulary words are repeated as the little bird approaches first a kitten, then a hen, dog, cow, car, boat, plane, and bull dozer (i.e., a snort), asking each in turn, if she is his mother.

Learning Opportunities: Read and reread the story. Use phonics, context, and picture clues to predict unfamiliar words. Write selected sight words on cards and sort according to short vowels (dog, hen, big, kitten, not, but, went, egg, ran) and long vowels (she, be, plane, fly, my, see, cat, came, home, tree). Review sight vocabulary by playing games such as Concentration and Bingo. Use the book as a LEA: retell the story, write it on a wall chart, and reread. Then circle and read target sight words such as *said*, *thing, are, then.* Cut apart the sentences, mix, and arrange the sentence strips in the correct order.

By the Same Author: *Go, Dog. Go!; Corre, Perro, Corre!; Big Dog . . . Little Dog.*

Title: *Bears in the Night* by Stan and Jan Berenstain (1971, 1987). New York: Random House.

Genre: fantasy

Interest Level: kindergarten–primary

Synopsis: After being tucked in bed, seven little bears crawl out of bed and out of the window when they hear a mysterious *Whooooo.* Spatial words and three word phrases are accompanied by humorous cartoon illustrations depicting the bears going *out, down, over, under, around, between, through, and up* Spook Hill. They quickly retrace their steps when confronted by a big owl. This book contains all short phrases and one sentence at the end of the story when the frightened bears tumble back into the window. Spatial words are repeated (with illustrations) throughout the story.

Learning Opportunities: Echo read and reread the story. Write spatial words on the chalkboard, wall chart, or on index cards. Reinforce spatial words in three dimensional and then two dimensional space. For example, ask students to put one hand *in, over, under* the other hand; raise one hand *up,* move the same hand *down,* put their arm *around* their waist, put their hands *between* their feet. Ask students to go *through* the doorway. As children follow each spatial demand, point to and read (with students) the corresponding word on the chalkboard, wall chart, etc. Then ask students to draw a stick figure *in, over,* and *under* a box; *between* two boxes; climbing *up* and *down* a tree. Match words on index cards to illustrations in the book. Read, trace, and spell (write) spatial words. Use this book to reinforce spatial words after reading *Go, Dog. Go!* by P. H. Eastman.

By the Same Author: *Bears in the Night; The Berenstain Bear Scouts and the Missing Merit Badges; The Berenstain Bears and the Messy Room; The Berenstain Bears on the Job; The Berenstain Bears on the Moon; The Big Honey Hunt* (contains following vowel patterns: op (Pop, stop), ot (lot, pot), ow (now, how), est (nest, rest), ad (mad, dad), ell (smell, well), or (more, store), ar (start, smart).

Title: *Brown Bear, Brown Bear, What Do You See?* By Bill Martin Jr., illustrations by Eric Carle (1992). New York: Henry Holt and Company.

Genre: picture book; concept book

Reading Level: NA

Interest Level: kindergarten–primary

Synopsis: Bright colorful collage illustrations accompany short, repetitive sentences. A red bird, yellow duck, blue horse, green frog, purple cat, white dog, black sheep, goldfish, teacher, and children introduce each four word question from the title. All animals, fish, and people are pictured at the end of the book on two colorful pages. This book provides opportunities for children to hear rhyming patterns and to develop vocabulary concepts by associating pictures (colors and animals) to corresponding words.

Learning Opportunities: Students and teacher read aloud simultaneously or echo read (teacher reads the phrase first and then the child rereads the same phrase). Copy the text on chart paper omitting animals and objects. Children substitute and draw a different animal or object for each phrase and read the phrase.

By the Same Author: *Fire! Fire! Said Mrs. McGuire; Polar Bear, Polar Bear, What Do You Hear?*

Title: *Clifford: The Big Red Dog* by Norman Bridwell (1963). New York: Scholastic Inc.

Genre: fantasy

Reading Level: 1

Interest Level: kindergarten–primary

Synopsis: Emily Elizabeth has a big red dog named Clifford. Clifford has amazing talents and some bad habits, too. However, he is an extraordinary dog. Short sentences, usually one or two on each page, easy vocabulary, repeated words, and full-page illustrations help readers become familiar with sight words. Clifford stories are also available in Spanish.

Learning Opportunities: Echo read and reread each short sentence to develop fluency. Find the information in the illustrations that is implied in the story. For example, why doesn't Emily Elizabeth need a tent when camping out with Clifford? Use picture cues, context cues, and phonics to identify unfamiliar words. Play word games (see Games, Part III) with sight words such as *house, good, very, but, too.* Use multisensory instruction to hear, see, trace, and spell high frequency sight words. Retell the story and use as a Language Experience Approach. Use a cloze activity with the language experience story and delete high frequency sight words. Students read the story and predict words to write in the blanks.

By the Same Author: *Clifford El Gran Perro Colorado; Clifford Va De Viaje; Las Buenas Acciones De Clifford; Los Trucos De Clifford: La Familia De Clifford; Clifford's Birthday Party; Clifford's Christmas; Count on Clifford; Clifford's Manners; Clifford's Tricks; Clifford, We Love You.*

Title: *Go, Dog. Go!* by P.H. Eastman (1961). New York: Random House.

Genre: fantasy

Reading Level: low 1

Interest Level: kindergarten–primary

Synopsis: Colorful dogs are engaged in many activities, with short sentences and words depicting each event. For example, red dogs are on a blue tree, a green dog is up, dogs stop at red lights and go with green lights. Spatial words (over, under, on, in, around), color words (red, blue, yellow, green), and nouns (sun, day, night, cars) are repeated and illustrated with humorous cartoon illustrations.

Learning Opportunities: Echo read and reread. Write color words and spatial words on index cards or wall charts. Reinforce color word concepts by matching crayons to a specific color word. Reinforce spatial words in first three dimensional and then two dimensional space. (See examples in *Bears in the Night*). Say, trace, and spell (write) reading vocabulary. Ask students to describe an illustration and then identify the specific sight word in the reading text, e.g., *red, blue, sun, cars, over, under, around*. Reread the story. Write simple sentences using reading vocabulary.

By the Same Author: *Are You My Mother? Big Dog... Little Dog: A Bedtime Story; Core! Perro Grande... Perro Pequeno: Big Dog... Little Dog.*

Title: *Green Eggs and Ham* by Dr. Seuss (1960). New York: Random House.

Genre: fantasy

Reading Level: 1

Interest Level: kindergarten–primary

Synopsis: "Sam-I-Am" tries to convince the Knox to like green eggs and ham in a house, with a mouse, in a box, with a fox (and on and on). Each event is repeated and added to subsequent events. There are at least seven rhyming patterns with one to three words building on that pattern: ox (box, fox); ouse (house, mouse), ere (there, where), am (Sam, ham), ee (tree, see, be), ain (train, rain) and oat (boat, goat). Zanny cartoon illustrations accompany and expand on each story event.

Learning Opportunities: Write word patterns and story words on index cards. Match word patterns (e.g., *am*) to story words (*Sam, ham*) (word sort activity). Generate additional rhyming words to go with each pattern. Write word patterns on the chalkboard from dictation (recall activity). Write a rhyming story with selected words. Reread the story. How did "Sam-I-Am" convince the Knox to eat green eggs and ham?

By the Same Author: *The Cat in the Hat; Fox in Sox; Oh, the Places You'll Go!; Horton Hatches the Egg; Hop On Pop; The Sneetches and Other Stories.*

Title: *Horton Hatches the Egg* by Dr. Seuss (1940; 1968). New York: Random House.

Genre: fantasy

Reading Level: 1

Interest Level: kindergarten–primary

Synopsis: Mayzie, a very lazy bird, coaxes Horton the elephant to sit on her egg while she is gone for a short while. The short while turns out to be 51 weeks! Poor Horton sits through rain, snow, ridicule from jungle animals and finally, capture and relocation to a zoo. Throughout trials and tribulations, the faithful elephant continues to sit on Mayzie's egg. This heartwarming story is full of rhythm, rhyming words, repetition, a wonderful theme, and full-page illustrations.

Learning Opportunities: Echo read or take turns reading each page with a partner. Choral read Horton's repeated phrase: *I meant what I said, and I said what I meant . . . an elephant's faithful one hundred per cent!* (unpaged). Compare and contrast Horton to Mayzie. Are there any similarities? What are the differences? Do you know anyone like Mayzie? Like Horton? Why do you think Dr. Seuss wrote this story? Make a story map and include (and sequence) the major events that Horton had to endure while sitting on Mayzie's egg. Write a short sequel about Horton and the egg.

By the Same Author: *Horton Hears a Who!; How the Grinch Stole Christmas! The Lorax; Daisy-Head Mayzie.*

Title: *King Bidgood's in the Bathtub* by Audrey Wood, illustrated by Don Wood (1985, Caldecott Honor Book). Orlando, FL: Harcourt Brace Jovanovich.

Genre: fantasy

Reading Level: 1

Interest Level: kindergarten–primary

Synopsis: Colorful, detailed illustrations by Don Wood depict a jolly King who won't get out of the tub! First the Knight, then the Queen, the Duke, the Court, and lastly the Page (who pulls the plug!) try to lure the King out of the tub. Wood's magnificent illustrations depict detailed and colorful costumes and laughing and disgruntled faces as each frustrated member of the Court ends up in the tub with the King. The illustrations and repetitive words and phrases (*Help! Help!, King Bidgood's in the bathtub, and he won't get out! Oh, who knows what to do?)* (unpaged) provide clues for struggling readers.

Learning Opportunities: Look at the hues of light reflected through the castle window and predict the time of day by the illustrations. Use the story to read, practice, and reinforce sight words (Knight, King, Queen, tub, battle, etc.), consonant blends (glub, plug, bright,) and short vowels (u—tub, plug, sun, lunch, yum; i—jig, fish; o—hot, got; a—bathtub, battle, dance). Write selected vocabulary words on index cards to sort into groups (e.g., short vowels, long vowels, consonant blends). Students must provide the reason for placing a word in a particular group (see Word Sorts, Part IV, Games).

By the Same Author/Illustrator: *The Little Mouse; The Red Ripe Strawberry and the Big Hungry Bear; Elbert's Bad Word; Heckedy Peg; The Napping House.*

Title: *Koala Lou* by Mem Fox (1988), San Diego: Harcourt Brace Jovanovich.
Genre: fantasy
Reading Level: low 4
Interest Level: kindergarten–primary
Synopsis: Koala Lou enters the Bush Olympics and competes in the gum tree climbing event to get her mother's attention. Her mother is too busy tending to younger brothers and sisters to say the phrase (repeated throughout the book) *"Koala Lou, I DO love you!"* as she used to do. Pamela Lofts' soft, detailed illustrations humorously portray Koala Lou working out in tennis shoes, lifting weights, and doing push-ups, as well as other fascinating Australian animals (kookaburra, emu, platypus, and Koala Klaws—her Olympic opponent).

Learning Opportunities: Listen to the story and predict what will happen in the race. Why did Koala Lou enter the Bush Olympics? Was it important that she win the race? Retell the story and use as a Language Experience Approach (LEA) (see Part I). Make up your own story changing setting and events. Include the phrase *Lou, I DO love you!*

By the Same Author: *Boo to a Goose; Time for Bed; Hattie and the Fox; Possum Magic; Wilfrid Gordon McDonald Partridge.*

Title: *Madeline* by Ludwig Bemelmans (1939). New York: Puffin Books.
Genre: fiction
Reading Level: 3
Interest Level: kindergarten–primary
Synopsis: This classic story is about spunky Madeline who lives with a governess (Miss Clavel) and eleven other little girls in a big old house in France. After having her appendix out, Madeleine proudly displays the scar on her stomach, her new toys, dollhouse, and candy to her eleven little friends. Now everyone wants her appendix out! This delightful story is composed of rhyming verse and repetition. Long sentences boost the reading level.

Learning Opportunities: Listen to the story and predict and supply the rhyming words and phrases. Echo read. To reinforce story comprehension, make a story map or color Madeleine on a large paper sack with construction paper arms and legs glued to the side and bottom of the sack. Write the sequence of events on one side and the characters on the other.

By the Same Author: *Madeline and the Bad Hat; Madeline and the Gypsies; Madeline's Rescue, Madeline's Christmas; Mad About Madeline: The Complete Tales.*

Title: *My Many Colored Days* by Dr. Seuss, paintings by Steve Johnson and Lou Fancher (1973, 1996) New York: Alfred A. Knopf.

Genre: picture book; feelings and moods

Reading Level: 1

Interest Level: kindergarten–intermediate

Synopsis: Rhyming verse describes feelings in terms of colors: how the writer feels on bright red days, orange days, purple days, gray, brown, and black days, and mixed-up days. Bright paintings and creative, bold print portray colors and feelings. This easy to read text has only a few phrases or short sentences on each page.

Learning Opportunities: Before reading about a particular color, predict your own feelings e.g., how do you feel on red days, gray days? Read one color poem and describe how the illustration and print (e.g., bold, little, big, wavy) make you feel? Do certain colors make you feel differently than the feelings expressed in the book? How? Why? On large newsprint, choose a color and write about your own feelings; use crayons, expressive lettering, and illustrate. Compare and share color feelings with peers. Combine all of the pages into one big book of feelings.

By the Same Author: *The Cat in the Hat; The Cat in the Hat Comes Back; One Fish Two Fish Red Fish Blue Fish; The Foot Book; The Shape of Me and Other Stuff.*

Title: *The Cat in the Hat* by Dr. Seuss (1957). New York: Random House.

Genre: fantasy

Reading Level: 1

Interest Level: kindergarten–primary

Synopsis: Two bored children are entertained and the gold fish terrorized by the Cat in the Hat and his two friends, Thing One and Thing Two. The clever story is full of rhyme, repetition, and only 223 different words. Miraculously, the Cat in the Hat cleans up his mess and disappears as mother walks in the door. The story contains lots of short and long vowel patterns (net, bet, at, hat, came, shame, game).

Learning Opportunities: Echo read or take turns reading each page. Why did Dr. Seuss write this story? Have you had similar experiences (bored on a rainy day)? What part did the fish play in the story? Thing One and Thing Two? Were the children part of the problem? Write words containing short and long vowel patterns on index cards and sort according to pattern (e.g., *net, bet* go in *et* pile). Play Story Jumble and sequence events (see Part III).

By the Same Author: *Hop on Pop; Fox in Socks; Mr Brown can Moo! Can You?*

Title: *The Gingerbread Boy*, illustrations by Scott Cook (1987). New York: Alfred A. Knopf.

Genre: folktale; cumulative story

Reading Level: NA (long sentences and repetitive words)

Interest Level: kindergarten–primary

Synopsis: This well-known cumulative folktale is about a little gingerbread boy who runs away from the little old man, the little old woman, a cow, a horse, a barn full of threshers, a field full of mowers, and is finally outwitted by a clever fox. The story repeats each phrase as the gingerbread boy says, *Run! Run! As fast as you can! You can't catch me, I'm the Gingerbread Man!* The joyful illustrations are muted in ginger tones and portray lively characters with a variety of expressions. Cumulative stories reinforce reading vocabulary and help students recall events because words and events are repeated as the story builds.

Learning Opportunities: Listen to the story and join in when you hear the repetitive rhyming phrase, *Run! Run! As fast as you can! You can't catch me, I'm the Gingerbread Man!* Retell the story sequence using a flannel board and flannel story characters. Make simple stick puppets (with tongue depressors) and act out the story.

By the Same Author: Retellings of this well-known folktale include: *The Gingerbread Boy*, retold and illustrated by Richard Egielski (1997); *The Gingerbread Man*, retold by Jim Ayleswood, illustrations by Barbara McClintack (1998); *The Gingerbread Man*, retold by Barbara Baumgartner (1998).

Title: *The Napping House* by Audrey Wood, illustrated by Don Wood ((1984). New York: Harcourt Brace Jovanovich. (ALA Notable Book for Children, *New York Times* Choice of Best Illustrated Children's Books of the Year.)

Genre: picture book; cumulative story

Reading Level: NA (repetitive words and long sentences)

Interest Level: kindergarten–primary

Synopsis: The cumulative story begins on a rainy day in a napping house where a granny is fast asleep and builds as the snoring granny is joined by a dreaming child, a dozing dog, a snoozing cat, a slumbering mouse, and finally—a wakeful flea. The flea bites the mouse and the count-down begins as each creature wakes the other and tumbles out of bed as the sun shines gloriously through the window. Don Wood's illustrations depict the colorful unfolding of the rainy day from dark blue and green hues to sunny light and a rainbow when the bed breaks and all go joyously out to greet the day.

Learning Opportunities: Listen to the story and predict what will happen as each creature wakes up. Retell the story, using book illustrations. Retell the story on a flannel board and sequence events with flannel pictures of a large bed, a granny, child, dog, cat, mouse, and flea. Make word cards of nouns (child, dog, bed, house, cat, flea), adjectives (dozing, dreaming, snoring, cozy, napping), verbs (bites, scares, claws, thumps, bumps, breaks), and spatial words (on, in). Read word cards, sort words into groups (see Word Sort, Part III), match word cards to those in the story, and arrange appropriate adjectives in front of nouns (e.g., snoring granny) and verbs after nouns (e.g., cat claws). Use the words to write a short story.

By the Same Author/Illustrator: *King Bidgood's in the Bathtub*; *Piggies*; *Heckedy Peg*.

Title: *The Very Hungry Caterpillar* by Eric Carle (1969). New York: Philomel Books, The Putnam Publishing Group.

Genre: picture book; concept book

Reading Level: 3

Interest Level: kindergarten–primary

Synopsis: Single sentences accompanied by full-page colorful collages show a young, hungry caterpillar emerging from an egg. He looks for food and finds one apple on Monday, two pears on Tuesday, three plums on Wednesday, four strawberries on Thursday, five oranges on Friday, a long list of sweets on Saturday, and has a stomachache Saturday night! On Sunday he eats a nice green leaf, builds a cocoon, and after two weeks emerges as a beautiful butterfly. The repetitive phrases reinforce vocabulary and prediction. The colorful fruit illustrations reinforce color words and the holes in the fruit provide tactile clues and reinforce number concepts. Days of the week are emphasized as children listen to and read about the events that occur on Monday through Sunday.

Learning Opportunities: Listen to the story and use the illustrations to retell the events. Share your experiences with butterflies and caterpillars. Use as a Language Experience Approach (LEA) (see Part I) and illustrate the story. Make a collage out of tissue paper and paint to resemble a butterfly.

By the Same Author: *The Very Quiet Cricket; Do You Want to Be My Friend? Draw Me a Star; The Grouchy Ladybug; 123 To the Zoo: A Counting Book.*

Picture Books/Picture Story Books/Wordless Picture Books

Title: *A Chocolate Moose for Dinner* by Fred Gwynne (1976). New York: Prentice-Hall Books for Young Readers, A Division of Simon and Schuster, Inc.

Genre: picture book

Reading Level: NA

Interest Level: primary–intermediate

Synopsis: Single sentences containing homonyms and figures of speech are surrounded by colorful, humorous illustrations that depict the literal meaning of the sentence. For example, *Daddy says lions pray on other animals,* shows three lions holding their hands in prayer while sitting on the back of a zebra, hippo, and rhinoceros (unpaged).

Learning Opportunities: Read and discuss how homonyms are used literally in Gwynne's book. Using *A Chocolate Moose for Dinner* as a guide, illustrate the literal meaning of other homonyms that come up in reading or in classroom reading and discussion. Write homophones (same sound but different meanings and spellings—be/bee, their/there) on index cards and create a card or board game. The player draws a card (*to/two*) and generates a sentence for each word.

By the Same Author: *The King Who Rained; The Sixteen Hand Horse.*

Title: *Abuela* by Arthur Dorros, illustrations by Elisa Kleven (1991). New York: Dutton Children's Books.

Genre: picture book; fantasy.

Reading Level: low 3

Interest Level: primary

Synopsis: Rosalba and her grandmother fly over New York City in vibrant patterns of color accompanied by descriptive language as in the following passage: *Abuela would wonder where I was. Swooping like a bird, I'd call to her* (unpaged). Spanish words and phrases fill the story as Rosabla talks to her Abuela: Then she'd see me flying. *Rosalba the bird. Rosalba el pajaro*, she'd say. *Ven, Abuela. Come Abuela,* I'd say. (unpaged.) Many sentences are short but multisyllabic words help to boost the reading level. Bright, colorful illustrations contain details of Rosabla's magic journey.

Learning Opportunities: Echo read and reread each page. Find information in the illustrations that support the story. Close your eyes and imagine

Rosalba and her grandmother flying above your city. Predict the meaning of Spanish words: read the preceding phrase, look for letter-sound clues and clues in the illustrations. Make a crossword puzzle of English and Spanish words that are in the story. Make up a story about flying with your own grandmother or grandfather (or another special person) over Chicago, New York, a nearby city, your town, or neighborhood. What sights would you see? What people would you visit? Use the story as a LEA.

By the Same Author: *Isla; Tonight is Carnival; Magic Secrets* (I Can Read Book); *Alligator Shoes* (Reading Rainbow).

Title: *Chicken Sunday* by Patricia Polacco (1992). New York: Putnam & Grosset Group.

Genre: autobiographical, picture book

Reading Level: 3

Interest Level: primary–intermediate

Synopsis: Three young friends, Stewart and Winston (African Americans) and the author (Russian American) pool their resources to buy an Easter hat for the boy's grandmother, Miss Eula Mae. When they go to the hat store, Mr. Kodinski mistakenly accuses them of throwing eggs at his shop window. The children prove their innocence by painting "Pysanky eggs" to sell to people who visit Mr. Kodinski's hat shop. The author uses descriptive vocabulary such as *Spaseeba* (thank you in Russian) and *Chutzpah* and figurative language—Miss Eula's voice was *like slow thunder and sweet rain* (unpaged)—to evoke rich images of story characters.

Learning Opportunities: Listen to the story and predict, validate, and modify predictions as the story enfolds. Make connections (inferences) between pictures and text. For example: Why did children throw eggs at Mr. Kodinski's shop window? Why did Miss Eula Mae say he had suffered enough? What information is revealed in the illustration of Mr. Kodinski and the three children having tea? Are there connections between the story and events that take place today? Discuss the author's use of language that evokes images. For example, why did the author compare Miss Eula's voice to *slow thunder and sweet rain*?

By the Same Author: *Pink and Say; Thank you, Mr. Falker; Babushka's Doll; Bee Tree; Rechenka's Eggs.*

Title: *Encounter* by Jane Yolen and illustrated by David Shannon(1992). New York: Harcourt Brace Jovanovich.

Genre: historical fiction

Reading Level: 2/low 3

Interest Level: primary–intermediate

Synopsis: An elderly Taino tribesman describes the tragic story about the encounter between Christopher Columbus and his people that occurred on San Salvador when he was a child in 1492. The story is documented by the author's research (see Author's Note at end of story). David Shannon's rich paintings realistically portray the Taino tribespeople and visually capture the author's eloquent writing. Readers experience events from the perspective of a young Taino child rather than from the European explorers' point of few.

Learning Opportunities: Discuss the illustrations and images evoked by Yolen's figurative language and David Shannon's paintings. For example, one detailed painting shows a young brown hand pulling at the explorer's white, translucent hand. The young boy describes the skin as *moon to my sun* (unpaged). In another passage the young Taino compares the speech of a pale-faced stranger to a dog's bark: *The stranger made a funny noise with his mouth, not like talking but like the barking of a yellow dog* (unpaged). What does the author mean? Why does the author use these comparisons? Take another historical event and rewrite it from a different perspective.

By the Same Author: *Owl Moon* (Caldecott Medal, 1962); *Favorite Folktales from Around the World; All Those Secrets of the World; And Twelve Chinese Acrobats; Animal Fare: Poems.*

Title: *Fly Away Home* by Eve Bunting, illustrated by Ronald Himler (1991). New York: Clarion Books. (An ALA Notable Book).

Genre: fiction

Reading Level: 2

Interest Level: primary–junior high

Synopsis: Andrew and his father are homeless and live in an airport. The touching story is told from Andrew's point of view. The boy compares his life to that of a bird who gets trapped in the main terminal. The illustrations are soft watercolors, evoking a gentle and sad feeling. Like many of Bunting's picture storybooks, many sentences are short, yet create powerful and moving images for the reader. In one moving passage, Andrew sees passengers waving good-by to family and friends and softly murmurs: *Everyone's going somewhere except Dad and me. We stay* (p. 15).

Learning Opportunities: Emphasize selected words from the story to reinforce reading vocabulary: compound words (airport, somewhere); word endings (ing—singing, flying, sliding, nothing, trying, disappearing, sitting, pushing, lying, bellowing); contractions (he's, it's, that's, I'm, can't). Support reading comprehension: develop a story map of literary elements that include characters, setting, problem, events, resolution. Discuss theme: Why did the author write the story? What did she want to say? How do you feel about the story? Did anything surprise you? How do the illustrations relate to the story (e.g., colors, realistic style)?

By the Same Author: *The Wall; Smoky Night; Summer Wheels; Going Home.*

Title: *Free Fall* by David Wiesner (1988). New York: Mulberry Books. (Caldecott Honor Book, ALA Notable Children's Book).

Genre: fantasy; wordless picture book

Reading Level: NA

Interest Level: primary-intermediate

Synopsis: This wordless picture book describes a boy's dreams through enchanting, realistic, and bizarre paintings. The first illustration shows the boy falling asleep with a book in his hands. In his room are books, maps, reptile toys, a chess set with knights, queens, kings, and a bowl of gold fish, all of which come to life in his dreams. As his dream is ending, he is soaring through space, riding on the back of a leaf that turns into a swan. He awakens as swans, ducks, and fish fade away on his quilt.

Learning Opportunities: Use as a Language Experience Approach (LEA) (see Part I) Look at the illustrations and tell (or write) a story to support the pictures. Write and illustrate your own *dream* story.

By the Same Author: *Tuesday; June 29, 1999; Hurricane.*

Title: *Grandfather's Journey* by Allen Say (1993). Boston MA: Houghton Mifflin. (Caldecott Medal Book).

Genre: autobiographical; picture book

Reading Level: low 4

Interest Level: primary-intermediate

Synopsis: This autobiographical story is about the author's grandfather who left home in Japan as a young man to see the world. Liking California, he made a second home there. Subsequent events such as the approach of WW II, prevent the grandfather from returning to California. The muted, realistic watercolors support the dignity of this immigrant story.

Learning Opportunities: Use as a listening activity. Predict what will happen to the grandfather as the story progresses. Develop an understanding and appreciation of figurative language. For example, what does the author mean when he compares life to leaves in a storm (p. 26)? Develop inference skills: Why did the author's grandfather never keep another songbird (p. 28)? Refer back to the story to support your answers.

By the Same Author: *Tree of Cranes; El Chino; The Lost Lake; A River Dream; Tea and Milk.*

Title: *Granpa* by John Burningham (1984). New York: Dragonfly Books, Crown Publishers, Inc.

Genre: fiction

Reading Level: 2

Interest Level: primary

Synopsis: A poignant story about friendship, love, and loss. Throughout the story a little girl and her "granpa" share experiences such as playing nurse and doctor with her dolls, telling stories, having tea in the garden, going to the beach, and ice skating. One day granpa can't come out to play. The soft, chalk illustration shows him in his chair, covered with blankets and surrounded by pills. The last illustration, with no text, pictures the little girl sadly perched on a chair, looking at the empty chair. Granpa's words are in bold print, the little girl's words are in italics. There are usually two sentences to a page, one comment from granpa and the other from the little girl. This story generates thoughtful discussions about the relationship between grandparents and grandchildren. There is much information in the illustrations that goes unsaid in the text. For example, only the illustration provides the reason why granpa can't come out to play. (A starred *Horn Book* review.)

Learning Opportunities: Read the story. Since the story is written in two parts, use as Reader's Theater with two students (or teacher and student) reading the part of the little girl or granpa. Discuss individual responses to the story. How did the story make you feel? Use the illustrations to make inferences; for example, at the end of the story why is an illustration (i.e., the empty chair) used rather than words? Why are some illustrations filled with colors and others are not? What is the relationship between the little girl and her granpa? Share the experiences you have had with your grandparent(s).

By the Same Author: *Cloudland*; *Hey! Get Off Our Train*.

Title: *Goggles* by Ezra Jack Keats (1969). New York: Collier Books, the Macmillan Company.

Genre: fiction

Reading Level: 2

Interest Level: primary

Synopsis: Peter and his friend Archie find a pair of motorcycle goggles and some "big boys" try to take them away. The dark palate illustrations (deep red, brown, gold, gray) depict alleys, apartment buildings, parking lot, and urban "hideouts" where Peter, Archie, and Willie (the dog) try to out run and out smart the bullies. Many pages have only two or three simple sentences. This book was an ALS Notable Children's Book (1969) and a Caldecott Medal Honor Book (1970).

Learning Opportunities: Develop fluency: echo read than reread the short story. Examine illustrations to infer time and place. Discuss Peter's problem and the resolution. What would students do in a similar situation?

By the Same Author: *The Snowy Day; Peter's Chair; Hi Cat; The Trip.*

Title: *I Like Me!* by Nancy Carlson (1988). New York: Viking Kestrel, the Penguin Group.

Genre: fantasy

Reading Level: 1

Interest Level: kindergarten–primary

Synopsis: This is a humorous story to boost "self concept" about a charming little pig who likes herself, her round tummy, curly tail, and tiny little feet! In fact, she is her best friend. When she feels bad, is sad, falls down, makes mistakes, she always finds something to boost her morale. The colorful, cheery pictures have lots of bright patterns (wallpaper, curtains, dresses, tile floors, table cloth) and cover three fourths of the page. The story has simple sentences in large, bold print. There are only 15 sentences in the book. The charming pictures illustrate phrases and sentences and help readers predict unfamiliar words.

Learning Opportunity: Read and reread to develop fluency. Use as a LEA activity; write your own story about what you do when you feel bad, sad, or make mistakes.

By the Same Author: *Harriet's Halloween Candy; A Visit to Grandma's.*

Title: *Jumanji* by Chris Van Allsburg(1981). Boston: Houghton Mifflin Company.

Genre: fantasy

Reading Level: high 3/low 4

Interest Level: primary–intermediate

Synopsis: Two bored siblings find a board game that becomes dangerous when they discover they cannot stop playing until one player reaches the Golden City and says "Jumanji." Lions, monkeys, snakes, and rhinos frighteningly come to life as the frantic children try to end the game before their parents return home. Surreal black and white illustrations depict frightened children and wild animals in a fantasy world where things are not as they should be. This was an ALA Notable Book and NY Times Best Illustrated Children's Book of the Year.

Learning Opportunities: Listen to the story and predict from the story and illustrations how the children will escape each game move (e.g., "lion attacks"—lion is pictured lying on the piano and licking his lips). Critique the story, e.g., does the author make the fantasy believable? How? Compare and contrast the black and white illustrations to color illustrations by the same illustrator or a different illustrator. (See Part III, compare/contrast map.) Write and make your own fantasy board game.

By the Same Author: *The Polar Express;The Mysteries of Harris Burdick; The Wreck of the Zephyr;The Widow's Broom;Two Bad Ants;Just a Dream.*

Title: *Miss Nelson Is Missing* by Henry Allard, illustrations by James Marshall (1977). Boston: Houghton Mifflin Company.

Genre: fiction

Reading Level: 2

Interest Level: primary

Synopsis: A teacher who has finally "had it" with her class leaves her students in the hands of the formidable substitute, Miss Viola Swamp, who hisses, snaps, and raps the desk with her ruler. The cartoon-like illustrations are clever, the first one depicting a frustrated Miss Nelson surrounded by horrible children making faces and throwing paper airplanes. The story often has two or three short sentences on a page. This story is available on audio cassette.

Learning Opportunities: Use the story for a Readers Theater (see Part IV, drama extensions). Select story characters (Miss Swamp, panicked children, Miss Nelson, Detective McSmogg) and read their dialogue from the book. Make character masks to represent characters. (Practice reading parts in pairs before performing in front of a group.) Use word identification skills (context clues, phonics) to predict and sound out unfamiliar words. Say, trace, and spell (write) unfamiliar sight words. Write your own episode of Room 207.

By the Same Author: *Miss Nelson Has a Field Day; Miss Nelson is Back*.

Title: *My House Mi Casa: A Book in Two Languages* by Rebecca Emberley (1990). Boston: Little, Brown and Company.

Genre: vocabulary concepts; picture book

Reading Level: NA

Interest Level: primary

Synopsis: Single words in English and Spanish label everyday objects that can be found in a house. Bright, colorful pictures illustrate each word. A single sentence or phrase referring to the particular room (e.g., bedroom, bathroom, hallway, kitchen, garden) appears at the bottom of the page.

Learning Opportunities: Read each sentence. Use picture clues and phonics clues to predict the word labels. Use each word in a short sentence that refers to your house. Categorize vocabulary into meaningful groups: Draw a semantic map with the name of a room in the middle of the circle and write (or draw) objects extending from the circle found in the room. Play Word Sort—write vocabulary words (e.g., couch, blankets, bed) and specific rooms on index cards. Player sorts words according to a specific room in which the object can be found. Some words may go in several rooms, e.g., chair. Draw a blueprint of your house and label (and draw) objects found in each room. Make your own "My House" book.

By the Same Author: *Taking a Walk; Caminando.*

Title: *Pink and Say* by Patricia Polacco (1994). New York: Philomel Books, a division of The Putnam & Grosset Group.

Genre: biographical; picture book (Civil War)

Reading Level: 3

Interest Level: primary-intermediate

Synopsis: This moving story is about friendship and the human tragedy of war. Polacco writes about her great grandfather, Sheldon Curtis (Say), and the young slave Pinkus Aylee (Pink), both fourteen year-old boys fighting for the Union in the Civil War. The boys meet when Pink finds the injured Say and takes him home to his mother, Moe Moe Bay, so that she can tend to the wound. The boys share special experiences: Pink can read and plans to teach Say after the war, and Say once shook the hand of President Lincoln. One of the many poignant parts occurs when confederate soldiers capture the boys and try to separate them. As each tries frantically to grasp the other's hand, Pink cries out: *Let me touch the hand that touched Mr. Lincoln, Say, just one last time* (unpaged.) The dramatic illustration shows the two boys frantically reaching for each other's hand as rough looking soldiers pull them apart. The story is written in first person from Say's point of view.

Learning Opportunities: Compare and contrast Pink and Say: For example, draw a Venn Diagram and contrast their families (Pink was born a slave), special talents (Pink can read), status as a soldier (Say deserted), and feelings about the war. Refer back to the story to support information. Discuss the impact of the illustrations and the artist's dramatic perspective (e.g., in one illustration the reader is looking down from above as Moe Moe Bay hustles the boys down to the cellar to hide from marauders that are approaching the house). Discuss the author's point of view (first person). How does this style of writing contribute to the meaning of the story? Why did the author write the story? What is the theme?

By the Same Author: *Thank you, Mr. Falker; Chicken Sunday; Bee Tree.*

Title: *Smoky Night* by Eve Bunting, illustrated by David Diaz (1994, a Caldecott Award Book). San Diego: Harcourt Brace & Company.

Genre: fiction

Reading Level: high 1/low 2

Interest Level: primary–intermediate

Synopsis: A fire, riot, and two lost cats bring two families together who live in the same apartment building but avoid each other because each feels the other is different. The story is written in first person from a young boy's point of view. The bold illustrations of brightly colored figures outlined in heavy black lines resemble stain glass windows. Frightened people rushing down apartment stairs, looters, people gathering in the church shelter, and two neighbors finding their lost cats are among the many striking illustrations that support the text. Collages of photographs (cardboard, tin foil, paint) surround the painted illustrations and highlight the urban theme. The text contains short sentences and dialogue with familiar words.

Learning Opportunities: Retell the story. Discuss characters, setting, events, and theme; for example, why did the author include a fire and riot to tell her story? What event or events bring the neighbors together? Could the story happen in any setting? Why is the story written in first person? Select an illustration and describe what information it portrays. Write about an event in first person that touches on some aspect of the story.

By the Same Author: *The Wall*; *Summer Wheels*; *Fly Away Home*.

Title: *Thank You, Mr. Falker* by Patricia Polacco (1998). New York: Philomel Books, a division of The Putnam & Grosset Group.

Genre: autobiographical; picture book

Reading Level: 3

Interest Level: primary–intermediate

Synopsis: This is an autobiographical story about the author/illustrator's difficulty learning to read. She describes school experiences such as feeling dumb, seeing wiggling shapes for words, and being teased by school peers. Things change in fifth grade when the new teacher, Mr. Falker, discovers Tricia's secret—that she pretends to read. Along with the reading teacher, Mr. Falker helps Tricia after school, first working with wooden blocks building letters, than words, and finally sentences. Polacco's expressive, detailed watercolors show a frustrated Tricia struggling to read in first grade, her red, tear-streaked face in third grade as children tease her and call her dummy, and a joyful Tricia (in fifth grade) as she begins to read words and sentences.

Learning Opportunities: Discuss the story events and Tricia's actions and feelings, such as her feelings toward school in first, third, and fifth grade; her relationship with her grandmother and Mr. Falker; her interest in drawing; of feeling "safe"; and the purpose of spooning honey on the cover of a book. Use a Venn Diagram to compare and contrast Tricia with yourself and include special talents, challenges, and important people in your life. Then write two short paragraphs, one on similarities and the other on differences, based on your compare/contrast map information. Select a favorite illustration and write about it. Select a favorite story part and illustrate it.

By the Same Author: *Pink and Say*; *Rechenka's Eggs*; *Chicken Sunday*.

Title: *The Giving Tree* by Shel Silverstein (1964). New York: Harper & Row.

Genre: fantasy

Reading Level: 1

Interest Level: all ages

Synopsis: This beautiful story about friendship, love, and giving is about a tree that gives all it has—its apples, limbs, and trunk—to a friend (i.e., little boy) to make him happy. Each time the boy receives a part of the tree, he goes away and the tree is lonely. Finally, the little boy returns an old man. With nothing left but a stump to give, the tree offers this and the old man wearily sits down. At last, the tree is happy. This moving story has little text and simple, descriptive, pen and ink drawings that spill over the two adjoining pages. Most pages have only a line or two of print.

Learning Opportunities: Look at the book cover and discuss what the story will be about. First listen to the story; then echo read or read the story. Reread the story. Discuss the illustrations and the information they add to the story. For example, what type of tree was the "Giving Tree"? (e.g., an apple tree, a big tree, a strong tree). Did the little boy love the tree? How do you know? What evidence do you find in the illustrations? Talk about the story. Why do you think the tree loved the little boy? Does the "Giving Tree" remind you of anyone you know? Does the little boy? Use a Venn Diagram to compare and contrast the little boy and the Giving Tree. Are there similarities? What are the differences? Why do you think the author wrote the story? How do you feel about the story?

By the Same Author: *Where the Sidewalk Ends; A Light in the Attic; Falling Up; The Missing Piece.*

Title: *The Girl Who Loved Wild Horses* by Paul Goble (1978, Caldecott Medal). New York: Aladdin Paperbacks, an imprint of Simon & Schuster.

Genre: Native American tale

Reading Level: high 4, low 5

Interest Level: primary–intermediate

Synopsis: A young Native American Indian girl loves and understands horses. During a storm, she clings to the back of a wild horse and is carried to a distant grazing land where she meets a spotted stallion, the leader of the wild horses. She disappears and is found a year later by hunters from her village. When she returns to her family, she becomes lonely and sick and tells her parents that she must return to run with the wild horses. Goble's detailed and vivid illustrations are full of bright colors, patterns, and circular, swirling, diagonal lines that create movement, excitement, and turmoil. Long flowing sentences boost up the reading level.

Learning Opportunities: Listen to the story and predict events as the story unfolds. Describe how the illustrations create movement and support the story. What does the author mean when he compares horses to a brown flood? Close your eyes and discuss the images you see and hear. Make a story map that includes characters, events, problem, resolution; use the map to retell the story.

By the Same Author: *Buffalo Woman*; *The Gift of the Sacred Dog*; *Star Boy*.

Title: *The Magic School Bus in the Time of the Dinosaurs* by Joanna Cole, illustrations by Bruce Degen (1994). New York: Scholastic.

Genre: picture book; informational book; science

Reading Level: 4

Interest Level: primary–intermediate

Synopsis: Ms. Frizzle, better known to her students as *The Friz*, takes her class on a field trip to see living dinosaurs. The magic school bus propels the students through time and space to experience first hand creatures living in the Triassic, Jurassic, and Cretaceous Periods. The short text includes two or three sentences per page. Cartoon illustrations of Ms. Frizzle and her class appear below the text and add more information to the story. Students' reports appear along the borders of each page providing still more information. This type of format may be too busy for some readers that have difficulty sorting out visual information. Others will enjoy the fun story, tons of information, and clever illustrations.

Learning Opportunities: Use a Semantic Feature Analysis to compare and contrast dinosaurs that live in the three time periods (see Part III, Learning Strategies, Vocabulary Concepts). Use the Frayer Model to list essentials, non-essentials, examples and non-examples of the prehistoric reptiles (see Part III, Vocabulary Concepts, Figure 4–2). Select a time period and write your own Ms. Frizzle dinosaur adventure. Include facts that you learned from reading. Illustrate your story.

By the Same Author: *The Magic School Bus at the Waterworks; The Magic School Bus Inside the Earth; The Magic School Bus Inside the Human Body; The Magic School Bus Lost in the Solar System; The Magic School Bus on the Ocean Floor.*

Title: *The Mysteries of Harris Burdick* by Chris Van Allsburg (1984). Boston: Houghton Mifflin Company.

Genre: fantasy

Reading Level: NA

Interest Level: all ages

Synopsis: This fantasy contains 14 mysterious black and white chalk drawings with only titles and captions opposite each illustration. According to the author, Harris Burdick left these drawings with the captions and titles in a publisher's office. Burdick was to return the following morning with the stories that went with the drawings. He never returned. Van Allsburg's surreal illustrations call out to the reader to finish the stories and solve the mysteries. For instance, one illustration depicts an angry man holding a chair over his head, ready to smash a small lump that is bulging under the carpet. The seven word caption alerts the reader that the strange event occurred again after two weeks.

Learning Opportunities: Read the captions and create (orally describe and/or write) a story to support the illustration and caption. Include characters, setting, at least three events, and a resolution or ending. Use the book with the Language Experience Approach (LEA) (see Part I, LEA).

By the Same Author: *Two Bad Ants; The Polar Express* (Caldecott Medal); *Jumanji*.

Title: *The Paper Princess* by Elisa Kleven (1994). London: Orchard Books.

Genre: fantasy

Reading Level: high 1

Interest Level: primary

Synopsis: A paper doll is carried away by the wind before a little girl can finish her. She flutters into a fairground, is crumpled up and thrown into a dustbin, then rescued by a blue jay, and finally reunited with the little girl. The whimsical illustrations are full of color, patterns, and story information. Only a few sentences or short paragraphs appear above or below an illustration. Descriptive words and figurative language are supported with the artist's colorful images.

Learning Opportunities: Discuss why the author compares her dress to a forest, her socks to starry skies. Find information in the illustrations that expand upon the story. Emphasize adjectives by substituting nouns to go with the descriptive words in the story: *fluffy* _____, *jingling* _____, *cloudy* _____, *crinkly* _____; *buttery* _____. Write your own story using descriptive adjectives and change one or more of the story elements, such as the setting, events, or characters. Write main events on sentence strips, jumble strips, and arrange (and read) strips in the correct order.

By the Same Author/Illustrator: *Snowsong Whistling*; *Abuela* (Illustrator, Author—Arthur Dorros).

Title: *The Snowy Day* by Ezra Jack Keats (1962, Caldecott Award). New York: Viking Press.

Genre: fiction

Reading Level: 2

Interest Level: primary

Synopsis: This simple, gentle story describes a day of making tracks, snowman, angels, and snowballs in the snow. Keats creates a colorful collage, winter wonderland of white snow mounds in front of orange, yellow, brown, and hot pink buildings. There are only one to three sentences per page.

Learning Opportunities: Use the story as a LEA activity. Retell the story or make up a story to accompany the illustrations. Strengthen phonics skills by emphasizing words with blends such as <u>cr</u>unch, <u>dr</u>ag, <u>tr</u>ack, <u>st</u>ick, <u>sn</u>ow, <u>tr</u>ee, <u>sm</u>ack, <u>pl</u>op, short vowels (dr<u>a</u>g, st<u>i</u>ck, pl<u>o</u>p), and long vowels (tr<u>ee</u>, l<u>i</u>ke). Make index cards of story vocabulary words and sort them according to consonant blends, short vowels, and long vowels (see Word Sorts, Part III). Explain why a particular word goes in a pile.

 By the Same Author: *Goggles*; *Peter's Chair*; *Whistle for Willie*.

Title: *The Steadfast Tin Soldier* by Hans Christian Andersen, retold by Katie Campbell and illustrated by David Delamare (1990). Morris Plains, NJ: The Unicorn Publishing House.

Genre: fantasy

Reading Level: 4

Interest Level: primary–intermediate

Synopsis: This is a retelling of the Hans Christian Andersen story about a steadfast tin soldier with one leg (their was no tin to finish his other leg) and a beautiful paper princess. Delamare's stunning paintings reflect light illuminating objects and show different perspectives such as the large, an evil looking goblin peering down on the small tin soldier, and the giant water rat perched on a ledge in a street drain above the tin soldier in a paper boat. Light is reflected on the top of the soldier's hat and shoulders as well as on the rat's hairy face and yellow eyes. The last full-page illustration shows twelve gossamer images of the paper princess filtering across a room brightened by a burning fire in the fireplace as the wind draws her into the fire. The formal text is enclosed on one side of the page surrounded by a deep yellow background with the colorful paintings on the other. While the estimated reading level of the story is high, the fascinating paintings with light and perspective and touching story present opportunities to develop visual literacy, listening skills, and creative writing.

Learning Opportunities: Write your own story to support the illustrations, then compare your version to the original. How do the illustrations (detail, light, and perspective) support the story? Rewrite the famous tale, changing an event to alter the outcome, or write a short critique of the book. Discuss theme and character motivation: What was the story about? Why did the author create a soldier with only one leg? Why do both characters end up in the fire? What is the story about (e.g., bravery, loyalty, love, carelessness)? Connect the story to current events. For example, are values represented in the fantasy reflected today?

By the Same Author: *The Little Match Girl* illustrated by Rachel Isadora. This is another example of a touching story with exquisite illustrations by Rachel Isadora, a Caldecott Honor Award artist.

Title: *The True Story of the Three Little Pigs* by Jon Scieszka, illustrated by Lane Smith (1989). New York: Penguin Books.

Genre: fantasy

Reading Level: 2

Interest Level: primary-intermediate

Synopsis: Scieszka retells the folktale of the Three Little Pigs from the wolf's perspective (i.e., by A. Wolf). The wolf was only borrowing a cup of sugar to bake a birthday cake for his granny when a sneeze buried the first little pig under a pile of straw! The witty cartoon illustrations match the hilarious text. For example, the innocent wolf, first pictured in a sweater, bow tie, and horn-rimmed glasses, is depicted at the story's end with a long white beard and striped prison attire. Many pages have two to four sentences; the longest page of text has 11 short sentences.

Learning Opportunities: Read the story and the original folktale version. Use a Venn Diagram to compare and contrast the two stories. Make a story map with characters, setting, events, resolution, and use as a prewriting organizer to write your own folk tale version; change the events and/or resolution. Play Story Jumble and sequence story events (see Games, Part III).

By the Same Author: *Squids Will Be Squids; Fresh Morals, Beastly Fables; The Not-So-Jolly Roger (The Time Warp Trio).*

Title: *The Wall* by Eve Bunting and illustrated by Ronald Himler (1990). New York: Clarion Books, a Houghton Mifflin Company imprint.

Genre: fiction

Reading Level: high 1/low 2

Interest Level: primary-intermediate

Synopsis: A father and son visit the Vietnam Veteran's Memorial to find the grandfather's name. The subtle dark watercolors reflect the quiet and solemn tone of Bunting's simple, yet powerful narrative. The illustrations provide numerous opportunities for discussion. For example, one illustration contrasts the figures of the little boy and his father with bowed heads facing the Wall to a group of noisy school girls walking past them. Another shows a veteran in a wheel chair staring at the names. Yet another pictures the little boy gently putting his school picture on the grass below his grandpa's name. The moving story is written in first person from the little boy's perspective.

Learning Opportunities: Discuss the story and theme. Why did the author write the story? What is the theme? Is there more than one? How do the illustrations support and extend the story? Select an illustration and write your own description to accompany the picture. Reread the story.

By the Same Author: *Smoky Night; Going Home; Fly Away Home; Summer Wheels.*

Title: *There's a Nightmare in My Closet* by Mercer Mayer (1968). New York: NAL Penguin Inc.

Genre: fantasy

Reading Level: 1

Interest Level: primary

Synopsis: A little boy tries to keep a ferocious nightmare in his closet, only to discover that the nightmare is as afraid as he is and wants to join him in bed! The story is written in first person from the little boy's perspective. There are only nine sentences in this clever story. The humorous illustrations show a huge monster tiptoeing across the room, perching on the edge of the little boy's bed, crying hysterically after being shot by the little boy with his toy gun, and finally nestled safely in bed beside the little boy.

Learning Opportunities: Read, predict events, and reread the story to develop fluency. Reinforce easy reading vocabulary (sleep, closet door, afraid, bed, shoot, light, around, began) and compound words (nightmare, sometimes) by rereading, writing words on a wall chart or index cards for discussion and review, and using them in a personal story about nightmares. Write a short story about what happens to the second nightmare.

By the Same Author: *Me Too; Little Critter's the Night Before Christmas; All by Myself.*

Title: *To Every Thing There Is A Season* illustrated by Leo and Diane Dillon; passages taken from the Book of Ecclesiastes (1998). New York: The Blue Sky Press, an imprint of Scholastic Inc.

Genre: traditional literature; Bible

Reading Level: NA

Interest Level: all ages

Synopsis: Passages from the Book of Ecclesiastes are illustrated in styles celebrating different cultures from around the world. The award winning artists majestically depict phrases with art work representing Ireland, Egypt, Japan, Mexico, Greece, Europe, North America, Ethiopia, Thailand, China, Russia, Australia, The Far North (from Siberia to Greenland), and The Middle East.

Learning Opportunities: Develop oral language and visual literacy: Look at each illustration and discuss the particular style that represents the culture; for example, what colors, shapes, and lines characterize Egyptian murals, Japanese woodblocks, or North American Pueblo drawings? Use a Venn Diagram to compare and contrast two styles of art from two different cultures. How do the paintings add meaning to the verses? Echo read and reread to develop fluency.

By the Same Illustrators: *Aida* (Leontyne Price); *Ashanti to Zulu: African Traditions; Honey I Love and Other Love Poems* (Eloise Greenfield); *Her Stories: African American Folktales, Fairy Tales, and True Tales* (Virginia Hamilton).

Title: *Tree of Cranes* by Allen Say (1991). Boston: Houghton Mifflin.

Genre: biographical picture book

Reading Level: 3

Interest Level: primary–intermediate

Synopsis: An eloquently written and illustrated autobiographical story about the author who celebrates his first Christmas in Japan. His mother decorates a small pine tree with paper cranes and candles, remembering the time she had lived in California as a small child. This story follows *Grandfather's Journey*, and is written in first person as the author recalls the time he was a small boy in Japan. Allen Say's realistic watercolors and gentle story inform readers about custom's in a different country. His distinctive watercolors depict the elegant simplicity of a Japanese home, garden, and hot bath.

Learning Opportunities: Read the story to students. Why did Allen Say write this story? What is the theme? Discuss characters' actions and emotions: How did the mother feel? Why did she want to decorate a tree? Discuss the realistic illustrations and the information that adds to the story. For example, what does a Japanese bath look like and how is it different from the ones we use? Compare and contrast Japanese and American customs (develop a Venn Diagram). Include other cultures (e.g., Mexico, Russia) if it is part of a child's heritage.

By the Same Author: *El Chino; Grandfather's Journey; How My Parents Learned to Eat; The Bicycle Man; Tea with Milk*.

Title: *Tuesday* by David Wiesner (1991, Caldecott Medal). New York: Houghton Mifflin.

Genre: fantasy; wordless picture book

Reading Level: NA

Interest Level: primary–junior high

Synopsis: This humorous, eerie story is about a frog invasion: frogs fly through the air on lily pads, drift through open windows (at 11:21 p.m.), work remote TV controls with their tongues, chase the family dog (4:38 A.M.), and as the sun comes up soar out of the house to return to the pond. The last page (next Tuesday, 7:58 p.m.) shows a shadow of a pig soaring through the air. The picture book has only four pages of words (or a phrase) that denote various times the story takes place. The artist uses cool colors, mainly blues and greens, to evoke a dream-like mysterious night quality.

Learning Opportunities: Use as a LEA (see Part 1). Tell the story, using the illustrations as prompts. Focus on the time and the sequence of events. Continue the story and write about a pig invasion (or another invasion), changing the setting (town, city, country) to match your own background experiences.

By the Same Author: *Free Fall; June 29, 1999.*

Title: *Yo! Yes!* by Chris Raschka (1993, Caldecott Honor). New York: Orchard Books.

Genre: fiction

Reading Level: NA

Interest Level: kindergarten–primary

Synopsis: An African American boy greets a sad-looking Caucasian boy with his head hung low. Two small words in red describe his lonliness. From then on the two consider a friendship with the last page showing both boys jumping in the air with wide grins and clasped hands, yelling enthusiastically. There are only 34 one syllable words with one or two word sentences. Words are written in large bold letters and are accompanied by expressive watercolors of the boys in muted backgrounds.

Learning Opportunities: Read and enjoy the short story and the expressive illustrations. Talk about how the color, size of print, and the bold illustrations contribute to the meaning of the story. Reread the story to reinforce sight vocabulary (yes, well, me, you, why, no).

By the Same Author: *Simple Gifts: A Shaker Hymn; Arlene Sardine; The Blushful Hippopotamus.*

Title: *Where The Wild Things Are* by Maurice Sendak. (1963, Caldecott Medal Book). New York: Harper and Row.

Genre: fantasy

Reading Level: 6

Interest Level: primary

Synopsis: Max is sent to bed after doing mischief (chasing the dog with a fork!) and telling his mother that he'd eat her up after she called him "Wild Thing." Then his bed becomes a forest and he sails away on a private boat to be king of the wild things. Sendak's imaginative, detailed illustrations carry the reader into Max's fantasy world. Long sentences boost the reading level.

Learning Opportunities: Listen to or echo read the story (with teacher, volunteer, support staff). Reread the story. Develop a story map to highlight characters, sequence of events, and the resolution. Retell the story using the map as a guide. Use a Venn Diagram to compare and contrast Max and the *wild things*. Write your own *wild thing* story and include descriptive vocabulary words such as *gnash, wild rumpus*.

By the Same Author: *In the Night Kitchen*; *Alligators All Around: An Alphabet*.

Easy Reading Books and Short Chapter Books

Title: *A to Z Mysteries: The Absent Author* by Ron Roy, illustrated by John S. Gurney (1997). (A Stepping Stone Book.) New York: Random House.

Genre: fiction; mystery

Reading Level: 2.5

Interest Level: primary–intermediate

Synopsis: When Drink invites his favorite mystery writer Wallis Wallace to visit Green Lawn, the author disappears and Drink and his friends, Josh and Ruth Rose, must solve the mystery. Comic black and white illustrations and short chapters keep the reader on track as Drink and his friends trace clues. The author sprinkles alliteration throughout with characters that include Ruth Rose, David Donald Duncan and Wallis Wallace. The humorous story has easy, short sentences, illustrated clues, ten chapters, and 87 pages.

Learning Opportunities: Keep track of clues and predict what will happen next based on story information. Back up predictions with illustrations and story information. The author gives his address at the end of the book. Write to Ron Roy and provide feedback about the book (e.g., did you like the book? Why? Would you suggest modifications in the next story? What about the illustrations?) Use alliteration to write new characters and extend the story.

By the Same Author: *The Bald Bandit—A to Z Mysteries; The Canary Caper; The Deadly Dungeon; The Empty Envelope.*

Title: *Aliens for Dinner* by Stephanie Spinner, illustrated by Steve Bjorkman (1994). (A Stepping Stone Book.) New York: Random House.
Genre: fantasy
Reading Level: 2
Interest Level: primary–intermediate
Synopsis: The earth is in terrible danger! Aric, a friendly, tiny alien that is commander of the Interspace Brigade, appears in a fortune cookie to ask for Richard's help in ridding the earth of the Dwilbs. The problem—the Dwilbs want to turn earth into a toxic waste theme park, putting the earthlings to work by selling tickets. The solution—bore the Dwilbs to death since they have a very short attention span and get bored easily! Another problem—how? A solution—Richard's boring principal, Mr. Felshin. There are 79 pages, 10 chapters, and clever illustrations. This book is an IRA/CBC Children's Choice Book.
Learning Opportunities: Represent story information in a Problem/Solution Map: trace the problem and solution sequence. Write a sequel to the story and describe what happens to Richard to force him to use the "Mind Control Inducer" (a parting gift from Aric that will cause brainlock for eight earth minutes!). Read the other books in the series (*Aliens for Breakfast; Aliens for Lunch*) and compare/contrast the plot and characters in the three books. Which book do you prefer? Why?
By the Same Author: *Aliens for Breakfast; Aliens for Lunch.*

Title: *Amelia Bedelia* by Peggy Parish, illustrated by Fritz Siebel (1963). New York: HarperCollins.
Genre: fiction; humor
Reading Level: 2
Interest Level: primary–intermediate
Synopsis: Amelia Bedelia is a maid for Mrs. Rogers and interprets cleaning directions in a very concrete manner! For example, to "change the towels" Amelia gets some scissors and begins snipping the towels; to dust the furniture she finds a box of dusting powder and dusts the furniture. Mrs. Roger's cleaning directions are written in large cursive print. This easy book has short sentences and numerous illustrations that depict Amelia Bedelia's literal interpretation of words.
Learning Opportunities: Predict how Amelia Bedelia will change Mrs. Roger's cleaning instructions. Keep a list of the homonyms and develop a card or board game. Select a card with a homonym and provide two interpretations (e.g., *dress*—dress a chicken or dress for dinner).

By the Same Author: *Thank You, Amelia Bedelia; Amelia Bedelia and the Surprise Shower; Come Back, Amelia Bedelia.*

Title: *Annie Bananie Moves to Barry Avenue* by Leah Komaiko, illustrated by Abby Carter (1996). New York: Bantam Doubleday Dell Publishing Group.

Genre: fiction; humor

Reading Level: 1.9

Interest Level: primary–intermediate

Synopsis: Libby and her new friend Annie Bananie start their own dog club with neighborhood girls Nia and Bonnie. In order for Libby to become president she must "prove her self worthy" by getting Grandma Gert (who hates dogs) to kiss Boris, Annie's large, loveable dog. The humorous story has short sentences, black and white watercolor illustrations, 11 chapters, and 85 pages.

Learning Opportunities: Develop a story map to review characters, sequence events, and describe the outcome or story resolution. Discuss characters: Are they real? Was the plot realistic? Do club members have to adhere to initiations or actions in which they prove themselves? Write about a similar time in your own background experience.

By the Same Author: *Earl's Too Cool for Me; Aunt Elaine Does the Dance from Spain.*

Title: *Ant Plays Bear* by Betsy Byars, illustrations by Marc Simot (1997). (Easy-To-Read.) New York: Viking.

Genre: fiction

Reading Level: 1

Interest Level: primary

Synopsis: There are four short stories about Anthony (Ant) and his older brother. Written in first person from the older brother's point of view, each story reflects the boys' warm friendship and humorous adventures. In the first story, *Ant Plays Bear,* Ant wants his older brother to pretend to be a bear until the "bear" begins to get into the role and growl! The charming stories have short sentences, repeated vocabulary, and colorful watercolor illustrations.

Learning Opportunities: Reread each short story for fluency. Read, trace, and spell unfamiliar sight words. Write reading vocabulary on a wall chart for discussion and review. Reinforce sight words by playing Concentration or Bingo (see Games, Part III). Each realistic story provides opportunities to write about similar experiences. For example, in the first story *Ant Plays Bear,* write about a time when a game got out of hand or became frightening.

By the Same Author: *My Brother Ant* (an ALA Notable Book, a Horn Book Fanfare Book); *The Golly Sisters Go West; Hurrah for the Golly Sisters; The Golly Sisters Ride Again; Summer of the Swans* (Newbery Award).

Title: *Bravo Amelia Bedelia* by Henry Parish, illustrated by Lynn Sweat (1997). New York: Greenwillow Books.

Genre: fiction; humor

Reading Level: 2

Interest Level: primary–intermediate

Synopsis: Amelia Bedelia's literal interpretations occur as she follows Mrs. Rogers to the school orchestra. Mrs. Rogers, Amelia Bedelia's employer, is in charge of picking up the new conductor at the station. Amelia Bedelia first tries to *pick up* the train conductor but he is too heavy. The music conductor is almost late for the concert since he was not the one *picked up*! Other humorous mishaps occur as Amelia is told to take up something in the *string section* (she looks for string in the storeroom) and to *play by ear* (the fiddle gets stuck on her ear). Lynn Sweat creates clever ink and watercolor drawings that compliment the humorous story.

Learning Opportunities: Predict how Amelia will interpret the conductor's instructions. Write homonyms on index cards. Play a word game where readers "draw" a card and give two interpretations of the homonym. Write a short story about Amelia in your own school setting using homonyms in the book. Add homonyms to word cards accrued from other Amelia Bedelia stories for practice and review. Make a picture dictionary using homonyms.

By the Same Author: *Good Driving Amelia Bedelia; Amelia Bedelia 4 Mayor.*

Title: *Cam Jansen and the Scary Snake Mystery* by David Adler, illustrated by Susanna Natti (1997). New York: Viking, Penguin Group.

Genre: fiction; mystery

Reading Level: 2

Interest Level: primary–iintermediate

Synopsis: Mrs. Jansen, her daughter Cam, and friend Eric visit the art museum. Cam's nickname derives from her photographic memory—like a camera. The mystery begins when a thief steals Mrs. Jansen's video camera. The "scary snake" that escapes from a bag on the museum steps is the motive for the robbery. A series of clues (sweatshirt, torn jeans, sunglasses, News Scoop Contest) lead to the culprit. There are 8 short chapters, 58 pages, and 20 detailed, pen and ink illustrations. The sentences are short, with easy vocabulary.

Learning Opportunities: Predict the meaning of each clue (Why is it important? What does it mean?). Study illustrations for added information. Develop a Problem/Solution map. Evaluate the story: Did you like it? Would you change any characters, events? Use a Venn Diagram to compare this story to one or more Cam Jansen mysteries: include characters, setting, mystery plot, resolution. Use information on the map to write a short comparison paragraph.

By the Same Author: *Cam Jansen and the Catnapping Mystery (Cam Jansen, No 18); Cam Jansen and the Ghostly Mystery (Cam Jansen, No 16); Cam Jansen and the Chocolate Fudge Mystery.*

Title: *Commander Toad and the Voyage Home* by Jane Yolen, illustrations by Bruce Degen (1998). New York: Putnam & Grosset Group.

Genre: fantasy; space

Reading Level: 3

Interest Level: primary–intermediate

Synopsis: Commander Toad, Mr. Hop (copilot), Lieutenant Lily (mastery of machinery), Young Jake Skyjumper (keeps eye on the dials), and Old Doc Peeper (keeps everyone healthy and happy) ride through the galaxy on their ship Star Warts to find new undiscovered worlds. When they decide to go HOME they find a strange planet, when in fact, it is the ancient burial grounds of Toad's ancestors. The clever story is full of Bruce Degen's humorous illustrations and Jane Yolen's playful language (e.g., *toad-um pole; froggiest notion*). There are 64 pages that include 23 full-page color illustrations.

Learning Opportunities: Look at the book cover and title. Predict what the story will be about. Predict and revise predictions as you read the story and look at the illustrations. Use context clues and phonics to identify unfamiliar words. Write unfamiliar words or words with specific patterns (e.g., compound words, words with prefixes) on a Word Wall or index cards to read, review, and use in writing. Discuss and explain the humor in *froggiest notion* (p. 44), *Star Warts* (the ship), *toad-um pole* (p. 57), *leapfrogging across the galaxy* (p. 64). What is the theme of the story? Where is HOME? What did you think about the story?

By the Same Author: *Owl Moon* (Caldecott Medal)*; Favorite Folktales from Around the World; Animal Fare: Poems.*

Title: *Emma's Magic Winter* by Jean Little, illustrations by Jennifer Plecas (1998). New York: HarperCollins Publisher.

Genre: fiction

Reading Level: 1

Interest Level: primary

Synopsis: Emma is too shy to read aloud in class. When Mr. Kent tells her it is her turn to read, she can only whisper. However, Emma has a wonderful imagination and pretends that her red snow boots are really magic boots that can do marvelous things. When Sally moves in next door with the same red boots, both girls become fast friends and invent stories about their magic boots. When Sally realizes that Emma can read aloud to her little brother Josh but is still too shy to read aloud in class, Sally helps Emma use her imagination to overcome her shyness. There are 7 short chapters, 64 pages, simple sentences, and short vocabulary. Colorful illustrations compliment this story of friendship and overcoming fear.

Learning Opportunities: Echo read or take turns reading each page with a partner. Look at the illustrations and discuss the information that is not presented in the story. Discuss how Emma feels when she is called to read in class. Have you had similar feelings? What does Emma do? Why can she read aloud to Sally's younger brother and not in front of her classmates? Predict the meaning of unfamiliar words using context and phonics clues. Use multisensory instruction for hard to learn sight words (i.e., hear, say, trace, and write words). Play words games (Bingo, Concentration) to reinforce sight words.

By the Same Author: *Lost and Found: Different Dragons; From Anna; Hey World, Here I am.*

Title: *Freckle Juice* by Judy Blume (1971). New York: Bantam Doubleday Dell

Genre: fiction; humor

Reading Level: 2

Interest Level: primary–intermediate

Synopsis: Andrew wants freckles like his classmate Nicky Lane. Then he won't have to wash behind his neck and be late for school. Sharon, a smart aleck classmate, sells Andrew her secret freckle juice recipe for 50 cents. The recipe, a concoction of grape juice, vinegar, mustard, mayonnaise, lemon juice, ketchup, olive oil, onion, pepper, and salt, only makes him sick. Andrew must figure out how to get freckles by the time he sees Sharon in school! The humorous story has 5 chapters, 47 pages, and clever pen and ink illustrations.

Learning Opportunities: Make a problem/solution map. What is Andrew's problem and how does he resolve it? What would you do? Sequence several events and illustrate them in comic book fashion (see pages 22–23 in book as a model). Make up a recipe for something you want. Select vocabulary words to uses in an "antonym" or "synonym" board game or card game. Write the words on index cards. Players draw a card and provide an antonym or synonym. Use story words such as *outside, down, secret, fair, inside, fast, open, unlock, few).*

By the Same Author: *Superfudge;Fudge-a-mania;Tales of a Fourth Grade Nothing; Otherwise Known as Shelia the Great.*

Title: *Frog and Toad Are Friends* by Arnold Lobel (1971, Caldecott Honor Book). (An I Can Read Book.) New York: Harper and Row.

Genre: fantasy; humor

Reading Level: 1

Interest Level: primary

Synopsis: There are five short stories in this gentle book about Frog and Toad. In the first story *Spring,* Frog tries to arouse his sleeping friend to enjoy the coming of spring with him. It is only April and Toad refuses to get up until it is at least May. Frog tears out the pages of the calendar until it says May, wakes up a sleepy Toad, who then climbs out of bed to experience spring with his friend. Lobel's simple illustrations humorously portray the likeable characters. The text has large type, short sentences, word repetition, and dialogue.

Learning Opportunities: Read simultaneously, echo read, and reread stories to develop fluency. Take parts of Frog and Toad and read the dialogue of a specific character (see Readers Theater, Part IV, Art and Drama Extensions). Study illustrations and predict what will happen to the two friends as the story unfolds. Use multisensory techniques and word games to reinforce unfamiliar sight words.

By the Same Author: *Frog and Toad Together; Days with Frog and Toad* (audio cassette and hardcover); *Dias Con Sapo Y Sepo/Days with Frog and Toad; Frog and Toad All Year.*

Title: *Henry and Mudge and the Long Weekend* by Cynthia Rylant, illustrated by Sicie Stevenson (1992). (Ready-To-Read, Level 2.) New York: Aladdin Paperback, imprint of Simon & Schuster Children's Publishing Division.

Genre: fiction; humor

Reading Level: middle 1

Interest Level: primary

Synopsis: Henry and his dog Mudge are bored on a gray, cold, wet day. Henry's mother suggests that they make a castle out of a refrigerator box in the basement. Henry and his parents become involved in the project, making turrets, buttresses, flags, and a drawbridge. Mudge just munches! Colorful full-page and half-page illustrations show the family cutting, pasting, and painting, with Mudge in the center of things. The short, 40-page story contains large print, short sentences, and dialogue.

Learning Opportunities: Echo read and reread to develop fluency. Write compound words (weekend, pancake, somebody), *ing* words (boring, closing, nodding, drooling, interesting, getting, exciting) and single syllable words (Mudge, gray, cold, wet, woke, push, sleep, kept) on a wall chart. Look for familiar phonic patterns in short words (oke, eep, ay); apply syllable generalizations to compound words and words with suffixes (ling words); look for chunks in long words (see Phonics Patterns, Part III). Play word games (Bingo, Concentration) with sight words (see Games, Part III). Develop a crossword puzzle with the vocabulary. Describe and write about a project you have made on a boring day (LEA activity, Part I, LEA Approach).

By the Same Author: *Henry and Mudge and the Sneaky Crackers (mystery); Henry and Mudge: The First Book of Their Adventures; Henry and Mudge and the Bedtime Thumps: The Ninth Book of Their Adventures (Ready-To-Read); Henry and Mudge in the Green Time, Vol 13; Missing May (*Newbery Award).

Title: *Hour of the Olympics* by Mary Pope Osborne (1998) (Magic Tree House #16; a Stepping Stone Book). New York: Random House.

Genre: fantasy; mystery; time travel

Reading Level: 2

Interest Level: primary–intermediate

Synopsis: Jack and Annie's mission is to save stories from ancient libraries for the magic tree house that is owned by Morgan le Fay, a magical librarian from the time of King Arthur. This time they are whirled back into the time of Plato and the Olympic Games in Greece to discover and bring back the story of Pegasus, the great winged horse. This is the fourth book in the series of *The Mystery of the Lost Libraries* (books 13-16). Osborne has written prior mysteries about *The Tree House* (books 1-4), *The Magic Spell* (books 5-8), and *The Ancient Riddles* (books 9-12). Following the Olympics' adventure, the author provides four pages of facts about characters and events that took place in ancient Greece such as the Olympics, Greek Language, Plato, Zeus, Pegasus, and Star Myths. The book includes short sentences, 10 chapters with black and white illustrations, and 70 pages.

Learning Opportunities: Read each chapter heading and predict chapter events. Modify and revise predictions as you read each chapter. Make a Venn Diagram and compare and contrast customs of ancient Greece and today (e.g., clothing, social customs, religion). Make a problem/solution map and note Jack and Annie's problems and how they solved the mystery of the lost story about Pegasus.

By the Same Author: *Vacation Under the Volcano (Magic Tree House #13); Day of the Dragon King (Magic Tree House #14); Viking Ships at*

Sunrise (Magic Tree House, #15); American Tall Tales; One World, Many Religions.

Title: *In a Dark, Dark, Room and Other Scary Stories* retold by Alvin Schwartz, illustrations by Dirk Zimmer (1984) (an I Can Read Book, Level 1). New York: HarperCollins.

Genre: fantasy; ghost stories

Reading Level: 1

Interest Level: primary

Synopsis: There are seven enthralling ghost stories, retold in short sentences and easy vocabulary, with colorful illustrations that portray scary events such as a man with three inch long teeth, a woman's severed head, and bones *with no skin o-n* (p. 60)! At the end of the 60-page book, the author tells a short history about each story.

Learning Opportunities: Develop fluency and intonation by echo reading and exaggerating scary parts (e.g., *Ooooh! AAAAAAAAAAAAh!* from *In the Graveyard*, pp. 18–23). Reread stories. After reading the six line poem *The Ghost of John* (p. 60), write another ghost poem using the same word pattern (on) or a different word family (e.g., the ghost of M<u>ary</u>, really quite sc<u>ary</u>).

By the Same Author: *Busy Buzzing Bumblebees; I Saw You in the Bathtub; There Is a Carrot in My Ear* (all Level 1 stories). *Scary Stories to Tell in the Dark; More Scary Stories to Tell in the Dark.*

Title: *It's a Fiesta, Benjamin* by Patricia Reilly Giff, illustrated by DyAnne DiSalvo-Ryan (1996). South Holland, IL: A Yearling Book, Dell Readers Service.

Genre: fiction; Mexican customs

Reading Level: 2

Interest Level: primary

Synopsis: The neighborhood is going to have a fiesta to raise money for a swimming pool. In the middle of all of the activities, Benjamin's little brother runs away and neighbors start to fight. All ends well with lessons learned by everyone. There are nine short chapters that include Benjamin's Spanish Notes (Spanish words and expressions with English translations) at the end of each chapter. For example, Chapter 2 is followed by words pertaining to the neighborhood (sidewalk, street, avenue, block), Chapter 3 has cleanup words (broom, trash can, detergent), and Chapter 4 includes family words (relatives, brother, sister, parents, cousins). There are 80 pages with full-page black and white illustrations.

Learning Opportunities: Make a Problem/Solution Map that lists the problems the neighbors encounter in preparing for the fiesta; include possible solutions and actual solutions. Discuss fiesta experiences (if relevant to the reader) and compare to those in the story. Discuss Spanish and English words from Benjamin's notes. Create a semantic word map (see Part III, Vocabulary) to develop vocabulary concepts of unfamiliar vocabulary. Use a category from Benjamin's notes (e.g., Ingredients) and develop a Semantic Feature Analysis to compare and contrast words listed in the category (see Part III, Vocabulary).

By the Same Author: *Kids of the Polk Street School; The Lincoln Lions Band; The Polka Dot Private Eye; The New Kids at the Polk Street School.*

Title: *Keep Your Eye On Amanda!* By Avi (1996, 1997), illustrated by David Wisniewski (Caldecott Medalist). New York: Avon Camelot Books.

Genre: fantasy

Reading Level: low 4

Interest Level: primary–junior high

Synopsis: When Amanda, a rambunctious young raccoon, falls in with a thief to rob neighboring houses, she gets herself into trouble and imperils the animals of the Park. To put an end to the robberies, Judge Peebles wants to get rid of all of the animals! When Amanda's older (but not so adventuresome) brother Philip tries to save her, he finds it more difficult than he thought. In Amanda's words, she doesn't want to be saved! *Like, dude, all you do is just sit around and go nowhere, like that train we live on. Well, I'm moving fast. Totally. You can just watch my moves* (p. 29). Each chapter ends in a cliffhanger. This book has been published in serial form in more than eighty newspapers. Avi notes that he has established a foundation called Breakfast Serials to bring good writing and illustrators to kids in today's newspapers.

Learning Opportunities: Predict and write your outcome after reading each cliffhanger chapter. Write your own next chapter before you read the author's version. Illustrate a favorite part. What is the theme of the story? Do you think the consequences fit Amanda's crime? Why or why not? Write a sequel about Amanda taking the train to Denver. Write your own short-story serial for publication in a newspaper.

By the Same Author: *Amanda Joins the Circus; Poppy; Poppy and Rye; Ragweed; What Do Fish Have To Do With Anything?*

Title: *Marvin Redpost: Is He a Girl?* (a First Stepping Stone Book) by Louis Sachar (1993). New York: Random House.

Genre: fantasy; humor

Reading Level: high 1

Interest Level: primary–intermediate

Synopsis: Ever since Marvin finds out from Casey that he'll turn into a girl if he kisses his elbow, he tries to do this very thing! After all, *There is nothing that Marvin Redpost can't do*! (p. 14). He is finally successful when he gets tangled up in his bed sheets, falls out of bed, and on the way down finds his elbow in kissing position. Is his voice changing? Why does he think like a girl? Can he get in an elbow-kissing position again to undo what he thinks he did? The funny, quirky story keeps the reader guessing. There are 12 chapters and 71 pages, with black and white illustrations throughout. The short sentences are filled with dialogue and familiar vocabulary.

Learning Opportunities: Look at the title? What do you think the story will be about? Read each chapter heading and predict what will happen. Continue to predict and revise your predictions as you read each chapter. Compare and contrast Marvin's behavior before and after he kisses his elbow. What changes occur? Why did the author include a character like Patsy Gatsby? Do you know anyone like Patsy? Did Marvin (the boy) change after he kissed his elbow the second time? Give reasons for your response.

By the Same Author: *Marvin Redpost: Why Pick on Me? Marvin Redpost: Kidnapped at Birth? Marvin Redpost: Alone in His Teacher's House.*

Title: *Mine's the Best* by Crosby Bonsall (1973, 1996) (My First I-Can-Read Book). New York: Harper Trophy, HarperCollins.

Genre: fiction; humor

Reading Level: NA

Interest Level: kindergarten–primary

Synopsis: Two boys meet on a boardwalk and begin arguing over whose balloon is the best. (They are identical except in color!) When a little girl shows up with a similar balloon and sticks out her tongue, the boys decide that their balloons were the best and walk away smiling, arms around each other. There are only 105 words and 28 sentences in this colorfully illustrated and humorous easy reading book. Many words are repeated and the short sentences contain from three to four words.

Learning Opportunities: Read and reread to develop reading fluency. Use the illustrations, beginning sounds, and familiar word patterns to recognize unfamiliar words. Enjoy and share information that is in the illustrations and not in the story. Use multisensory instruction to reinforce reading vocabulary. Write vocabulary words on index cards or on a Word Wall and generate rhyming words for word patterns: *Mine*—fine, line; *spots*—dots, pots, lots; *best*—rest, pest; *ride*—side.

By the Same Author: *The Case of the Dumb Bells; The Case of the Scardy Cats; The Case of the Cats Meow.*

Title: *Molly's Pilgrim* by Barbara Cohen (1983). New York: Bantam Skylark.

Genre: historical fiction; prejudice

Reading Level: middle 2

Interest Level: primary–intermediate

Synopsis: Molly and her family have moved to America from Russia. Molly's classmates make fun of her dress and speech. Elizabeth, who laughs most of all says: *You talk funny, Molly. You look funny, Molly (p. 2)*. For Thanksgiving, Miss Stickley asks her students to bring a pilgrim doll to class. Molly's mother makes a lovely Russian doll for the assignment. When Molly brings the doll to class classmates snicker and Elizabeth exclaims: *That's not a Pilgrim. That's some Russian or Polish person. What does a person like that have to do with Pilgrims?* (p. 34). Miss Stickley places the Russian doll on a prominent place on her desk and helps her class understand the true meaning of Thanksgiving. The simple, short story (41 pages) is written in first person from Molly's point of view. There are a few unfamiliar words that provide good opportunities for prediction and discussion (*shaynkeit, Malkeleh, paskudnyaks*).

Learning Opportunities: Use the sentence context to predict the meaning of the following words: *Nu, shaynkeit, Nu Malkeleh* (p. 22), *paskudnyaks* (p. 13). Develop a story map to recall characters and organize story events. Look at the illustrations: When does the story take place (time) and where does it take place? How does this setting affect the story? Could the story happen today? Discuss the characters and their actions. For example, why did Elizabeth make fun of Molly? Why was Molly embarrassed by her mother's doll? Why did Molly's mother make the doll? Have you experienced any of these same feelings? What is the theme or themes? Why do you think the author wrote the story?

By the Same Author: *The Christmas Revolution; The Orphan Game.*

Title: *Mr. Putter and Tabby Walk the Dog* by Cynthia Rylant, illustrated by Arthur Howard (1994). Orlando, Florida: Harcourt Brace and Company.

Genre: fiction; humor

Reading Level: low 2

Interest Level: primary

Synopsis: Mr. Putter with his cat Tabby, offers to walk Mrs. Teaberry's dog, Zeke, while she recuperates from an injured foot. On the walks Zeke tugs, wraps his leash around trees (and Mr. Potter), and chases big dogs. Mr. Putter and Tabby are exhausted. What can Mr. Putter do? The solution is one most dog owners will predict. The limited text on each page is around three sentences and phrases are repeated throughout the story. The expressive, colorful illustrations show the humorous interaction between the superior cat, a frustrated Mr. Potter, and a silly, enthusiastic dog. The author has written other delightful adventures about Mr. Putter and Tabby.

Learning Opportunities: Echo read, read simultaneously with a peer, teacher, or support staff, and reread to develop fluency. Make a problem/solution map to reflect Mr. Putter's problems and his solutions for walking Mrs. Teaberry's unruly dog. Use a multisensory approach to learn unfamiliar sight words such as *again, through, around, with* (see Part IV, Sight Words).

By the Same Author: *Henry and Mudge* books; *Poppleton and Friends; Appalachia: The Voices of Sleeping Birds; Bear Day; Cat Heaven; A Fine White Dust.*

Title: *Muggie Maggie* by Beverly Cleary (1990). New York: Avon Books.
Genre: fiction; humor
Reading Level: 4
Interest Level: primary - intermediate
Synopsis: Maggie is in the third grade and refuses to learn cursive. She would rather print and use her computer. Her contrary ways lead to a parent/teacher conference, a visit to the principal and school psychologist, and her dad putting the computer off limits. When Maggie's teacher Mrs. Leeper makes Maggie a message monitor, Maggie discovers she must be able to read cursive if she is to read the messages (some include her name!). The short chapter book has 8 chapters, 70 pages, and realistic black and white illustrations.

Learning Opportunities: Discuss detail and inference type questions: How does Maggie's mother dot her i's and her father make his u's? Why does the author refer to her parents' cursive writing habits? What does Maggie's teacher do about her refusal to learn cursive? Why does Maggie feel trapped when she wants to learn cursive? Why do Maggie's feelings change toward learning cursive? Create semantic word maps to discuss unfamiliar vocabulary. Play synonym or antonym word games: write selected vocabulary words on index cards. Students select a card and provide an antonym or synonym. Use words such as *indignant, virtuous, accurate, motivated.*

By the Same Author: *Beezus and Ramona; Henry and Beezus; Henry and Ribsy; Ramona the Brave; Ramona Forever.*

Title: *Nate the Great and the Tardy Tortoise* by Marjorie Weinman Sharmat and Craig Sharmat, illustrated by Marc Simont (1995). New York: Bantam Doubleday Dell Books.
Genre: fiction; mystery

Reading Level: high 1

Interest Level: primary

Synopsis: Nate the Great and his dog Sludge try to find the home of a lost tortoise who appears in their yard nibbling at the garden flowers. Following clues and searching the neighborhood, Nate relentlessly searches for the tortoise's home. The book has 42 pages and colorful, watercolor drawings of clues for the reader to follow. The sentences are short and many words are repeated (e.g., *A bite here. A bite there. He started to eat a daisy. A bite here. A bite there.* [p.3]).

Learning Opportunities: Predict the meaning of each clue. Reread the story to develop fluency. To reinforce sequencing skills, play Story Jumble. Write main events (mystery clues) on sentence strips. Arrange jumbled strips in the correct order and then read the sentences (see Part III, Games).

By the Same Authors: *Nate the Great and the Mushy Valentine.* **By Marjorie Weinman Sharmat:** *Nate the Great; Nate the Great Goes Undercover; Nate the Great and the Lost List; Nate the Great and the Missing Key; Nate the Great and the Boring Beach Bag; Nate the Great and the Halloween Hunt.*

Title: *Owl At Home* by Arnold Lobel (1975) (An I-Can-Read Book, Level 2). New York: HarperCollins Children's Books.

Genre: fantasy; humor

Reading Level: middle 1

Interest Level: primary

Synopsis: The author/illustrator tells five short stories that describe gentle owl's problems. These include: accommodating an aggressive house-guest, Winter *(The Guest);* seeing two strange bumps in his bed *(Strange Bumps)*; making tear-water tea *(Tear-Water Tea)*; being upstairs and downstairs at the same time *(Upstairs And Downstairs)*; and, finding, losing, and finding again a friend *(Owl and Moon)*. Soft watercolor illustrations portray the slightly befuddled owl and the various events that take place in and around his home. The book has 64 pages, large print, numerous illustrations, and simple, declarative sentences. Each humorous story describes everyday experiences that seem to complicate the life of friendly, trusting Owl.

Learning Opportunities: Predict events based on illustrations, prior reading, and background experience (see Part III, DR-TA, Inference Skills). Discuss the problem presented in each story and possible solutions (especially stories 1, 2, and 3—*The Guest, Strange Bumps, Upstairs And Downstairs*). Compare stories. Which one was a favorite? Why? Make a Description Map of Owl (see Part III, Text Relationships, Description Map). Reread stories to develop fluency. Write sight words on index cards for review, to use with Bingo board game, and to play Concentration (see Part IV, Games). Use multisensory instruction to reinforce mastery of hard to learn sight words (e.g., another, there, shout) (see Part III, Sight Words).

By the Same Author: *Frog and Toad Are Friends; Frog and Toad Together; Days With Frog and Toad* (audio cassette); *Fables; The Arnold Lobel Book of Mother Goose.*

Title: *Poppleton and Friends* by Cynthia Rylant, illustrated by Mark Teague (1997). New York: The Sky Blue Press, Imprint of Scholastic.

Genre: fantasy; humor

Reading Level: 2

Interest Level: primary

Synopsis: Three humorous stories describe Poppleton's day at the beach (*The Shore Day*), his problem with dry skin (*Dry Skin*) and wanting to live longer (*Grapefruit*). Friends Hudson and Cherry Sue are there to provide advice and company. Artist Mark Teague's illustrations are expressive and comical. A favorite picture shows Poppleton trying to eat a grapefruit as his lips turn inside out! The book is written in large print and has 48 pages. Rylant's stories include descriptive words and phrases such as *dry as a dandelion* (p. 24), *dry as a desert* (p. 27), worthwhile themes (friendship), and problems to solve.

Learning Opportunities: Use context clues, picture clues, and phonics to predict unfamiliar words. Predict what will happen to Poppleton as he tries Cherry Sue's solutions for his dry skin. Make a Problem/Solution Map (see Poppleton example, Figure 3–10, Part III, Text Relationships). Enjoy Teague's illustrations and discuss information in pictures that add to story content.

By the Same Author: *Poppleton; Henry and Mudge; Mr. Putter and Tabby; Missing May* (Newbery Medal); *A Fine White Dust* (Newbery Honor Book).

Title: *Rats on the Range and Other Stories* by James Marshall (1993). New York: Puffin Books, Penguin Group.

Genre: fantasy

Reading Level: 2

Interest Level: primary–intermediate

Synopsis: Eight clever short stories describe the comical adventures of Miss Mouse and Tomcat, Pig, the Waldo Rat family, and Buzzard Watkins. Humorous lines crop up in each witty adventure. For example, when Pig treats Miss Lola to chocolate eclairs and a mud bath, she sighs, *"You really know how to entertain a girl." And Pig was in heaven* (p. 33). In the first story ("Miss Mouse"), a clever and industrious Miss Mouse outsmarts and befriends tomcat when she becomes his housekeeper. Realizing that he cannot live without her, tomcat reluctantly gives up his taste for mouse meat! Each delightful story is about 10 pages, a good length to read at one sitting.

Learning Opportunities: Make a problem/solution map describing the problems and resolutions in "Miss Mouse."Talk about the clever language and what it implies, such as when Miss Mouse leaves and there is no one to read tomcat stories. He finds *a day without one of Miss Mouse's stories was a day without sunshine* (p. 21). Does the author make tomcat (and other characters) believable? In what ways? Illustrate each chapter (there are no illustrations). Illustrate and sequence major story events in a can (see Illustrate Stories in a Can, Part III, art extensions).

By the Same Author: *George and Martha; The Cut-Ups; Four on the Shore (Puffin Easy to Read, Level 3); Fox and His Friends (Puffin Easy to Read, Level 3).*

Title: *Rosie's Big City Ballet* by Patricia Reilly Giff (1998). New York: Puffin Books, Penguin Group.

Genre: fiction; ballet

Reading Level: 3

Interest Level: primary–intermediate

Synopsis: Rosie O'Meara wants to be a real ballerina. When her older friend takes her to a big city ballet production of *Romeo and Juliet,* the "Juliet" understudy tells Rosie that she will be a ballet dance but she must believe in herself. This important theme occurs throughout the story. Rosie is disappointed when she doesn't get a dancing role, but a bigger surprise awaits her at the end of the book. The story is full of ballet terms such as *pas de chat, en haut, pirouette,* and *corps de ballet.* There are 10 chapters, 73 pages, full-page black and white illustrations, and pages from Rosie's Notebook with definitions of dance terms (pp. 74–75). The story is written in first person from Rosie's point of view.

Learning Opportunities: Make a story map that includes characters, setting, problem, events, and resolution. Discuss the theme. Why did the author write the story? Evaluate the story. Were the characters believable? Did you like the story? Would you change anything? What about the dancing terms? Did they add or detract from the story? Why? Write Chapter 11, taking up where the story leaves off.

By the Same Author: *Kids of the Polk Street School; It's a Fiesta, Benjamin; The Lincoln Lions Band; The Polka Dot Private Eye; Lily's Crossing* (Newbery Honor).

Title: *Sarah, Plain and Tall* by Patricia MacLachlan (1985, Newbery Medal). New York: A Charlotte Zolotow Book, Harper Trophy, A Division of HarperCollins.

Genre: historical fiction; frontier

Reading Level: 3

Interest Level: primary–intermediate

Synopsis: Anna and Caleb's mother died giving birth to Caleb, and the house is quiet and empty. Papa puts an add in the paper for a wife and Sarah Elisabeth Wheaton reponds from Maine, writing that she will stay for a month to see how things work out. Sarah sings, teaches the children about the sea that she loves, and brings laughter and beauty back into the prairie house. When the month is over, Sarah puts on her yellow bonnet, hitches the horse to a wagon, and leaves for town. The anxious family fears that she will not return. This simple, moving story is told in first person from Anna's perspective. It has 58 pages and nine chapters, each about six pages long.

Learning Opportunities: Make a character map and describe Anna, Caleb, Sarah, and Papa. Make a story map and list characters, setting, story events, conflicts, and resolutions. Discuss higher-level questions: Why did Anna and Caleb want Sarah to stay? Why were they afraid that she might leave? What was the relationship between Papa and Sarah? How did prairie life differ from living in Maine? Find references in the story to support your answers. Evaluate the story: Were the characters real? What did you think about the story? What did the setting have to do with the story? Why did the author write from Anna's point of view? Extend the story and write a chapter beginning where the story left off. Write an acrostic poem about Sarah.

By the Same Author: *All the Places to Love; Arthur, for the Very First Time; Through Grandpa's Eyes; Skylark; Seven Kisses in a Row.*

Title: *Summer Wheels* by Eve Bunting, illustrated by Thomas B. Allen (1992). San Diego: Harcourt Brace Jovanovich.

Genre: fiction; understanding differences; bikes

Reading Level: 1

Interest Level: primary–intermediate

Synopsis: An old man, called the Bicycle Man, fixes broken bikes and then loans them to kids in the neighborhood to ride free of charge. There are only two rules: the bikes must be returned by 4:00; and, if the bike is broken, the rider must fix it. Lawrence and his friend Brady, friends of the Bicycle Man, visit him daily and ride his bikes. When a stranger who calls himself Abraham Lincoln checks out a bike and doesn't return it, the two boys try to find him and retrieve the bike. This is a heart-warming story about a boy's need to love and be loved, an understanding old man who "bends" the rules, and two friends who learn to befriend someone different than they. Bike enthusiasts will enjoy the bike vocabulary, e.g., *cherry pickers* (bouncing on back wheels) and *Vander rolls* (throwing yourself over the handlebars). There are 45 pages and six short chapters with 13 full-page illustrations. Allen illustrates the book in soft, subtle chalk drawings. Like many of Eve Bunting's books, the story is written in first person.

Learning Opportunities: Discuss characters and their motivations. For example, why did the new boy tear up the bike? What was he afraid of? Why did Lawrence and Brady mistrust him in the first place? Why did the Bicycle Man fix bikes and then sign them out free of charge? Why did he care about what happened to Abraham Lincoln? Support answers with story information (see Higher-Level Questions, Part III). Use a Venn Diagram and compare and contrast Lawrence and Brady with Abraham Lincoln. Develop a character map and describe the Bicycle Man, Lawrence, Brady, and Abraham Lincoln.

By the Same Author: *The Wall; Fly Away Home; Smoky Night; Going Home; Goose Dinner* (An I-Can-Read Book).

Title: *The Cut-Ups Crack Up* by James Marshall (1992). New York: Puffin Books, Penguin Group.

Genre: fiction; humor

Reading Level: 1

Interest Level: primary

Synopsis: Spud Jenkins and Joe Turner want to impress classmates Charles Andrew and Mary Frances. The adventure begins when the boys video tape themselves sitting inside Principal's Spurgles brand new red sports car. When the car accidentally starts up, the boys are in for trouble! The easy reading book contains short sentences, hilarious illustrations, and a fun story.

Learning Opportunities: Read the story and use the context, phonics, and syllabication to read long words (e.g., repugnant, blissfully, mechanical). Predict the meaning of unfamiliar vocabulary words. Why did the author use "repugnant" to describe Bessie? What picture clues provide information about Principal Spurgle's character and personality? Retell the story. Play Story Jumble: write story events on strips, mix, and arrange in the correct order. Read other stories about the Crack-Ups and compare the characters, problem, events, and resolution.

By the Same Author: *The Cut-Ups; The Cut-Ups Carry On; The Cut-Ups Cut Loose: The Cut-Ups at Camp Custer.*

Title: *The Golly Sisters Go West* by Betsy Byars, illustrations by Sue Truesdell (1985, An I-Can-Read Book, Level 3). New York: Harper and Row.

Genre: historical fiction; humor

Reading Level: 1

Interest Level: primary–intermediate

Synopsis: May-May and Rose, two zanny sisters, go west to dance and sing. Six short chapters have individual stories about the sisters beginning their singing and dancing career. In the first chapter, *The Golly Sisters Go West*, May-May and Rose cannot get their horse to go! Finally remembering the horse word for go (Giddy-up!), they begin their adventures. (They must also remember the horse word for stop!) The silly cartoon illustrations fit Byars' clever writing. This is the first of three comical books describing the adventures of the Golly sisters. The books contain large print, 64 pages, numerous colorful illustrations, and easy words with many words repeated.

Learning Opportunities: Reread each short chapter for fluency. Write unfamiliar sight words (e.g., Chapter 1—*there, ready, around;* Chapter 2—*blue, can, both, first;* Chapter 3—*third, fourth, about*) on a wall chart or on index cards. Use a multisensory approach and listen to, pronounce, trace, and spell the words from memory. Play word games (Bingo, Concentration, Board Games). Select three or four major events and Illustrate the story in a can (see art extensions). Pick a favorite illustration and write about it. Write your own Golly Sisters' adventure.

By the Same Author: *The Golly Sisters Ride Again; Hurray for the Golly Sisters; Tornado; A Herculeah Jones Mystery: Death's Door; The Summer of the Swans* (Newberry Award Book); *Coast to Coast; Wanted . . . Mud Blossom.*

Title: *The King's Equal* by Katherine Paterson (1992, a Trophy Chapter Book). New York: Harper Trophy, a Division of HarperCollins.

Genre: fantasy

Reading Level: 3

Interest Level: primary–intermediate

Synopsis: A wise and gentle dying King tells his greedy son that he will wear his crown only when he marries a princess who is his equal in beauty, intelligence, and wealth. So starts the search for the King's Equal. A mysterious wolf with strange powers and a beautiful and kind peasant girl save the Kingdom and help the prince find true wealth. Detailed black and white illustrations support the mystery and beauty of this engaging tale by Newbery Award author Katherine Paterson. There are six chapters and 56 pages, with full-page illustrations beginning each chapter. The book was a 1993 Teachers' Choice (IRA) and a 1992 Irma Simonton Black Award (Bank Street College of Education).

Learning Opportunities: Develop a story map to trace characters and events. What is the theme of the story? Why did the author write the fairy tale? Discuss detail and inference questions: Who is Rosamund? What did Rosamund do that impressed the wolf with her kindness? Who was the wolf? What events changed the prince? How did he change? Illustrate your favorite part of the story. Write a sequel to the story that includes the Wolf. Create masks of the prince, Rosamund, the goats, Wolf, the old King, and the councilors, and act out the story.

By the Same Author: *Bridge to Terabithia* (Newbery Award); *Jacab Have I Loved* (Newbery Award); *Jip, His Story; The Master Puppeteer* (National Book Award); *The Great Gilly Hopkins* (National Book Award).

Title: *The Seven Treasure Hunts* by Betsy Byars (1991). New York: Harper Trophy, a division of HarperCollins.

Genre: fiction

Reading Level: high 1

Interest Level: primary–intermediate

Synopsis: Jackson and his best friend Goat hide treasures for the other to find. To find the treasure, each boy must follow a list of treasure clues. The first treasure hunt is fun, but the second treasure hunt turns disastrous when Jackson mistakenly eats Rachel's chocolate popsicle. Goat's older sister Rachel (known as the ogre) is furious and gets even by burying Jackson's treasure where Goat will never find it. The story is written in first person from Jackson's point of view. There are 7 chapters and 74 pages in this humorous story about two good friends and an disagreeable sister.

Learning Opportunities: Using Goat's clues—*4 to the right, 6 to the left, 7 across, 1 ahead, 2 sideways, look up* (p. 4)—predict where the treasure will be. Continue the story. What will the boys do tomorrow? Goat's sister Rachel has a *haglike grin* (p. 55) and *crocodile smile* (p 58). Draw a picture of Rachel. Compare Jackson and his friend Goat. What do the boys have in common? How are they different? Make up a list of clues for your own treasure hunt.

By the Same Author: *The Golly Sisters Go West; Hooray for the Golly Sisters! The Golly Sisters Ride Again; Herculeah Jones Mysteries.*

Title: *The Time Warp Trio: The Not-So-Jolly-Roger* by Jon Scieszka, illustrated by Lane Smith (1991). New York: Penguin Group.

Genre: fantasy; humor

Reading Level: 2

Interest Level: primary–intermediate

Synopsis: Joe, Sam, and Fred find themselves 275 years in the past on a deserted island because Fred wished for buried treasure. The boys are in the midst of pirates lead by the notorious, singing Blackbeard. The only way to get home and escape demise (walking off a gang plank, digging their own graves!) is to find "The Book," a birthday present from magician Uncle Joe, with mysterious powers. The comical story is written in first person (Joe's point of view), and contains 10 short chapters, 57 pages, and witty cartoon illustrations by Lane Smith.

Learning Opportunities: Use context clues, phonics, and syllabication strategies to decode unfamiliar words. Predict how the boys will escape each harrowing episode. Make a story map of each chapter to keep track of main story events (see Part III, chapter map of *Hatchet*). Research Blackbeard. Was there such a pirate? What was he like? Select a time and write about another humorous travel adventure that propels Joe, Sam, and Fred into the future or the past.

By the Same Author: *The Good, the Bad, and the Goofy; Knights of the Kitchen Table; Your Mother was a Neanderthal, 2095 (Time Warp Trio Books); The Frog Prince—Continued; The True Story of the 3 Little Pigs.*

Title: *Tornado* by Betsy Byars, illustrated by Doron Ben-Ami (1996). New York: HarperCollins Children's Books.

Genre: fiction; dogs

Reading Level: middle 2

Interest Level: primary–intermediate

Synopsis: When a family is huddled in a storm shelter during a tornado, Pete, the farmhand, tells stories about his dog Tornado that he found during a similar storm. There are 7 short chapters, 49 pages, and soft black and white chalk drawings. Each chapter tells a different story about Tornado. Dog lovers will particularly enjoy these gentle, realistic stories.

Learning Opportunities: Compare and contrast several stories. Develop a Venn Diagram and list similarities and differences in characters and events. Share your own background experiences that relate to a particular chapter such as being in a storm or special adventures with a dog or other pet. Retell a favorite chapter and extend the story.

By the Same Author: *The Golly Sisters Ride Again; Hooray for the Golly Sisters; The Golly Sisters Go West* (I-Can-Read Books); *A Herculeah Jones Mystery: The Dark Stairs, Dead Letter, and Death's Door.*

Novels

Title: *A Fine White Dust* by Cynthia Rylant (1986, a Newbery Honor book). New York: Simon and Schuster Children's Books Publishing Division.

Genre: fiction; identity

Reading Level: 3

Interest Level: intermediate–junior high

Synopsis: Pete knew he loved the church. When the Preacher Man comes to town Pete believes that he is being called to follow the revivalist in his mission. His good friend Rufus is suspicious of the Preacher Man from the start, but cannot dissuade Pete from his mission. This is a poignant story about growing up and finding oneself. Older struggling readers will find authentic characters, a gripping story, mature theme, and familiar vocabulary. The story is written in first person from Pete's point of view.

Learning Opportunities: Discuss Rylant's use of similes to create images. On page 42, Pete describes the interaction between his friend Rufus and the Preacher Man *like a tornado, hot air hitting cold and just plain getting out of hand.* Use Think Alouds (see Part III, Thinking Aloud) to model developing images, making predictions, linking story information to prior knowledge, and using syllabication strategies to decode polysyllabic words. Use a Venn Diagram and compare and contrast Pete and Rufus, their personality, strengths, beliefs. Ask higher-level questions: Why did Pete want to go with the Preacher Man? Why did Pete's parents not attend church on a regular basis? What was the relationship between Pete and his mother, his dad? Did Pete change at the end of the story? Did Rufus? What type of man was the Preacher Man? Find evidence in the book to support your interpretations. Write a personal response after reading the book. Discuss the theme(s). Why do you think the author wrote the book?

By the Same Author: *Missing May* (Newbery Medal); *Henry and Mudge series; Poppleton and Friends books; Mr. Putter and Tabby books* (easy reading books).

Title: *Adam Zigzag* by Barbara Barrie (1994). New York: Bantam Doubleday Dell.

Genre: fiction; reading difficulties

Reading Level: 3

Interest Level: junior high–high school

Synopsis: Adam is bright, popular, and can play the guitar. He also has a reading disability (dyslexia); when he reads the letters zigzag across the page. By the end of 6th grade Adam can read and write just enough to get by. Teachers think he is lazy and he falls in with the wrong peer group. Adam's parents send him to a private high school for learning disabled students where caring teachers help him acquire learning strategies and achieve success. The book is written in first person from the perspective of Adam and his older sister Caroline. Short chapters (two to three pages) alternate between Adam's story and Caroline's.

Learning Opportunities: Compare and contrast Adam and Caroline. Record information on a comparison/contrast map. Discuss higher-level questions: Why did Adam fall in with the wrong peer group? How did he change over the course of the story? What was the relationship between the brother and sister? How did Adam cope with his dyslexia? What strategies did he use? Support your answers by sharing information from the book. Describe your reactions to the story.

By the Same Author: *Lone Star.*

Title: *An Island Like You: Stories of the Barrio* by Judith Ortiz Cofer (1995). New York: Penguin Group.

Genre: fiction; short stories (ALA Best Book for Young Adults)

Reading Level: low 6

Interest Level: junior high–high school

Synopsis: Twelve poignant short stories tell about the adventures, conflicts, relationships, and problems in the lives of Arturo, Rita, Yolanda, Doris, and other teenagers that live in the Puerto Rican barrio of Paterson, New Jersey. In each short story the author paints a moving and realistic picture of her protagonist. For example, in "The One Who Watches," Doris compares herself to her colorful friend: *See, I'm not flashy like Yolanda. I'm practically invisible. My hair is kinky, so I keep it greased down, and I'm short and plain. Not ugly, not beautiful. Just a nothing. If it wasn't for Yolanda, nobody would know I'm around* (p. 74). A frightened Doris is confronted with guilt and her own insecurity when she sees her friend shoplift in the presence of security guards.

Learning Opportunities: Write a response after reading a particular story. How did you feel after reading the story? What did you think about the characters? What motivates or makes Yolanda (Doris, Arturo, Rita) act and react to his or her situation? What would you do in a similar situation? What influences do family and peers have? Have you experienced similar feelings? Write another chapter building on a certain character and story. Write from the point of view of the main character.

By the Same Author: *Silent Dancing: A Partial Remembrance of a Puerto Rican Childhood.*

Title: *Baseball Pals* by Matt Christopher (1956, 1984). New York: Little, Brown and Co.

Genre: fiction

Reading Level: 2

Interest Level: primary–intermediate

Synopsis: When Jackie is elected captain of the baseball team, he feels that he can play any position he wants. He has always wanted to pitch and asks his best friend Paul, who is a strong pitcher, to play in the outfield. When Paul decides to pitch for a competing team, Jackie realizes that friendship may be more important than being pitcher. There are 17 chapters, 97 pages, and lots of baseball action.

Learning Opportunities: What is the problem and how does Jackie resolve it? Do you think that Jackie eventually would have been a good pitcher? Find evidence to support your answer. What did Jackie's father mean when he said, *Now, hold your horses* (p. 40). Illustrate the idiom. Make a character map and include Jackie, Paul, Mr. Nichols, Mr. Todd, and Ervie. What was the theme of the story?

By the Same Author: *Challenge at Second Base; Soccer Soup; At the Plate With—Ken Griffey, Jr.; Michael Jordan; Tiger Woods; Mo Vaughn.*

Title: *Brian's Return* by Gary Paulsen (1999). New York: Delacorte Press.
Genre: fiction; survival; identity
Reading Level: 5
Interest Level: intermediate–junior high

Synopsis: This book, the last in the series about Brian and his adventures in the wilderness, begins two years after *Hatchet* and describes Brian's difficulty adjusting to home and school surroundings. In high school, a class bully picks a fight with Brian. Brian savagely defends himself like he did in the wilderness. Because of his violent response, Brian is sent to Caleb, a family counselor. Both Caleb and Brian realize that Brian misses the wilderness and must return to discover what he left behind. Once there, Brian writes Caleb and his brief letters begin each chapter. This is a short book, 18 chapters and 115 pages.

Learning Opportunities: Read aloud Brian's letters to Caleb that describe the sunset, ice, and sky (p. 20-21). Close your eyes and image the colors and sounds. Describe what pictures you see in your mind. Discuss characters and character motivations: What made Brian return to the wilderness? Who was Billy and what did he represent? How did Brian change over the course of the book? What was the theme of the book? Compare and contrast *Hatchet* and *Brian's Return*. Draw a Venn Diagram and note the similarities and differences. Extend the story—write about Brian's life five years from now. Evaluate the story—did you like the author's resolution? How did this book compare to *Hatchet* or *Brian's Winter*? Did you learn anything new? Would you change anything?

By the Same Author: *Hatchet; The River; Brian's Winter; Brian's Return; Nightjohn; Dogsong.*

Title: *Bridge to Terabithia* by Katherine Paterson (1977). (Newbery Award) New York: Harper Trophy, a division of HarperCollins.

Genre: fiction; friendship; loss; identity

Reading Level: high 4

Interest Level: intermediate–junior high

Synopsis: Jess Aarons, a runner and an artist, befriends newcomer Leslie Burke, a tomboy from the city with spunk and imagination. Both, in various ways, are school outcasts. Together they create a magic kingdom called Terabithia, where they share dreams and secrets. To get to Terabithia they must swing from a rope attached to a tree on the bank of the creek. Spring rains make the trip dangerous because of the overflowing creek. Jess plans to meet Leslie in Terabithia, but instead accepts an invitation from his teacher to visit Washington, D.C., secretly relieved that he doesn't have to cross the high creek. When Jess arrives home, he learns that Leslie has been drowned crossing the creek. The author's moving descriptions of character relationships and motivations bring this extraordinary story to a close. There are 13 chapters and 128 pages. The book is filled with image building language and well-developed, complex characters such as Jess, Leslie, and Janice Avery, the school bully who is abused by her father.

Learning Opportunities: Discuss how the author develops images by using figurative language as in the following passage: *Jess's feelings about Leslie's father poked up like a canker sore* (p. 68). Write predictions about what will happen in the oncoming chapter and provide reasons for your predictions. After reading, verify or modify predictions. Develop vocabulary by selecting a few words from each chapter that relate to students' experiences yet ones with which they are not familiar (e.g., Chapter 2— *nauseatingly, pudgy, hypocritical*). Develop a word map listing word attributes (see Part III, Vocabulary). To read long words use syllabication rules and structural analysis (e.g., find word stems and apply the rules of 3's and 2's) (see Word Identification, Part III). Use vocabulary words in writing character sketches. Develop a character map that includes Jess, Leslie, Janice Avery, and May Belle (Jess's little sitter). Write a letter to Janice Avery or Jess. Write or discuss personal responses to the story. Discuss the theme(s). Why did the author write the story?

By the Same Author: *Jacob Have I Loved; Jip: His Story; Lyddie.*

Title: *Bunnicula: A Rabbit Tale of Mystery* by Deborah and James Howe, illustrated by Alan Daniel (1979). New York: Avon Books, a division of Hearst Corporation.

Genre: fantasy; humor

Reading Level: 3

Interest Level: primary–intermediate

Synopsis: The Monroe family goes to a Dracula movie and finds a rabbit whom they bring home as a pet. The friendly family dog (Harold) and suspicious cat (Chester) view the newcomer differently. Harold finds a friend in the fluffy animal, while Chester believes Bunnicula to be a vampire. Chester has read all about supernatural matters; and after the rabbit arrives, vegetables are mysteriously drained of color and show the markings of two fangs, closely resembling the rabbit's teeth. There are 9 chapters, 98 pages, and humorous pen and ink drawings. Harold tells the story in first person, from his rational point of view.

Learning Opportunities: Develop a problem/solution map that describes the problem and the different attempts by Harold and Chester to resolve the mystery. Discuss higher-level questions. Examples from this story are included in Part III, Higher-Level Questions. Write main events on sentence strips, mix, and play *Story Jumble*. Write a sequel that continues the relationship between Bunnicula, Harold, and Chester.

By the Same Author: *Holiday Inn; The Celery Stalks at Midnight.*

Title: *Crash* by Jerry Spinelli (1996). New York: Alfred A. Knopf.

Genre: fiction; peer relations; friendship

Reading Level: 3

Interest Level: intermediate–high school

Synopsis: John Coogan (i.e., "Crash") and his best friend Mike like to play pranks on Penn Webb because he is different: he is small, a Quaker, a vegetarian, too nice and friendly, and a cheerleader to boot. Penn, named by his great, great grandfather who won the Penn Relays in 1919, is training to win the relay race because his 95 year-old great, great grandfather will be visiting. Crash discovers the meaning of loyalty and friendship from Penn and his own grandfather "Scooter," who comes to live with the family. The story is written in first person from Crash's point of view. There are 49 short chapters (3–4 pages each) and 182 pages, with short sentences and familiar words. This is an American Library Association (ALA) Best Book for Young Adults and an International Reading Association (IRA) Children's Choice.

Learning Opportunities: Predict events and refer back to the story to back-up or modify predictions. Discuss the characters Crash, Penn, and Mike. What are similarities and differences in their behavior? What makes them act the way they do? How does Crash grow and develop in the story? Why did he befriend Penn? How does his grandfather's illness change his family? Relate the story to life experiences. For example, do you know anyone like Crash, Penn, or Mike? Develop a character map of the three boys. Create a bio-poem about Crash or Penn (see Part III, Writing Poetry).

By the Same Author: *Maniac Magee* (Newbery Medal); *Wringer; There's a Girl in My Hammerlock; Who Put That Hair in My Toothbrush?*

Title: *Dead Letter: A Herculeah Jones Mystery* by Betsy Byars (1996)

Genre: fiction; mystery

Reading Level: high 2, low 3

Interest Level: intermediate–junior high

Synopsis: When Herculeah finds a disturbing letter inside the lining of a coat she has just bought at a second hand store, her hair begins to frizzle and the danger begins. In trying to solve the accidental death of horse-woman Amanda Cole, she is almost run down by a menacing black car, attacked by a killer Doberman, and locked up in a dark stable to await the return of the killers. Meat, her good friend and protector, follows her to Elm Street in hopes that he won't be too late! This readable, fast-paced thriller has 27 short chapters and 147 pages. Vivid passages, descriptive language, and colorful characters add to the suspense of the story.

Learning Opportunities: Trace the clues that guide Herculeah to Elm Street. How does Meat help to solve the mystery? Compare and contrast Meat and Herculeah. What are similarities and what are differences. Make a character map and include the following characters: Meat, Herculeah, Mim and Chico Jones, Mr. Gamballi, Roger Cole, Sam, and Cobby. Use structural analysis and context clues to predict the meaning of unfamiliar multisyllabic words such as *defiance, paranoid, premonition.*

By the Same Author: *The Seven Treasure Hunts; The Golly Sisters Go West; Summer of the Swans* (Newbery Award); *The Pinballs; Coast to Coast; Mud Blossom.*

Title: *Dear Mr. Henshaw* by Beverly Cleary, illustrated by Paul O. Zelinsky (1983, Newbery Award Book). New York: Dell, a division of the Bantam Doubleday Dell Publishing Group.

Genre: fiction; family problems; corresponding with an author

Reading Level: high 4

Interest Level: intermediate–junior high

Synopsis: Leigh Botts is a sixth grader who has moved to a new town. His teacher makes the class write to an author to improve writing skills. Leigh has written two-sentence correspondences to Mr. Henshaw since second grade and asks the author to answer 10 questions for his school assignment. The author responds with questions for Leigh to answer (e.g., who is he, what is his family like). The relationship develops, as well as Leigh's writing skills, as he shares his sad and angry feelings about his parents divorce, his dad's absence, living in a new town, and having his lunch periodically stolen at school because his mom includes delicious tidbits from her catering job. The story is written in first person in the form of Leigh's diary entries. Paul Zelinsky's (Caldecott artist) realistic pen and ink drawings add to the emotional impact of the book. There are 134 pages with diary entries ranging from one paragraph to several pages.

Learning Opportunities: Develop a time line to record Mr. Henshaw's correspondence and help sequence important events that happen to Leigh. Discuss a variety of questions. Include literal (What was in the lunch box?) and inference questions (Why did Leigh say he hated his father?). Write a story sequel that contains diary entries. For example, hat does Leigh do in 7th grade, or what becomes of him when he finishes school? Write your own diary entry about a school episode, friend, pet. Keep a list of descriptive vocabulary to discuss and to use in writing (e.g., *quilted down jacket* [p. 44]; *I hope the thief drooled* [p. 46]; *ordinary light switch, little battery and cheap doorbell* [p. 95]).

By the Same Author: *Ramona Quimby, Age 8; Henry and Ribsy; The Mouse and the Motorcycle; Runaway Ralph.*

Title: *Disappearing Acts: A Herculeah Jones Mystery* by Betsy Byars (1998). New York: Viking, the Penguin Group.

Genre: fiction; mystery

Reading Level: high 2, low 3

Interest Level: intermediate–junior high

Synopsis: Herculeah Jones and her friend Meat are sleuths when it comes to solving mysteries. This time Meat finds the dead body and eventually the murderer. Hurculeah, however, discovers the secret of Meat's father, who has been missing ten years. The book contains easy words, short sentences and chapters, and frequent dialogue. The author's vivid description of characters and events help build the suspense. For example, at the end of Chapter 6, Meat finds a dead body in the washroom and backs out of the area: *Something seemed to be stuck in his throat. It felt like a rock but Meat knew it was something worse. Meat knew it was a scream and that it wouldn't go down, and he hoped it wouldn't come up* (p. 25).

Learning Opportunities: Keep track of clues and write predictions based on the story information. Discuss descriptive language and the images that it evokes, as in the following passage: *He was the slowest runner he knew. And tonight he seemed to be running in molasses, his feet sticking to the pavement* (p. 38). Use a Venn Diagram and compare and contrast Meat and Herculeah. What are the similarities and differences in behavior, appearances, family, etc. (see Part III, Text Structure)? Develop a problem/solution map that includes the problem(s) and actual solutions. Extend the story— develop another adventure involving the two friends, or continue where the story leaves off. Evaluate the story—did the author make the characters believable? Was the plot realistic? Did you like the resolution? Would you have changed anything?

By the Same Author: *Summer of the Swans* (Newbery Award); *The Night Swimmers* (American Book Award); *The Pinballs; Coast to Coast; Mud Blossom.*

Title: *Don't you dare read this, Mrs. Dunphrey* by Margaret Peterson Haddix (1996). New York: Alladdin Paperbacks, an imprint of Simon and Schuster. Winner of the International Reading Association (IRA); an American Library Association (ALA) Quick Pick.

Genre: fiction; coping; abuse; family; school

Reading Level: 4

Interest Level: junior high–high school

Synopsis: Sixteen-year-old Tish is required to keep a journal for her English teacher, Mrs. Dumphrey. The teacher will not read any entry that has "do not read" and Tish makes certain that her journal has *do not read!* Tish and her younger brother live with their mother. Her father has been absent for two years. When he returns he continues to first charm, then abuse the family. After staying a short time, her father leaves and her mother tries to find him, leaving Tish to take care of her younger brother, cook, clean, and find money to pay the bills. Her life becomes desperate when she loses her job, cannot pay the electricity bill, water bill, and taxes, and sees her brother growing emotionally and physically ill. Finally, she allows Mrs. Dumphrey to read her journal. This is a gripping story written in first person (i.e., Tish's diary entries) with strong character portrayals and complex family relationships. The author uses experiences from her life as a reporter when she worked on a series about abused and neglected children and as a community college teacher where she required journal entries from her students.

Learning Opportunities: Discuss characters: Tish, her mother, father, her brother, Mrs. Dumphrey. What problems do each face? How do they resolve them? How would you resolve them? Describe how Tish's behavior changed throughout the story—towards school, her teachers (Mrs. Dumphrey, Mr. Sarcusi), her mother, father, brother, and grandparents. Why was crocheting so important to Tish? Select particular entries to discuss and describe the images that they create. For example, when Granma and Tish crocheted every night, Matt hid in the yarn between them. *He said in the yarn, he couldn't hear anything* (p. 43). What did he mean? How did he feel? Discuss the theme(s). Why do you think the author wrote this story? Write a personal response after reading the story. What did you like about the book. Did anything bother you? What entries were especially meaningful to you? Continue the story and write journal entries from Tish's

point of view describing her new school and life with her grandparents.
By the Same Author: *Running Out of Time.*

Title: *Egg-Drop Blues* by Jacqueline Turner Banks (1995). New York: Houghton Mifflin.
Genre: fiction; reading problems; family
Reading Level: 5
Interest Level: junior high–high school
Synopsis: Judge Jenkins, who has a reading disability (dyslexia), talks his twin brother Jury into entering the Einstein Rally and the science egg-drop event, to earn extra points to raise his grades. The winner will drop an egg from a distance of 12 feet—keeping the egg intact! Additional problems include accepting his parent's divorce and his new stepmother. The book is written convincingly in first person, with Judge describing his reading problems such as having difficulty reading small words like *they, and, this, that* (p. 10), and shifting tasks: *My problem is shifting. If I'm distracted, it takes me a while to mentally get back to whatever it was I was doing* (p. 52). The book has 120 pages, 11 chapters, and familiar vocabulary. The long sentences boost the estimated reading level. This book is third in a series about the Jenkins twins, African American middle-school boys. The others include *Project Wheels* (1993) and *The New One* (1994).
Learning Opportunities: Compare and contrast the two brothers by writing similarities and differences in a Venn Diagram. Discuss Judge's strengths and his learning problems. What conflicts does he face? How does he use his strengths to win the egg-drop event? What are the main events in the story? What is the theme(s)? Why did the author write the story? Write a bio-poem about Judge (see Part III, Writing Poetry).
By the Same Author: *Project Wheels; The New One.*

Title: *Encyclopedia Brown and the Case of the Mysterious Handprints* by Donald J. Sobol, illustrated by Gale Owens (1985). New York: Bantam Books.
Genre: fiction; mystery
Reading Level: 4
Interest Level: primary–junior high
Synopsis: Encylopedia Brown is ten-year-old LeRoy Brown whose father is the Idaville police chief. LeRoy is called Encyclopeida by his friends because he never forgets what he hears or reads. Each chapter is a different case that Encyclopedia must unravel such as the case of the blonde wig, the missing tools, the angry girl, and the albatross. Before he announces his solution, the reader is asked to figure out **WHY?** (written in bold type) at

the end of each chapter. If the reader is stumped, the author gives a page number that locates the solution for each chapter mystery. Readers can predict outcomes and then check their predictions by looking up the designated page. There are ten short chapters, each four to five pages plus an illustration, and ten different mysteries. It is the reader's job to solve the mystery; Encyclopedia discovers the important clues.

Learning Opportunities: Read each chapter, keep track of clues, and predict the mystery outcome. Check responses. Write your own mystery and end your story with the same **WHY?** for classmates to solve. Compare and contrast two favorite mysteries or one you liked and one you did not like as well.

By the Same Author: *Encyclopedia Brown, Boy Detective, #1; Encyclopedia Brown Keeps the Peace, #6; Encyclopedia Brown and the Case of the Two Spies, #19.*

Title: *Fourth Grade Rats* by Jerry Spinelli, (1991). New York: Scholastic.
Genre: fiction; humor; identity
Reading Level: 3
Interest Level: primary–junior high
Synopsis: The rhyme kids say is as follows: "*First grade babies! Second grade cats! Third grade angels! Fourth grade . . . RRRRRATS!*" (p. 1). Suds would rather remain a third grade angel but is now in fourth grade. His friend Joey thinks being a "rat" is the next thing to being a man. With the goading of his friend, Suds pushes kids off swings, gets a detention from school, rings doorbells, keeps his room messy, and talks back to his mother in an effort to become a "rat." He finally realizes that it is not as much fun as he thought and certainly no way to become a man. Realistic pencil drawings depict Suds' adventures in and out of school. The story is written in first person, from Suds' point of view. There are 14 short chapters, 84 pages, and a variety of sentence lengths, with frequent short sentences filled with dialogue.

Learning Opportunities: Compare and contrast the two friends. Use a compare/contrast map (e.g., Venn Diagram). Ask higher-level questions: Why did Suds want to remain a third grade angel? Why did Joey want to be a fourth grade rat? Why did the author end the story with Suds' father crying over ET? (Find book references to support your answers.) What was Suds' problem? How was it resolved? Develop a problem/solution map (see Text Structure, Part IV). Discuss the theme. What was the story about? Evaluate the story: Was it realistic? Were the characters believable? Relate the story to your own experiences. Were you ever involved in any pranks? How did you feel? Find and discuss descriptive words, phrases, and idioms. For example, what did the author mean when he said, *Mrs. Peterson glared daggers at Joey* (p. 44)? Make a list of descriptive words (e.g., baby, sniffles,

shrugs, dorky, ticklish) and use them to describe a story character or someone you know.

By the Same Author: *Maniac Magee; School Daze #1: Report to the
Principal's Office; School Daze #2: Who Ran My Underwear Up the Flag-
pole?*

Title: *Freak the Mighty* by Rodman Philbrick (1993). New York: The Sky
Blue Press, an imprint of Scholastic.

Genre: fiction; friendship; loss; identity

Reading Level: 4

Interest Level: junior high–high school

Synopsis: Maxwell Kane (Max) is a big, gentle, teenager who has a learning
disability and thinks he is dumb. Max lives with his grandparents Grim and
Gram in a basement room that is his own private "down under" where no
one can bother him. Kevin, the Freak, is small with physical defects and
wears a leg brace. He lives with his mother, whom he calls the Fair Gwen,
nicknamed after Guinevere in the Legend of King Arthur. Unlike Max, he
has a quick mind, a fierce spirit, and a big imagination. The boys become
inseparable best friends, each sharing their strength with the other—Kevin,
his brains and bravery, and Max, his strength. The conflict mounts and the
story darkens as Max's father Killer Kane, who is in prison for killing his
mother, is released on parole at Christmas and comes back to kidnap his
son. The book, written in first person from Max's retrospective point of
view, is an exciting story and a sensitive portrayal of friendship and loss. It is
an American Library Association (ALA) Best Book for Young Adult Readers.

Learning Opportunities: Discuss characters. Compare and contrast Kevin
and Max. What were their strengths, their weaknesses? Why did they become such good friends. What was Kevin's relationship to his mother, the
Fair Gwen? Why was this important to the story? What were Gram and Grim
like? Why were Max and his grandparents afraid of his father? (Find information in the story to support your discussion.) Develop a compare/contrast
map of the two friends. Write a paragraph or develop a bio-poem of your
best friend, Max, or Kevin (see Part III, Poetry). Talk about the resolution or
ending. Why did the author resolve the conflict in the way he did? Illustrate
your favorite part of the story. Rewrite the ending or write a short sequel to
the story. Write your own dictionary of vocabulary words, using *Freak's Dictionary* (pp. 167–169) as a guide. For example, select a long word, look it up
in the dictionary, and then write your own personal definition. Read the
sequel, *Max the Mighty* (1998). Develop a Venn Diagram and compare and
contrast the two stories, the characters, and plot. How are the stories similar?
How are they different? Which book did you prefer and why?

By the Same Author: *The Fire Pony; Max the Mighty.*

Title: *Freaky Friday* by Mary Rodgers (1972). New York: Harper Trophy, a division of HarperCollins.

Genre: fantasy; humor; mother/daughter relations

Reading Level: 3

Interest Level: intermediate–junior high

Synopsis: Thirteen-year-old Annabel wakes up on a Friday morning to discover that she is in her mother's body. She recently had an argument with her mother in which she angrily retorted that her mother always told her what do to but there was nobody telling her mother what to do! Now they have switched bodies and Annabel finds out that having responsibilities isn't as much fun as she thought. She forgets a parent school conference, argues with and then fires the cleaning lady, and thinks she is responsible for her brother's kidnapping. The book has 11 chapters, 145 pages, and is written in first person from Annabel's point of view.

Learning Opportunities: Make a problem/solution map: list Annabel's problems, attempted and actual solutions. Include cooking, the broken washing machine, Mrs. Schmauss, the school conference with the psychologist, the client dinner, and her brother and mothers' disappearance. Would you have solved any problem differently than Annabel? Develop chapter maps and list characters, problems, and sequence events. Pretend that you have traded places with one of your parents and write about your own "Freaky Friday." Discuss the theme. What is the story about? Is the theme important today? 30 years ago? 100 years ago?

By the Same Author: *A Billion for Boris*; *Summer Switch* (both books are about the Andrews family).

Title: *From the Notebooks of Melanin Sun* by Jacqueline Woodson (1995). New York: Scholastic. (Coretta Scott King Honor Book, ALA Best Book for Young Adults).

Genre: fiction; identify; family and peer relations; homosexuality

Reading Level: low 4

Interest Level: junior high–high school

Synopsis: Melanin, going on fourteen, expresses his thoughts and secrets through his notebooks, because he has difficulty finding words when he talks out loud: *And when I can't speak it, I write it down. I wish I was different. Wish I was taller, smarter, could talk out loud the way I write things down* (p. 2). His notebook thoughts are interspersed throughout the short chapters in italics. Melanin is close to his mamma, EC, and when his mother shares her secret, Melanin faces conflicts within himself and with others (his buddies, his girlfriend Angie, his mother, and Kristen), as he struggles to make sense of his world. This short powerful book addresses differences, prejudice, caring, and family love.

Learning Opportunities: Write a personal response in your notebook. What did you like about the book? What questions do you have for the author? Who were Melanin's true friends? Why do you think so? Do you know anyone like Melanin, Ralph, Angie, or Sean? What did Melanin's mom mean when she said, *Because I've raised you to care* (p. 59)? Why do you think the author wrote the book?

By the Same Author: *I Hadn't Meant to Tell You This; Last Summer with Maizon; Maizon at Blue Hill.*

Title: *Hatchet* by Gary Paulsen (1987). New York: Penguin Group.

Genre: fiction; survival; divorce

Reading Level: 4

Interest Level: intermediate–junior high

Synopsis: Brian's parents are divorced and he is on the way to visit his father in a small, single engine plane when the pilot has a heart attack and dies. The plane crashes in the Canadian wilderness and Brian must learn to survive with the hatchet his mother gave to him for the trip. Each chapter ends in a cliff hanger as Brian encounters animals and endures hunger, cold, and illness. Paulsen uses short sentences, repeats words to evoke an emotional impact, and writes in first person, propelling the reader into hazardous circumstances as Brian uses his wit and camping experiences to survive.

Learning Opportunities: Develop a story map or chapter map to record and remember events (see chapter map of story, Part III). Predict what will happen in the following chapters, using prior chapter clues. Make a bio-poem of Brian (see Part III, Poetry, Brian's bio-poem). Write a sequel or short chapter that carries on where the book left off. Use first person and Paulsen's writing style (i.e., word repetition, short, choppy sentences). Discuss Brian's conflicts with nature and in dealing with his parent's divorce. How did he resolve each? Read the sequels, *Brian's Winter, Brian's Return*. Compare the three stories (i.e., characters, plot, resolution, writing style). Which story did you prefer? Why?

By the Same Author: *Nightjohn; The Car; The River; Brian's Winter; Brian's Return.*

Title: *Henry and Ribsy* by Beverly Cleary (1954). New York: Dell, a division of Bantam Doubleday Dell.

Genre: fiction; humor

Reading Level: 4

Interest Level: primary–intermediate

Synopsis: Henry wants to go salmon fishing with his dad and Mr. Grumbie.

His dad agrees on one condition—that Henry can keep Ribsy out of trouble until the scheduled fishing trip in two months. After several misbehaviors, Henry and Ribsy are allowed to go fishing. Ribsy gets into more trouble in the fishing boat when he causes Mr. Grumbie to lose his salmon by jumping out of the boat to escape the wiggling fish. The well-meaning dog redeems himself when he discovers a struggling, large Chinook salmon at the edge of a small stream for Henry to bring back to shore. The book has 7 chapters, 192 pages, black and white cartoon illustrations, and familiar words. While the book builds toward the big fishing trip, each chapter includes an adventure in itself.

Learning Opportunities: Develop a chapter map of characters, problems, and events for selected chapters. Develop a problem/solution map for the last two chapters: *Ribsy Goes Fishing; Henry's Adventure.* Decode polysyllabic words (e.g., *lubricated, gloomily, imagination*); find the stem and use the rules of 2's and 3's, identify familiar word chunks in long words, or use syllabication generalizations (see Part IV, Syllabication). Use a semantic word map to discuss and develop vocabulary concepts for unfamiliar words. Share and write about your dog (or pet) adventures.

By the Same Author: *Ribsy; Ramona the Pest; Ramona Quimbly, Age 8; Dear Mr. Henshaw; Henry and Beezus; Ramona the Brave.*

Title: *Holes* by Louis Sachar (1998, National Book Award, Newbery Award). New York: Frances Foster Books, Farrar, Straus and Giroux.

Genre: fiction; juvenile delinquency; friendship; buried treasure

Reading Level: high 3, low 4

Interest Level: junior high–high school

Synopsis: Stanley Yelnats, in middle-school and overweight, is sent to Camp Green Lake Juvenile Correctional Facility for a crime for which he was falsely accused. Each day the boys must dig one hole that is five feet deep and five feet across. Stanley meets and befriends Zero, who helps dig Stanley's holes in exchange for reading lessons. For four generations Stanley's family has had bad luck, since his great-great grandfather (Elya Yelnats) failed to keep a promise and received a curse on himself and on future generations of Yelnats. The author alternates between Stanley's present-day story and that of his great-great-grandfather Elya Yelnats and the legendary outlaw schoolteacher, Kate Barlow. The exciting and offbeat story (e.g., Stanley's father is trying to discover a cure for foot odor) has colorful, menacing characters (the evil Warden uses poisonous fingernail polish), an exciting plot (camp survival and escape), and familiar vocabulary.

Learning Opportunities: Develop a story map to keep track of the two ongoing stories (i.e., Stanley and Elya Yelnats). Include time, place, characters, and events. Develop a character map to describe and remember characters (see Part III, character map, that includes an example from *Holes*). Discuss higher-level questions:What were Elya Yelnats' problems and how did they affect Stanley? What was meant by "finding refuge on God's Thumb?" Why did Zero want to learn to read and why did people ridicule him? How did Stanley change over the course of the story? How do *holes* relate to the overall story and theme? Draw an illustration of Camp Green Lake or of a favorite part. Select a descriptive passage and image the smells, sounds, and how characters feel and look (see Mental Imagery, Part III, passage example from *Holes*).

By the Same Author: *Sideways Stories from Wayside School; There's a Boy in the Girls' Bathroom; Dogs Don't Tell Jokes.*

Title: *How to Eat Fried Worms* by Thomas Rockwell (1973). New York: Dell Publishing Company.

Genre: fiction; humor

Reading Level: middle 2

Interest Level: primary–junior high

Synopsis: Billy bets Alan fifty dollars that he can eat one worm a day for 15 days. After Billy chews, gulps, and swallows ten worms with various sauces (ketchup, mustard, horseradish), his mother helps out by preparing a recipe from her French cookbook,"Alsatian Smothered Worm." As Billy is nearing his 15th worm, his anxious betting opponents create obstacles that will prevent him from winning the bet. The hilarious book has 24 short chapters, from one to three pages. Clever pen and ink illustrations add to the fun of Billy's adventures and eventual triumph.

Learning Opportunities: Predict how Billy will eat another worm. Use a Semantic Feature Analysis (SFA) to develop vocabulary concepts: list the different food products, spices, and sauces that Billy uses to eat fried worms (e.g., ketchup, horseradish, mustard, grated cheese, parsley, salt, pepper, butter, cornmeal) and compare and contrast these words by noting common features (e.g., color, taste, texture) (see SFA Vocabulary Concepts, Part III). Select a descriptive passage and image how Billy looks and feels when he sees, touches, chews, and swallows a worm. Page 27 includes a rich description of worms—*gaggles of worms, drowned worms dying up on sidewalks, squirming worms on fishhooks, soggy worms in dead fish's mouths).* List descriptive words that the author uses to evoke images of color, taste, and feeling. Use these words to describe some of your own experiences. Use syllabication generalizations, structural analysis, and the rules of 2's and 3's, or find familiar word chunks to decode unfamiliar long words (e.g., *breathlessly, sizzling, minibike, shirttail).*

By the Same Author: *How to Fight a Girl; How to Get Fabulously Rich.*

Title: *I Hadn't Meant to Tell You This* by Jacqueline Woodson (1994). New York: Delacorte Press. (Coretta Scott King Honor Book).

Genre: fiction; friendship; prejudice; parental abuse; loss.

Reading Level: 4

Interest Level: junior high–high school

Synopsis: A poignant, moving story about the strong friendship between two seventh graders who come from different races and social class. Marie is African American, smart, popular, and her father is a university professor. Lena is poor, white, and ridiculed for her shabby clothes, stringy dirty hair, and speech. *"I'm whitetrash," Lena said flatly, as though she had said this a hundred thousand times before or maybe heard it from a hundred thousand people* (p. 19). When Marie promises to keep Lena's secret, she realizes that in keeping it she will lose her best friend. The powerful story and richly drawn characters allow readers to consider friendship, loyalty, and the price of keeping secrets.

Learning Opportunities: Write a personal response to the story. What questions would you ask the author? Would you have ended the story differently? Why or why not? Compare Marie and Lena. Why did they become such good friends? Would you have kept Lena's secret? What other choices did Marie have? What choices did Lena have? Write a sequel to the story.

By the Same Author: *From the Notebooks of Melanin Sun; Lena; Maizon at Blue Hill.*

Title: *James and the Giant Peach* by Roald Dahl, illustrated by Nancy Ekholm Burkert (1961). New York: Puffin Books, Viking Penguin.

Genre: fantasy

Reading Level: 4

Interest Level: primary–junior high

Synopsis: James, who is orphaned when his parents are eaten by an angry rhinoceros, lives with his two mean aunts that use him as a servant. His life changes when a little man gives him magic green crystals that James accidentally drops under a peach tree, creating a giant peach. James discovers that Old-Green-Grasshopper, Ladybug, Earthworm, and Centipede live inside the giant peach and embarks on an exciting adventure with his insect friends when the peach, with them in it, rolls down the hill and out to sea. The story is full of descriptive language. For example, when the giant peach rolls over James' two greedy aunts the author writes: *And behind it, Aunt Sponge and Aunt Spiker lay ironed out upon the grass as flat and thin and lifeless as a couple of paper dolls cut out of a picture book* (p. 40). There are 39 chapters, 119 pages, and black and white magical illustrations scattered throughout the story.

Learning Opportunities: Develop a story map and include characters, main events, problem, and resolution. Make and revise predictions as you finish each chapter. Use a cloze activity to foster prediction. For example, select a short passage and delete selected words for students to provide; use phonics clues and provide the beginning letter or letters (if word begins with a digraph or blend). Discuss Dahl's descriptive vocabulary and figurative language such as the example on page 40. Illustrate a favorite part of the story (see Sketch to Sketch activity in Part IV, Art Extensions). Make a character map of James, his two aunts, and his insect friends.

By the Same Author: *The Minpins; Charlie and the Chocolate Factory; Matilda; The Witches.*

Title: *Maniac Magee* by Jerry Spinelli (1990, Newbery Award). Boston: Little Brown and Company.

Genre: fiction; identity, adventure

Reading Level: 4

Interest Level: junior high–high school

Synopsis: Maniac Magee, born Jeffrey Lionel Magee, is an orphan. After eight years of living with his quarreling Aunt and Uncle who refuse to speak to each other, Maniac leaves home and school. He runs, and in running, meets people whom he changes and who change him. There are 45 short chapters, 184 pages, interesting and well-developed characters, and fast-paced events.

Learning Opportunities: Image characters, such as old man Grayson. What did he look like, act like? How did Maniac teach Mr. Grayson to read? What did Mr. Grayson teach Maniac? Compare and contrast Amada and Maniac. What are similarities and differences? Write a bio-poem about Maniac Magee (see Poetry, Part III). Discuss the theme of the story. What is the story about? What makes this story a fantasy? Write the main events on paper strips and play Story Jumble (see Games, Part III).

By the Same Author: *Space Station Seventh Grade; Who Put That Hair in My Toothbrush?; Fourth Grade Rats; The Library Card.*

Title: *Matilda* by Roald Dahl (1988). New York: Penguin Group.

Genre: fantasy; humor

Reading Level: 5

Interest Level: primary–junior high

Synopsis: Matilda is brilliant but her parents think she is lazy, stupid, and a bother. Matilda's father, Mr. Wormwood, is a shady car salesman that cheats customers. Her mother sits in front of the "telly" all day. Miss Trunchbull, the evil nasty headmistress, makes Matilda's life miserable, as well. Only Miss Honey, Matilda's kindergarten teacher, appreciates her brilliant mind. When Matilda takes on magic powers that enable her to move objects—Miss Trunchbull is in for a surprise! The story is long, 240 pages, but full of rich character descriptions, comical pen and ink illustrations, and a fast-moving plot.

Learning Opportunities: Make a problem/solution map that describes Matilda's problems with her parents and Miss Trunchbull and how she resolves them. Read specific character descriptions, close your eyes, and image how the characters look in your head. For example, image The Trunchbull when she tries to force Bruce Bogtrotter into eating an entire cake. *Her great horsy face had turned the colour of molten lava and her eyes were glittering with fury* (p. 133). Develop a character map. Compare and contrast Miss Trunchbull and Miss Honey. What do they have in common? How do they differ?

By the Same Author: *Charlie and the Chocolate Factory; James and the Giant Peach; The Minpins.*

Title: *More Scary Stories to Tell in the Dark* by Alvin Schwartz, illustrated by Stephen Gammell (1984). New York: Harper and Row.

Genre: folklore; scary stories

Reading Level: 4

Interest Level: intermediate–high school

Synopsis: The book contains over 28 short scary stories, a poem, and a song collected from folklore. Each story, accompanied by expressive and gruesome black and white drawings, is only two or three pages long. For example, *The Cat's Paw*, retold from a widespread witch tale, is only six short paragraphs. Jed Smith shoots off a paw of a black she-cat stealing the meat in his smoke house. The wiggling, bloody paw turns into a woman's foot before his eyes! Jeff thinks she is a witch until his neighbor comes running to his house exclaiming that his wife has been shot in an accident and has lost a foot! At the end of the book the author provides sources of his selections with variants and related information.

Learning Opportunities: Change the characters but use the same problem to write a different variant. Select certain stories to retell, changing inflections and tone to create a scary tale. Illustrate a story. Compare two ghost stories by listing similarities and differences on a Venn Diagram.

By the Same Author: *Scary Stories to Tell in the Dark: Collected from American Folklore; Tomfoolery: Trickery and Foolery with Words; Flapdoodle: Pure Nonsense from American Folkore.*

Title: *Nightjohn* by Gary Paulsen (1993). New York: Bantam Doubleday Dell, (ALA Best Book for Young Adults; IRA–CBC Children's Choice).

Genre: historical fiction; slavery

Reading Level: high 4

Interest Level: intermediate–junior high

Synopsis: *Nightjohn* is a riveting, historical fiction book about slavery, self-esteem, and the power of reading. Nightjohn is a slave who has escaped North to freedom but returns to teach other slaves how to read. The story is told in first person from the point of view of twelve-year-old Sarny, a slave who accidentally betrays Nightjohn when she excitedly draws her first word *Bag* in the dust, unaware that Mr. Waller (the cruel slave owner) is looking on. Mammy and Nightjohn pay a terrible price for Sarny's mistake. The author notes that except for variations in time, character identification, and placement, the events actually happened. The powerful short story has 7 chapters, 90 pages, and a two-page epilogue.

Learning Opportunities: Develop a story map that depicts characters, setting (time/place), problem, events, and resolution. Discuss story elements: Who are the main characters? What are the problems and forms of conflict in the story? Discuss the theme or themes. Why was reading so important? Why were slaves not allowed to read? Is reading valued today? Use the story map and retell the story. Extend the story—write about Sarny as a grown-up woman. Use first person and tell the story from Sarny's perspective.

By the Same Author: *Sarny; Hatchet; The River; Brian's Return; The Car; Dogsong.*

Title: *Poppy* by Avi (1996), an ALA Notable Book, a Booklist Editors' Choice. New York: Avon Books.

Genre: fantasy; forest mouse adventure, suspense

Reading Level: high 4

Interest Level: intermediate–junior high

Synopsis: Poppy, a forest mouse, and her family live in Gray House. In order to leave the area, they must receive permission from Mr. Ocax, a great horned owl who lives at the edge of Dimwood Forest. Poppy's adventuresome boyfriend, Ragweed, is quickly eaten in the first chapter when he takes Poppy to dance on romantic Bannock Hill without asking for the Owl's permission. Poppy barely escapes and races back to tell her father Lungwort. The mice do not realize that Mr. Ocax is waiting for an opportunity to catch Poppy, too. The problem becomes more complex when Longwort tells his family that they are growing too big to remain at Gray House and will starve unless they move to New House. When Longwort and a quivering Poppy ask the owl permission, it is denied. Poppy must go alone to New House to discover why Mr. Ocax denied the request. The brave little mouse encounters an unexpected friend, the porcupine Ereth, as well as frightening encounters with Mr. Ocax as she makes her way across Dimwood Forest to New House. There are 20 exciting chapters, each about five to six pages, and 160 pages. Avi's rich character descriptions and dialogue easily carry the reader to a believable, fantasy world. For example, *Mr. Ocax's eye—flat upon his face—were round and yellow with large ebony pupils that enabled him to see as few other creatures could* (p. 1). Ereth's expletives include delightful alliterations: *bee's burp, frog flip, bug's bathwater, weasel wonk, lice lips.*

Learning Opportunities: Take one of many descriptive passages and share your images of Ragweed, Poppy, Mr. Ocax, or Ereth. Develop a story map to keep track of characters and events. Create a character map that includes Mr. Ocax, Ereth, Poppy, Ragweed, and Longwort. Discuss higher-level questions: Why did Mr. Ocax say he was protecting the mice from dangerous animals? What effect did Mr. Ocax have on the mice? Why did the author sacrifice Ragwood in the first chapter? How does Avi use language to develop his characters (Ereth, Ragwood, Poppy, Mr. Ocax)? What is the theme or themes of the story? Evaluate the fantasy: Were the characters believable? If so, how did the author make them believable? Did you like the story? Did anything bother you? Continue where the author left off and write a short chapter about Poppy and her family.

By the Same Author: *The True Confessions of Charlotte Doyle; What Do Fish Have To Do With Anything And Other Short Stories; Finding Providence: The Story of Roger Williams (An I-Can-Read Book); The Man Who Was Poe; Poppy and Rye (Sequel); Ragweed.*

Title: *Ramona Quimby, Age 8* by Beverly Cleary (1981). New York: Avon Books.

Genre: fiction; humor

Reading Level: 3

Interest Level: primary–junior high

Synopsis: This is a heart-warming, humorous story about eight-year-old Ramona, her junior high school sister Beezus, and her parents, who are working to support Mr. Quimby's education to become a teacher. Ramona's problems include entertaining Willa Jean after school, breaking a raw egg over her head during school lunch time (she thought her mother had hard boiled it), throwing up in class in front of her classmates, and believing that her teacher doesn't like her. The story is full of humorous events and believable characters. Realistic situations include getting angry at parents, worrying about whether Mrs. Quimby will lose her job when she stays home to take care of a sick Ramona, and having to stay with Willa Jean and her grandmother after school until her parents get home from work.

Learning Opportunities: Make a character map and include Ramona, Beezus, Mr. and Mrs. Quimby, Mrs. Whaley, Willa Jean, and Yard Ape. Develop a problem/solution map and list Ramona's problems, her solutions, and your solutions. What did Ramona mean when she said that she no longer felt like a real person (p. 70)? Have you felt this way? Why did Ramona dislike her teacher and what did she do about it? What would you have done? Why did the old gentleman pay for the Quimby's dinner at the Whopperburger Restaurant? Illustrate your favorite part of the story. Write a bio-poem about Ramona.

By the Same Author: *Beezus and Ramona; Ramona and Her Father; Ramona and Her Mother; Ramona the Brave; Ramona Forever.*

Title: *Running Out of Time* by Margaret Peterson Haddix (1995). New York: Simon and Schuster.

Genre: fantasy; time travel; suspense

Reading Level: 4

Interest Level: intermediate–junior high

Synopsis: Jessie and her family live in Clinton. The time is 1840. Unknown to the children, it is actually 1996. Clinton is a reconstructed, frontier village where tourists observe frontier life through concealed windows. When the village was first reconstructed, Jessie's parents and other village adults chose to live and raise their children in the simple life of 1840 rather than to remain in 1996. When an outbreak of diphtheria causes the illness and death of village children, Jessie's mother tells Jessie the truth and urges her to escape to the outside world to get medicine. The exciting story builds to a frantic climax as Jessie confronts danger and betrayal as she races with time to bring back the life-saving medicine. There are 24 chapters, five to eight pages long, and 184 pages. The descriptive passages and authentic characters make the reader feel a part of life in the 1800's and share Jessie's bewilderment when she encounters an alien world of cars, traffic lights, pay phones, and television.

Learning Opportunities: Discuss the similarities and differences in living in Clinton and in the present time. Use a Venn Diagram to describe living conditions, food, medicine, dress, school, activities. Find specific passages, such as Dr. Fister's prescriptions of making a *poultice of chokeberries to rub on your neck three times a day* (p. 1). Make a story map to remember story characters and to record and sequence important events such as Jessie's escape from Clinton, her encounter with Mr. Neely, her escape, and the news conference. Discuss higher-level questions: Why were the "Clinton people" closing the multimillion dollar tourist village? Describe the double identity of Mr. Neely. How did Jessie convince the reporters that she was from Clinton? What part did her sister Katie play in the conflict? Were Jessie's parents and other Clinton parents responsible? What is the theme of the story? How did the writer make the characters' convincing?

By the Same Author: *Don't you dare read this, Mrs. Dunphrey.*

Title: *Scorpions* by Walter Dean Myers (1988, Newbery Honor book). New York: Harper Trophy, a division of HarperCollins.

Genre: fiction; peer pressure; friendship

Reading Level: high 3, low 4

Interest Level: intermediate–junior high

Synopsis: Jamal's older brother Randy is in prison for armed robbery. Randy has been the leader of a gang called the Scorpions and now Jamal must take his place. Tito, Jamal's gentle Puerto Rican friend, tries to protect Jamal from the danger of receiving, keeping, and using a gun. Gang pressures and jealousies, school troubles, and loving family relationships are part of this tough, moving, and realistic story. There are 20 chapters and 216 pages filled with short paragraphs and gritty, realistic dialogue. The book has won numerous awards including: Newbery Honor, Notable Children's Book (ALA), Best Book for Young Adults (ALA), and Reluctant Young Adult Readers (ALA).

Learning Opportunities: Compare and contrast Jamal with his brother and with his best friend Tito. Develop a problem/solution map, listing problems, possible solutions, and Jamal's solutions. Predict what will happen when you finish reading a chapter. Back up predictions with story information. Make a character map to clarify and review characters. Include Jamal, Tito, Mack, Indian, Angel, Mama, Sassy, and Randy. Discuss the author's theme and resolution. Would you have resolved the story in a different way?

By the Same Author: *Slam; Shadow of the Red Moon; The Glory Field; Malcolm X: By Any Means Necessary; Somewhere in the Darkness: Fallen Angels.*

Title: *Slam* by Walter Dean Myers (1996, Coretta Scott King Award). New York: Scholastic Press.

Genre: fiction; basketball; identity

Reading Level: mid to high 4

Interest Level: intermediate–high school

Synopsis: "Slam", Greg Harris, is 17 years old and a whiz on the basketball court. However, he has problems in math and in taking orders from his basketball coach. Slam knows the game and wants to play it his way. Problems arise when his attitude gets the best of him, math becomes more difficult, and he discovers that his best friend may be dealing in drugs. There are 266 pages and 21 chapters in this realistic, fast-paced story about self-worth, responsibility, and friendship.

Learning Opportunities: Discuss higher-level questions: Why did Slam refuse the math tutor? What were Slam's academic strengths? Why did he have difficulty in math? What were the dynamics between the two schools and how was Slam affected? Discuss Slam's feelings toward school: *When you have a lot of hard classes, one after the other, getting out of school at the end of the day is like getting out of a torture chamber or something* (p. 18). Connect the story to life experiences. Evaluate the story: Were the characters authentic? Would you have changed anything?

By the Same Author: *Hoops; Scorpions; Somewhere in the Darkness: Fallen Angels; The Glory Field; Malcolm X: By Any Means Necessary.*

Title: *Song of the Trees* by Mildred Taylor (1975). New York: Bantam Books.
Genre: historical fiction; family relations; racism
Reading Level: 5
Interest Level: intermediate–junior high
Synopsis: Cassie Logan loves the trees in the timber land owned by her father. Times are hard for the African American family in rural Mississippi during the depression. Cassie's father has gone to Louisiana to lay track for the railroads in order to pay the bills, leaving Cassie, her brothers, mother, and grandmother (Big Ma) to take care of the farm. While he is away, Mr. Andersen, a greedy, adjacent land owner, tries to pressure Big Ma into selling the land. Pa returns to defend his property and plans to dynamite the timber rather than sell it to Mr. Andersen. The book is short, with only 52 pages, and told from Cassie's point of view. While many sentences are long, they contain rich, descriptive passages that evoke strong visual and auditory images. For example, in the following passage Pa has forced his enemies to leave his land: *Then, when the sound of the last wagon rolling over the dry leaves could no longer be heard and a hollow silence filled the air, he slowly removed his hands from the plunger and looked up at the remaining trees standing like lonely sentries in the morning* (p. 52).
Learning Opportunities: Develop a story map with setting (time, place), characters, problem, sequence of main events, and resolution. Discuss higher-level questions: How did Papa get the land? Why did Mr. Andersen feel he should have it? Would Mr. Andersen feel differently if the Logans were not African American? What does the setting (time and place) have to do with the story? Decode polysyllabic words: use syllabication generalizations, structural analysis, e.g., find word stems and apply the rules of 2's and 3's, or find familiar chunks in long words (e.g., *impatiently, emerged, listlessly, restless, lumberman*). Use context, structural analysis (root words, affixes), and semantic word maps to discuss, understand, and develop vocabulary. Read descriptive passages, close your eyes, and describe the images you see in your head. Discuss the meaning of the author's descriptive similes such as in the following passage where trees are compared to defeated

warriors: *Those trees that remained standing were like defeated warriors mourning their fallen dead* (p. 35). Brainstorm other comparisons that could be made.

By the Same Author: *Roll of Thunder, Hear My Cry; Let the Circle Be Unbroken.*

Title: *Stone Fox* by John Reynolds Gardiner (1980). New York: Harper Trophy, HarperCollins Publisher.

Genre: legend; dog sled race

Reading Level: 3

Interest Level: intermediate–junior high

Synopsis: Ten-year-old Willy and his dog Searchlight live with his grandfather. When the grandfather cannot pay the farm taxes, he becomes ill and no longer has the will to live. Willy and Searchlight enter the National Dogsled Races to win the prize money and save the farm and his grandfather's life. Although Willy knows the terrain and Searchlight is strong and brave, they are no match for the Indian Stone Fox and his beautiful team of Samoyeds. This simple, moving story is short and has 10 chapters and 81 pages.

Learning Opportunities: Make a story map, listing characters, setting, problem, resolution. Compare and contrast Willy and Stone Fox. Show similarities and differences on a Venn Diagram. Connect the story to life events. Do you know anyone like Little Willie, grandfather, or Stone Fox? Make an illustration that describes what the story means to you. Discuss the theme. What is the story about? Extend the story by writing what happens to Willy after the race.

By the Same Author: *Top Secret; General Butterfingers.*

Title: *That Was Then, This Is Now* by S. E. Hinton (1971). New York: Puffin Books, the Penguin Group.

Genre: fiction; peer relations; friendship; identity

Reading Level: 4

Interest Level: intermediate–high school

Synopsis: Sixteen year-old Byron and his foster brother Mark have been best friends since childhood. Mark is easy-going, with no concept of right or wrong, whereas Byron is aware of consequences. Both are tough and are use to defending themselves and each other in a rough, urban neighborhood. What was once a "one-for-all, all-for-one" relationship unravels when Byron discovers that Mark has been dealing in drugs. Written in first person from Byron's perspective, the novel explores the personality and conflicts of both boys as they are pulled into ominous circumstances that they cannot seem to control. There are 159 pages, familiar vocabulary, realistic characters, and a gripping story that leaves the reader with much to contemplate.

Learning Opportunities: Compare and contrast the two brothers. Read descriptive passages and image how the brothers look and act. How did their personalities propel them into hazardous circumstances? Use chapter information and your own experiences to discuss character actions and events. For example, what were the major events that started the boys on their collision course? How did the episode with Angela backfire? After Byron found out about Mark's drug activity, was he justified in his actions? Could the conflict have been resolved in another way? How did each brother change? Discuss the theme of the book. Why did the author write this story? Write your own personal reaction.

By the Same Author: *The Outsiders; The Puppy Sister: Tex; Rumble Fish.*

Title: *The Box Car Children: The Panther Mystery* by Gertrude Chandler Warner (1998). Morton Grove, ILL: Albert Whitman & Company.

Genre: fiction; mystery

Reading Level: 3

Interest Level: primary–junior high

Synopsis: Benny (age 6), Violet (10), Jessie (12), and Henry Alden (14), lived in a box car after their parents died. Now they live with their grandfather. The mystery begins when the grandfather hears that Andrew Belden, the son of his friend, is missing. The young Belden is a wild life ranger in the Everglades National Park and is trying to track a panther that a poacher intends to capture and sell to the zoo. The grandfather and children must locate the cat in order to find the missing ranger. The story has short paragraphs, easy vocabulary, and 10 chapters that are full of clues.

Learning Opportunities: Predict, check, and revise predictions. List and sequence clues. Use decoding strategies (context, phonics, syllabication) to decode unfamiliar words. Discuss characters. Are they believable? What does each character add to the story? Discuss and write unfamiliar words on index cards or a Word Wall (e.g., poaching, airboat) and use in story discussion. Develop semantic word maps to broaden vocabulary concepts (see Part IV, Vocabulary Concepts). Read another *Boxcar* mystery and compare the two stories: characters, events, time, setting. Illustrate a favorite part. Redesign the cover.

By the Same Author: *The Boxcar Children Mysteries: The Mystery at Peacock Hall; The Windy City Mystery; The Black Pearl Mystery; The Cereal Box Mystery.*

Title: *The Giver* by Lois Lowry (1993). New York: Houghton Mifflin. (Newbery Award)

Genre: fantasy; communal society; suspense

Reading Level: high 4, low 5

Interest Level: intermediate–high school

Synopsis: Jonas lives in a futuristic community of sameness (no color, no pain, no love) where in the annual Ceremony, 12-year-old children are assigned life roles. Jonas is given the prestigious assignment of Receiver of Memories, to become the trusted elder who alone is allowed to remember past memories. Through daily sessions with his revered mentor, The Giver, Jonas experiences color, pain, happiness, and love, and discovers the insidious meaning of community *release*. Jonas' harrowing escape with the newborn infant Gabe and suspenseful ending require the reader to decide the outcome for themselves. The story has 23 chapters and 180 pages. The descriptive passages, realistic characters, and spell-binding plot allow the reader to participate in a world of conflicting values.

Learning Opportunities: Compare characters: how are Jonas and his friends Ashner and Fiona alike and different? Make a story map and list important characters and main events. What is the climax and resolution? What conflicts does Jonas experience? How does he resolve them? Discuss higher-level questions: What events make Jonas question the integrity of his parents? How did his relationship with The Giver affect his relationship with his parents and his sister? What events lead to Jonas' attempted escape? How does Jonas feel about The Giver, Fiona, and Gabe? Develop a bio-poem of Jonas. Write a short sequel to describe what happens to Jonas and Gabe.

By the Same Author: *Number the Stars* (Newbery Award); *The One Hundredth Thing About Caroline; All About Sam; Anastasia Again.*

Title: *The Hundred Dresses* by Eleanor Estes, illustrated by Louis Slobodkin (1944). New York: Scholastic.

Genre: fiction; prejudice; friendship

Reading Level: 4

Interest Level: primary–intermediate

Synopsis: Wanda Petronski doesn't have any friends. Children laugh at her name, her accent, and her old clothes. However, she tells her ridiculing classmates, Peggy and Maddie, that she has 100 dresses hanging in her closet! The girls laugh, only to discover after Wanda moves away (and wins the school's drawing contest), that she has 100 magnificent drawings of dresses hanging side by side in her closet. Mr. Petronski has moved his unhappy children to the city where *No more holler Polack. No more ask* *why funny name* (p. 46). Peggy and Maddie regret their actions and write Wanda a letter telling her of her drawing prize. The short, moving story has 7 chapters and 79 pages. Long sentences boost the reading level.

Learning Opportunities: Discuss the similarities and differences between Wanda and Maggie and Peggy. Why was Wanda the brunt of class jokes? What were the events that contributed to Wanda's leaving school? Why did she give her drawings to Maggie and Peggy? Support your response with book information. Are there similar events that happen today? Why did the author write the book? After reading each chapter, jot down unfamiliar long words (e.g., *unexpectedly, approving, intruder*). Use syllable generalizations, structural analysis, or find familiar word patterns to decode and understand polysyllabic words (see Word Identification, Part III). Make word webs to discuss and develop vocabulary concepts; for example, write root words in the center of a web with affixes extending from it such as approve—disapprove, approving, approved.

By the Same Author: *Moffats; The Witch Family; The Curious Adventures of Jimmy McGee.*

Title: *The Puppy Sister* by S. E. Hinton (1995). New York: Bantam Doubleday Dell.

Genre: fantasy; humor

Reading Level: 2

Interest Level: primary–intermediate

Synopsis: Aleasha is a new pet puppy. She loves Nick, Mom, Dad, and even the cat, but wants to become a real part of the family, and that means being human. Through pure desire and perseverance, she gradually changes into a little girl, and after a check up with Dr. Steven, finds that she will be perfectly normal except for her exceptionally strong toes, pointed ears, and affectionate and enthusiastic personality. The clever story is told from Aleasha's point of view and has 11 chapters, 122 pages, and black and white realistic illustrations.

Learning Opportunities: Predict, validate, or modify your predictions based on story information. Develop a story map, with characters, problem, main events (describe the changes as Aleasha changes into a human), and the outcome. Extend the story—write another chapter about the problems Aleasha encounters as Nick's little sister. Evaluate the story. Did you like it? Although a fantasy, were the characters believable? Would you change anything?

By the Same Author: *The Outsiders; That Was Then, This is Now; Rumble Fish; Tex; Taming the Star Runner.*

Title: *The Purloined Corn Popper: A Felicity Snell Mystery* by E.W. Hildick (1997).Tarrytown, NY: Marshall Cavendish.

Genre: fiction; mystery

Reading Level: 3

Interest Level: intermediate–junior high

Synopsis: Felicity Snell is a junior high librarian and former private detective.When someone steals Mrs. Kowalski's corn popper that contains her "tip" savings from the beauty shop (over $200), Mrs. Kowalski directs her son and his friend Freddie to the library to enlist the help of Miss Snell.The book is full of illustrated clues that provide additional information to the story such as the drawing of a footprint that includes the length of foot, width of sole, width of instep, and width of heel.There are 29 short chapters, 158 pages, and lots of clues leading to the "perpetrator": *But it's all beginning to tie in.The sugar.The footprints.The timetable.The weather.A good map of the neighborhood might just clinch it* (p. 100).

Learning Opportunities: Study the illustrations to infer information that is not evident in the story. Keep an ongoing list of clues to help predict the outcome after each chapter. Develop a problem/solution map:What is the problem? How does each clue add to the solution? Read another mystery story (e.g., *The Boxcar Children)* and illustrate the clues in the same detailed manner as in this story.

By the Same Author: *The Serial Sneak Thief.*

Title: *The Skirt* by Gary Soto (1992). New York: Bantam Doubleday Dell.

Genre: fiction; Mexico traditions; family; friendship

Reading Level: 4

Interest Level: primary–intermediate

Synopsis: Miata brings her mother's *folklorico* skirt to show off to her fourth grade friends before the big dance on Sunday.The precious skirt had belonged to her mother when she was a little girl in Mexico.Absentmindedly, Miata leaves the skirt on the school bus.A distraught Miata convinces her friend Ana to help her retrieve the skirt by crawling under the fence in the school parking lot and searching each bus.Their plan is foiled by unexpected visitors.The author includes Spanish words and phrases, realistic characters, and a story that celebrates cultural traditions and families. It is short, with 8 chapters and 74 pages.

Learning Opportunities: Develop a problem/solution map that describes Miata's problem, suggested solutions, and the actual solution (see Part III, Text Relationships). Keep a word dictionary of Spanish words and English equivalents. Predict unknown words using context and phonics clues.Write about a similar circumstance when you forgot or lost something special.

By the Same Author: *Too Many Tamales; Chato's Kitchen; Baseball in April; And Other Stories.*

Title: *Tunes For Bears To Dance To* by Robert Cormier (1992). New York: Dell Publishing.

Genre: fiction; prejudice; identity

Reading Level: 5

Interest Level: junior high–high school

Synopsis: Henry and his parents move to a new town to escape memories of his brother's death. Here he meets and befriends Mr. Levine, an elderly survivor of the Holocaust, and Doris, the quiet, timid daughter of Mr. Hairston, an abusive father and the grocer for whom Henry works. Henry's job becomes more important with his father out of work and clinically depressed over his brother's death. Mr Levine who befriends Henry, is carving a delicate miniature wooden replica of his childhood village that will be displayed at City Hall. The tension mounts as Mr. Hairston assures Henry that he can keep his job and that Henry will receive a stone monument for his brother's grave in return for one favor: the smashing of Mr. Levine's miniature village. Henry struggles with his conscience as he sneaks into the Craft Center at City Hall with a mallet. Cormier's powerful short story has 101 pages, convincing characters, intriguing story, and resolution that generates discussion and contemplation.

Learning Opportunities: Describe characters (look for details). Read selected passages that describe Henry, Doris, and Mr. Hairston. Image the characters and describe how you "see them" in your mind. Discuss character motivations. For example, why does Mr. Hairston hate Mr. Levine and abuse his own family? Why does Henry finally decide to smash the village and what actually happens? Why does Doris remain faithful to her father? What makes Mr. Levine rebuild his village? Support these inferences with text information. Discuss the author's poignant climax and resolution: the accident at the Craft Center, the family's move back to Frenchtown, the gift from Mr. Levine. Discuss the author's use of descriptive words and similes. For example, what did Cormier mean when he described the sound of the hammer smashing the village as *enormous, like a bomb falling and exploding* (p. 75). What was the theme or themes of the book? Write your reactions to the story. Would you have changed anything? Write a bio-poem describing Henry (see Writing Poetry, Part III).

By the Same Author: *I Am the Cheese; The Chocolate War; Beyond the Chocolate War.*

Title: *Wayside School Gets a Little Stranger* by Louis Sachar (1995). New York: Avon Books.

Genre: fiction; humor

Reading Level: 4

Interest Level: primary–junior high

Synopsis: Wayside School, a 30 story building with one room on each floor (except there is no 19th floor) is ready to reopen after having been closed for 243 days of school repairs. The story is full of wacky characters, bizarre problems, and events that find a way of relating to other events! Eccentric characters include Louis, the yard teacher; Dr. Pickle, a psychiatrist who becomes the school counselor because he is not allowed to practice psychiatry (he hypnotizes people with disturbing results); Mrs. Drazil, the substitute teacher with the strange blue notebook; and Mr. Gorf, the substitute who has three nostrils. There are 30 chapters, 168 pages, and clever black and white cartoon illustrations.

Learning Opportunities: Retell each chapter and predict the outcome of the subsequent chapter. Make a story map to remember characters and sequence story events. What problems do the characters have? How are they resolved? Describe and illustrate your favorite character. Why does the author use the number *three,* e.g., three nostrils, ears, etc.? Extend the story—make up and write about another Wayside School teacher with *three* of something. Write about what happens if Mrs. Drazil comes back. Evaluate the story—do you like the author's style of writing, his characters, and the problems he creates? Why or why not.

By the Same Author: *Sideways Stories from Wayside School; Wayside School is Falling Down; Holes* (National Book Award, Newbery Award).

Title: *What Do Fish Have To Do With Anything And Other Stories* by Avi (1997). Cambridge, MA: Candlewick Press.

Genre: fiction (short stories)

Reading Level: high 2, low 3

Interest Level: intermediate–junior high

Synopsis: This book is a collection of seven short stories, all with different, intriguing stories and mature themes. "Pets," for example, is a ghost story about two cats who die of distemper and come back to reclaim their gentle mistress. "The Goodness of Matt Kaizer" is about a minister's son who thinks he is bad, a father who thinks he is good, and the dying father of a classmate who thinks he is an angel. Avi's realistic characters, fascinating stories, and descriptive language capture the reader from the beginning. Older readers with decoding problems will feel comfortable with the low reading level, readable print, and individual stories, each about 24 pages.

Learning Opportunities: Read "What Do Fish Have To Do With Anything?" What is the theme? What is the significance of the title? What does the author mean when he writes: *His eyes, like high beams on a car flashed up at Willie, then dropped* (p. 16). What part does the beggar play in the story? To what does Willie compare his mother? Why? How did you feel about the story? Write a short story about what happens to Willie and his mother, starting where the story leaves off.

By the Same Author: *Poppy; Finding Providence: The Story of Roger Williams (an I-Can-Read Book); The Man Who Was Poe; Devil's Race (Trophy Chiller).*

Title: *Who Stole The Wizard of Oz?* by Avi (1981). New York: Alfred. Knopf.

Genre: fiction; mystery

Reading Level: 3

Interest Level: primary–junior high

Synopsis: Becky is a suspect when five old children's books are stolen from the Checkertown library. In order to clear her name, she and her twin brother Toby must find the robber. The twins follow a series of clues beginning with Gertrude Tobias, the name found in most of the children's books that had been donated to the library. Avi's descriptive characters and suspenseful story provide numerous opportunities for imaging his colorful characters and predicting the culprit and his or her motive. The fast paced, readable story has 116 pages, 17 chapters, and is written from Toby's point of view.

Learning Opportunities: As you read the story, make a list of clues along with your predictions, paying special attention to Chapters 3, 8, 9, 11, and 12. After reading, make a character map and include Mrs. Brattle, Gertrude Tobias, Miss McPhearson, Miss Chesterton, Becky, Toby, and Gramp. Make a story map and identify the setting, main characters, problem, significant events, and resolution. Why did the author compare Mrs. Brattle to a sparrow, her office to a bird's nest (see pp. 11–12) and Miss Chesterton to a kitten (p. 41)? What did Gramp mean when he said, *Curiosity killed the cat* (p. 39)? Why was Alice against the Red Queen? Illustrate your favorite part. How did you feel after reading the book? Write a short sequel from Miss Chesterton's or Miss McPhearson's point of view.

By the Same Author: *The True Confessions of Charlotte Doyle; Poppy; What Do Fish Have To Do With Anything And Other Stories.*

Title: *Wringer* by Jerry Spinelli (1998, Newbery Honor Book). New York: HarperTrophy, a division of HarperCollins.

Genre: fiction

Reading Level: 3

Interest Level: intermediate–junior high

Synopsis: A spell binding and thought provoking story about a young boy's struggle against peer pressure and his own conscience. Palmer will become a Wringer when he is ten, a boy who wrings the necks of injured pigeons during the annual Pigeon Day shoot. Wanting to be part of the gang, he goings along with two bullies, Beans and Mutto, only to discover that his neighbor Dorothy is his true friend. When a wild pigeon befriends Palmer, he must find a way to save "Nipper" from the cruel antics of Mutto and Beans and the annual Pigeon Day shoot when he will be ten years old, a "wringer." As the climax hurtles to a riveting peak, Palmer discovers that Nipper is one of the captured pigeons that will be released from a cage, only to be shot down by eager sharpshooters. Spinelli's story about morals and group pressure contains easy vocabulary, short sentences of dialogue, an important theme, and good story.

Learning Opportunities: Develop a character map that includes Palmer, Beans, Mutto, Henry, Palmer's Mom and Dad, and Dorothy. Write a bio-poem about Palmer (e.g., fears, loves). Describe how Palmer changes throughout the story. What is the relationship between Palmer and his Dad? Find evidence in the story to support your view. Why did the author write the story? Did you identify with any of the story characters? How do you feel about the story? Write a short sequel that continues the story after Palmer leaves the shooting field.

By the Same Author: *Crash; Maniac Magee; Who Put That Hair In My Toothbrush?; Fourth Grade Rats.*

Poetry

Title: *A Pizza the Size of the Sun* by Jack Prelutsky, illustrations by James Stevenson (1994, 1996). New York: Greenwillow Books.

Interest Level: primary–intermediate

Synopsis: This collection is full of funny, short, rhyming poems with clever, black and white cartoon illustrations by James Stevenson. The poems are easy to read and many have only four lines, perfect for reading aloud.

Learning Opportunities: Read aloud "Milk!" (p.114). What is the humor in this poem? Read and reread "Chipmunk, Chipmunk" (p.115). What words rhyme? What other words have the same ending patterns? Pick out your favorite poem to share with a classmate. Choral read the rhyming refrains from "Rat for Lunch!" (pp. 126–127).

By the Same Author: *The New Kid on the Block; Something Big Has Been Here; The Dragons Are Singing Tonight; Monday's Troll.*

Title: *beast feast* poems and paintings by Douglas Florian (1994, an ALA Notable Children's Book). New York: Voyager Books, Harcourt Brace & Company.

Interest Level: primary–intermediate

Synopsis: The poet/painter includes engaging, full-page watercolor paintings and descriptive, humorous poems about 21 *beasts* that include a Walrus, Barracuda, Anteater, Boa, Toad, and Bat. Some poems are only two lines while others are longer. All rhyme and leave the reader with a chuckle and information about the fascinating subject. Several colorful watercolors hide words in intricate designs for readers to find.

Learning Opportunities: Listen to and read *The Grasshopper.* Look at the full-page illustration and find the hidden words written in the grass. What do they have to do with the poem? List facts that you have learned about the grasshopper. The poem is written from the perspective of the grasshopper. Select another *beast* and write a short poem or story in first person, as if you were the insect or mammal. Be sure to include at least three facts. Illustrate your poem or story. Read and reread the four line poem *The Whale.* What information is in the illustration? Listen to *Ants.* What hidden words are contained in the ant tunnel illustration?

By the Same Author: *Insectlopedia: Poems and Paintings; An Auto Mechanic (How We Work); Bing Bang Boing: Poems and Drawings.*

Title: *Cool Melons—Turn To Frogs! The Life and Poems of Issa* translated by Matthew Gollub, illustrations by Kazko Stone, calligraphy by Keiko Smith (1998). New York: Lee & Low Books.

Interest Level: primary–intermediate

Synopsis: Matthew Gollub translates over 30 haiku poems by the famous Japanese poet Kobayaski (Issa) Yataro that were written over the span of his lifetime, one written when the poet was only six years old. Gollub also includes a short biography and introduction to each poem. The simple verses are easy to read and are accompanied by gentle watercolor and colored pencil illustrations. Calligraphy on the borders of each page represent the poem in Japanese.

Learning Opportunities: Infer the meaning of the poems. Describe what the poem means to you. What feelings does the poet create? Gollub notes that there is never one correct way to interpret haiku because the poems tend to be simple and understated (see author's note at close of book). Close your eyes and image the sights and sounds of the poem. Share your images. Enjoy the detailed illustrations. How does the illustrator create a Japanese setting? How does she use watercolor and chalk to represent the feelings conveyed by the poet? Compare the poet's life to his poems. How do the poems represent his life experiences? Do the poems represent life experiences of today?

By the Same Author: *The Moon Was at a Fiesta; The Twenty-Five Mixtec Cats.*

Title: *Everett Anderson's Goodbye* by Lucille Clifton, illustrations by Ann Grifalconi (1983, a Coretta Scott King Award, an NCTE Teachers' Choice). New York: Henry Holt and Company.

Interest Level: primary

Synopsis: The gentle verse takes the reader through the five stages of grief that Everett Anderson experiences after his father dies. The soft, black and white chalk drawings encompass the feelings of denial, anger, bargaining, depression, and acceptance. The meaningful verses (10 sentences) are easy to read and contain word repetition and rhyme.

Learning Opportunities: Listen to and/or read the verses. Look at the illustrations. Share your feelings about the book and illustrations (if you choose). How does the artist's choice of materials (chalk) and color (black and white) compliment the text? How would color effect the mood of the book?

By the Same Author: *Everett Anderson's Friend; Everett Anderson's 1-2-3; Everett Anderson's Christmas Coming; The Boy Who Didn't Believe in Spring.*

Title: *Extra Innings: Baseball Poems* selected by Lee Bennett Hopkins, illustrated by Scott Medlock (1993). New York: Harcourt Brace & Company.

Interest Level: primary–intermediate

Synopsis: This collection of 19 poems includes ball players (*Casey at the Bat; Mighty Joe DiMaggio*), umpires (*The Umpire*), pitches, e.g., fastball, curveball, and Little League outings. The poems vary in length. Some, like *Casey at the Bat* are long with 13 stanzas, while others are short. For example, *Great Pitches* describes seven kind of pitches in seven short verses. All are great fun for baseball lovers.

Learning Opportunities: Listen to the first six stanzas of *Casey at the Bat*. Predict what will happen when the ballplayer gets up to the plate. After you hear the rest of the poem check your predictions. What information in the poem made you predict the outcome? Have you watched a similar game where the hero has struck out? Read *The Baseball*. Close your eyes and image baseballs that *conquer space like a rocket in a race* (p. 19). To what else could baseballs be compared? Why does the poet compare the baseball to a rocket? Read *Great Pitches* (p. 22). Find the rhyming words. Select two or three pitches (e.g., fastball, curveball, spitball) and write your own one-line poem using the same or different rhyming words. Select a favorite to read and reread. Share it with a partner or friend.

By the Same Author: *Sports! Sports! Sports!; Munching: Poems About Eating.*

Title: *For Laughing Out Loud—Poems to Tickle Your Funnybone* selected by Jack Prelutsky, illustrated by Marjorie Priceman (1991). New York: Alred A. Knopf.

Interest Level: primary–intermediate

Synopsis: Noted writers such as Judith Viorst, Ogden Nash, Jack Prelutsky, Jane Yolen, and Arnold Lobel make up this humorous collection of over 130 poems. Most of the poems are short (*The Water's Deep* has four short lines and one sentence), cover a variety of subjects, and all are accompanied by clever cartoon, watercolor illustrations.

Learning Opportunities: Reinforce phonic patterns with rhyming verse. For example the limerick, *I Wish that My Room Had a Floor* (Gelett Burgess, p. 34), has one sentence, five lines, and two rhyming patterns—*or* (floor, door, bore) and *ound* (ground, around). Write the rhyming words on index cards, shuffle, and sort them into word families. Write your own limerick using the same five line, rhyming format.

By the Same Author: *The New Kid on the Block; Something BIG Has Been Here; Read-Aloud Rhymes for the Very Young; Poems of A. Nonny Mouse; Random House Book of Poetry for Children.*

Title: *For the Love of the Game—Michael Jordan and Me* by Eloise Greenfield, illustrations by Jan Spivey Gilchrist (1997). New York: HarperCollins.

Interest Level: primary–intermediate

Synopsis: The poet celebrates the human spirit by writing about Michael Jordan's extraordinary talents and encouraging children to embrace their own special talents. Figurative language, rhyme, and word and phrase repetition describe Jordan's magical actions on the court and inspire children to follow their own heart's dream. Soft, watercolor illustrations realistically depict the athlete and two children as they contemplate and celebrate life choices. An eagle motif appears throughout the book, hiding in the background or becoming part of the action (e.g., wings attached to Jordan's back). The verse is written in bold type that seldom takes up more than one fourth of the page.

Learning Opportunities: Discuss the theme. Why did the author write about Michael Jordan and his love of basketball? To what does she compare the *game?* How does the poem make you feel? Discuss the illustrations. Why does the artist include an eagle in most of the illustrations? How do the illustrations (color, lines, shapes) compliment the words? Discuss the poet's use of figurative language and the images she creates. For example, what does Eloise Greenfield mean when she writes about tree roots that trip and holes that swallow? Why does she compare Jordan's landing after making a basket to a plane gliding smoothly to the ground? To what would you compare Michael Jordan's basketball jumps?

By the Same Author: *Honey, I Love and Other Love Poems; Me and Neesie; Africa Dream* (Coretta Scott King Award).

Title: *Honey, I Love and Other Love Poems* by Eloise Greenfield, illustrations by Diane and Leo Dillon (1972). New York: Harper and Row.

Interest Level: primary

Synopsis: A small book of 15 poems describe everyday experiences such as loving (*Honey I Love*), receiving a keepsake (*Keepsake*), feeling pretty (*I Look Pretty*), jumping rope (*Rope Rhyme*), and riding on a train (*Riding on the Train*). The poems are filled with alliteration, word repetition, rhythm, and rhyme. The soft, realistic black and white chalk illustrations and child-like brown and white drawings capture the range of emotions that are encompassed in this powerful little book.

Learning Opportunities: Listen to *Riding on the Train,* close your eyes, and image what the poet is describing. What words does the author use to evoke sounds and sights of riding on a train? Why does she describe rain-drops as crawling backwards on the window? Think of your own words to describe riding on the train. How does the poem make you feel? Read *Things.* Why does the poet compare a poem to candy and a sandhouse? How are they alike and how are they different? Why does the poet think a poem is so special?

By the Same Author: *Africa Dream; For the Love of the Game; Mary McLeod Bethune; Me and Neesie; Rosa Parks.*

Title: *If I Were In Charge of the World* by Judith Viorst (1984). New York: Atheneum.

Interest Level: primary

Synopsis: Forty poems are included in ten categories: wishes and worries; cats and other people; night; spring fever; facts of life; fairy tales; words; thanks and no thanks; wicked thoughts; and good-byes. Most poems are humorous, but a few have more serious themes such as in *Mending* (p. 26), where the poet describes the pain in mending a broken heart. All are meaningful and reflect ordinary experiences and feelings. Poems range from four lines to five stanzas and intricate black and white pen illustrations accompany most poems.

Learning Opportunities: Read or listen to *If I Were In Charge Of The World* (p. 203). Write a poem using the same language pattern. In the first stanza list what you would cancel; in the second stanza list what you would have if you were in charge of the world. For example, "If I were in charge of the world I'd cancel . . ."; "If I were in charge of the world there'd be . . ." Read *Since Hanna Moved Away* (p. 34). Why does the poet describe the sky as a grouchy gray and velvet that feels like hay? Have you had similar feelings? Read or listen to *Mending* (p. 26). How does the poem make you feel? Close your eyes and image the giant hand, the gentle hand. Why do you think the poet wrote this poem?

By the Same Author: *Alexander and the Terrible, Horrible, No Good, Very Bad Day; The Tenth Good Thing About Barney; Alexander, Who Used to Be Rich Last Sunday.*

Title: *Insect Soup: Bug Poems* by Barry Louis Polisar, illustrations by David Clark (1999). Silver Spring, MD: Rainbow Morning Music.

Interest Level: primary

Synopsis: Short, rhyming poems describe actual insects in witty, unusual ways. The comical, colorful illustrations by David Clark portray fleas with razor sharp teeth and bulging eyes, an oriental cockroach eating fish with chopsticks, and a disgusting brown tick licking its chops as it starts to dig into a fury beast. The poems are typed in bold print and have from one to four stanzas.

Learning Opportunities: Read and reread the short poems for fluency. Identify rhyming patterns (e.g., tick, sick, thick, quick; odd, bod) and use them in your own poem. Write rhyming patterns on index cards, mix, and sort into patterns. Select an insect in the book with which you are familiar and compare your experiences to the poet's description. Choose an insect that isn't represented in the book and illustrate it in the same comical manner. Describe the humor in the illustrations and the connection with the poems.

By the Same Author: *The Trouble With Ben; The Haunted House Party; Don't Do That; A Child's Guide to Bad Manners: Ridiculous Rules and Inadequate Etiquette.*

Title: *Lunch Money and Other Poems About School* by Carol Diggory Shields, illustrations by Paul Meisei (1995). New York: Puffin Books, Penguin Group.

Interest Level: primary–intermediate

Synopsis: Everyday school events are represented in 40 halarious poems. Subjects include *Lunch Money; Math My Way; Recess Rules; I'm Doing My Homework;* and *Book Report.* Clever, detailed cartoon illustrations add humor and information to the witty poems. The poems are filled with rhyming words, word repetition, and familiar vocabulary.

Learning Opportunities: Read *Math My Way* (p. 13). Why is two plus two twenty-two? Look at the illustrations. What information adds humor to the poem? Read *And the Answer Is … ?* (p. 11). Close your eyes and image how the boy feels. How does the poem make you feel? Read *I'm Doing My Homework (p. 38-39).* Infer—why does she like doing her homework? Find the rhyming words.

By the Same Author: *I Am Really a Princess; I Wish My Brother Was a Dog.*

Title: *Life Doesn't Frighten Me* by Maya Angelou, paintings by Jean-Michel Basquiat (1993). New York: Stewart, Tabori & Chang.

Interest Level: all ages

Synopsis: Short rhymes and bold, colorful paintings depict frightening shadows, barking dogs, ghosts, strangers, and bad dreams. However, a magic charm and reassuring refrain (i.e., the title of the book) leaves readers in charge of their own fears. One or two lines of big print are accompanied by expressive, child-like paintings awash with color and emotion. Two page biographies of Maya Angelou and Jean-Michel Basquiat follow this powerful poem.

Learning Opportunities: Listen to the verse and join in the refrain. Look at the paintings. How do they express the poet's feelings? How do the paintings make you feel? How does the poem make you feel? Make a list of things that don't frighten you.

By the Same Author: *I Know Why the Caged Bird Sings; All God's Children Need Traveling Shoes.*

Title: *Mine, All Mine: A Book About Pronouns* written and illustrated by Ruth Heller (1997). New York: Grosset and Dunlap.

Interest Level: primary–junior high

Synopsis: The clever poems are part of a series on parts of speech that include collective nouns, verbs, adjectives, nouns, and adverbs. The rhyming poems and humorous illustrations explain how and when to use various types of pronouns. Blue type and enlarged letters focus the reader's attention on pronouns.

Learning Opportunities: Read a poem about a particular pronoun. Look at the illustrations. Read the poem again. To what word and subject (in the illustration) does the pronoun refer? Use the pronoun in your own sentence. Write and illustrate a pronoun book.

By the Same Author: *A Cache of Jewels and Other Collective Nouns; Kites Sail High: A Book About Verbs; Many Luscious Lollipops: A Book About Adjectives; Merry Go Round: A Book About Nouns; Up, Up and Away: A Book About Adverbs; Behind the Mask: A Book About Prepositions.*

Title: *Reach for the Moon* by Samantha Abeel, watercolors by Charles Murphy (1994, IRA distinguished book award). Duluth, MN: Pfeifer-Hamilton.

Interest Level: intermediate–high school

Synopsis: Samantha, a junior high student with learning disabilities in spelling and math, writes eloquently about her experiences. In descriptive, image-building verse she describes her learning problems and other topics. Colorful, expressive watercolors accompany poems that include *Quilt, Leaves in the Fall, Sunrise, What Once Was White,* and *Self Portrait.*

Learning Opportunities: Read or listen to *Self Portrait.* How does the poem make you feel? What feelings do you think the author experiences? What does she say about numbers? Read the *Quilt.* How do you feel about this poem? To what does she compare her grandmother's quilt? Look at the watercolor illustration. How does the illustration convey the message of the poem?

By the Same Author: None at this time.

Title: *Sports! Sports! Sports! A Poetry Collection* selected by Lee Bennett Hopkins, illustrations by Brian Floca (1999). New York: HarperCollins.

Interest Level: primary

Synopsis: This collection contains forty rhyming and free verse poems about sports including ice hockey, football, baseball, track, running, soccer, diving, and ice skating. It is an I-Can-Read Book with large print, familiar words, and short image-building poems. Colorful, watercolor cartoon illustrations spill over two pages. Poets include Nikki Grimes—*Fast Track,* Lee Bennet Hopkins—*High Dive,* Rebecca Dotlich—*Hoop Dream,* and Carl Pech—*Fly Balls.*

Learning Opportunities: The short poems provide practice for developing fluency. Read and reread your favorite sport poem. Read *Fly Balls* by Carl Pech (p. 9). Why does the poet compare the ball player to a spider? What words in the poem make you think of spiders? Read *Play Ball* by Lillian Fisher (pp. 12–13). How does the poem make you feel? Make a list of rhyming words in three or four poems. Write the words on index cards, shuffle, and sort into word groups that have the same rhyming pattern. Write your own sports poem using some of these word patterns.

By the Same Author: *Blast Off! Poems About Space; More Surprises; Questions; Weather; Good Rhymes, Good Times; Morning, Noon and Night-time, Too.*

Title: *The Dream Keeper and other poems* by Langston Hughes (1932, 1994). Illustrated by Brian Pinkney (1994). New York: Alfred A. Knopf.

Interest Level: intermediate, junior high, high school

Synopsis: The original collection was published in 1932. The new 1994 collection includes scratch-board illustrations by Brian Pinkney and seven more poems that are appropriate for children. The inspiring, powerful, and moving poems are full of comparisons, descriptive language, and meaning. Many poems are short, three to eight lines, and are easy to read. All are rich in meaning and imagery. *Dreams* emphasizes the importance of dreams and the devastation when dreams die (p.4). *Poem* is a short, sensitive poem about death and losing a friend (p. 12). *Mother and Son* (p.64) is longer, but inspiring and motivating: the poet describes a mother's advice to her son and compares life's difficulties to climbing stairs with tacks and splinters. The poems provide multiple opportunities for imaging, discussing descriptive words, metaphors and similes, making inferences and discussing themes, and developing fluency (rereading and reading aloud to share favorites).

Learning Opportunities: Read *Winter Moon*, a three line poem (p. 4). Image the moon that the poet describes. Draw the moon. What words does he use to create images? What other words can you think of to describe the moon? Reread the poem. Read *Dreams*, an eight line poem. Reread it several times. To what does the poet compare broken dreams? How does the poem make you feel? Draw the images that the poet creates. Draw your own dreams. Think of two or three words or phrases that describe fulfilled dreams.

By the Same Author: *The Selected Poems of Langston Hughes; The Big Sea* (an autobiography).

Title: *The Owl and the Pussycat* by Edward Lear (1812–1888), illustrated by Jan Brett (1991, 1996). New York: Putnam & Grosset Group.

Interest Level: primary

Synopsis: Edward Lear's rhyming, rhythmical poem about two lovers, the owl and the pussycat, who sail out to sea is illustrated in detailed, tropical colors by distinguished artist Jan Brett. The two-page illustrations are accompanied by only two to four lines of Lear's magical verse. Lear repeats phrases and includes wonderful words (*runcible spoon; mince and slices of quince)* that Brett gloriously illustrates.

Learning Opportunities: Echo read and reread each page. Look at the detailed illustrations and predict the meaning of unfamiliar vocabulary words: What is a *runcible spoon,* a *bong-tree*? Can you find these words in the dictionary? Where does the poem take place? In the South Pacific, the North Atlantic? How do you know? What colors does the artist use that provide clues? How does the poem make you feel? Write and illustrate a short story that describes the characters, setting, and events of the poem.

By the Same Author: *Complete Nonsense of Edward Lear; A Book of Nonsense (Everyman's Library Children's Classics).*

Title: *The Way I Feel Sometimes* by Beatrice Schenk de Regniers, illustrated by Susan Meddaugh (1988). New York: Clarion Books, Ticknor & Fields, Houghton Mifflin.

Interest Level: primary

Synopsis: The poet expresses ordinary feelings in amusing rhyme and free verse poems that describe: *Feeling Mean, Mostly; Feeling Better; Feeling Wishful; Feeling OK, After All.* Soft, watercolor illustrations compliment the humorous verse. For example, the poet suggests that on days you wake up feeling MEAN you read aloud *Mean Song* (pp. 10–11) three times in a row!

Learning Opportunities: Select a poem to read or to listen to. How does it make you feel? Read *Mean Song* (pp. 10-11). What words does the poet use to describe her feelings? What words rhyme? Read or listen to *I Wish* (p. 31). What is the poet trying to say? Have you had similar feelings? Read *When I Tell You I'm Scared* (pp. 24–26). Describe and illustrate your imaginary "ghosts." What does the poet think about being scared? Make a list of rhyming words and add additional words to your list that rhyme. Create a poem of your own.

By the Same Author: *David and Goliath; Jack and the Beanstalk Retold in Verses for Boys and Girls to Read Themselves; May I Bring a Friend?; So Many Cats!; Everyone Is Good for Something.*

Title: *Where the Sidewalk Ends* poems and illustrations by Shel Silverstein (1974). New York: Harper and Row.

Interest Level: primary–intermediate

Synopsis: Humorous poems (*The Gypsies Are Coming; Smart; Sarah Cynthia Sylvia Stout Would Not Take The Garbage Out*) and thought-provoking verse (*No Difference; The Search*) contain rhyming words and alliteration. The whimsical drawings include imagery creatures, dancing pants, a two-faced head, and a crocodile in a dentist's chair.

Learning Opportunities: Rhyming poems create endless opportunities to reinforce phonics patterns. For example, read *Sarah Cynthia Sylvia Stout Would Not Take The Garbage Out* (pp. 70–71). Find words that rhyme with the following words: *Stout, pans, ceilings, peas, floor, bones, toast, hall, dry, fate.* Find words that rhyme but that have different spellings (e.g., *peas/cheese; peel/meal*). Write the words on index cards, shuffle, and sort into rhyming piles or write patterns on a Word Wall. Make up your own poem. Read *No Difference* (p. 81). Why did the poet write this poem? Read *Band-Aids* (p. 140). How many Band-Aids are represented in the poem? Pick a favorite poem to reread to a small group.

By the Same Author: *A Light in the Attic; Falling Up; The Missing Piece; The Giving Tree.*

Nonfiction

Title: *A Fair Bear Share* by Stuart J. Murphy (1998). New York: HarperTrophy.

Genre: picture book; math (regrouping)

Reading Level: 1

Reading Interest: primary and up

Synopsis: A mother bear asks her four little cubs to gather nuts, berries, and seeds so that she can bake her special Blue Ribbon Blueberry Pie. When the pie is baked, each bear will get a fair bear share. Three little bears (and eventually the fourth little bear) gather nuts, berries, and seeds that are grouped by tens. All in all, 82 berries, 91 seeds, and 52 nuts go into a delicious blueberry pie. Soft, water color illustrations of bear activities and regroupings help readers visualize math concepts. The clever story has short sentences and introduces readers to math vocabulary.

Learning Opportunities: The author presents book activities at the end of the story that include reading the story and describing what is going on in each picture, asking questions, retelling, and linking book activities to the real word such as creating an inventory of kitchen cabinets and circling the tens (p. 32). He also suggests activities that extend the concepts when riding in the car, taking a walk, or grouping with crayons, markers, and colored pencils (p. 34).

By the Same Author: *The Best Bug Parade* (comparing sizes); *The Best Vacation Ever* (collecting data); *Betcha!* (estimating); *Divide and Ride* (dividing); *Too Many Kangaroo Things to Do!* (multiplying).

Title: *All-Time Great World Series* (All Aboard Series) by Andrew Gutelle, illustrated by Bart Forbes (1994). New York: Grosset & Dunlap.

Genre: short chapter book; information; baseball

Reading Level: 3

Interest Level: primary–intermediate

Synopsis: The short chapter book describes four stories about the most exciting World Series. These include the 1924 series with pitcher Walter Johnson (Washington Senators), the 1977 series with Reggie Jackson (New York Yankees), the 1986 series with pitcher Roger Clemens (Boston Red Sox), and the 1991 series with pitcher John Smoltz (Atlanta Braves) and best player Kirby Puckett (Minnesota Twins). There are 48 pages filled with colorful illustrations and fascinating photographs of Walter Johnson, Freddie Lindstrom, Reggie Jackson, and Babe Ruth. Each chapter is about 11 pages with fairly large print. This is a book for baseball enthusiasts.

Learning Opportunities: Share your background experiences about the World Series. Read the chapter title and predict what information will be in the chapter. Summarize what you learned in each chapter. Reread if you need to fill in information. Make a time line of the four World Series. Include important players. Use a Venn Diagram and compare two of your favorite World Series that were described in the book. Make a list of long words and use syllabication strategies to sound out words (see Part IV, syllabication).

By the Same Author: *Baseball's Best: Five True Stories (Step into Reading); 9 Puzzle-Mysteries (Lunchbox Libraries, Vol. 2: Read While You Eat); Cobi Jones Soccer Games; I Can Do That: A Book About Confidence.*

Title: *Anno's Math Games III* by Mitsumasa Anno (1982, 1991, 1997). New York: A PaperStar Book, The Putnam & Grosset Group.

Genre: picture book; math (geometry concepts, mazes)

Reading Level: high 2

Interest Level: intermediate

Synopsis: Kriss and Kross, two little people, introduce the reader to mathematical concepts and abstract thinking through a series of games involving changing shape (manipulating string), exploring triangles (folding colored tissue paper), making mazes (making a cat's cradle with string), and following and comparing directions (right and left). Easy to follow directions and detailed illustrations present math games that reinforce concepts, develop abstract thinking, and require following directions.

Learning Opportunities: Fold colored tissue paper into triangles to make a penguin, a cat's face, or monster face (pp. 40–49). Write the directions for a friend to follow. Follow directions on pp. 54–55 to find your way through mazes. Write a short story to accompany a particular maze. Draw a maze for a friend to follow. Use string and follow the directions on p. 67 to make a cat's cradle. Teach a friend how to make a cat's cradle. With one piece of string see how many designs you can make.

By the Same Author: *Anno's Math Games, Anno's Math Games II, Anno's Mysterious Multiplying Jar.*

Title: *Antics! An Alphabetical Anthology* written and illustrated by Cathi Hepworth (1992). New York: G. P. Putnam's Sons.

Genre: picture book; alphabet book; humor

Reading Level: NA

Interest Level: primary–junior high

Synopsis: Hepworth's alphabet book is filled with twenty-six witty illustrations of ants depicting words that contain **ant** as part of the spelling. For example, the first word **Ant**ique appears below a colorful illustration of a wrinkled, gray-haired ant knitting in a rocking chair and listening to a victrola. Interesting words (e.g., Vigil**ant**es, **Pant**aloons, Quar**ant**ine) and fascinating, colorful ants emphasize the possibilities of creating words that contain the same syllable.

Learning Opportunities: Predict the next alphabet word. For example, what word starts with **B** and contains the syllable **ant**? Predict the meaning of unfamiliar words such as Flamboy**ant** using the picture clues (e.g., this word is illustrated by a fashionable ant wearing a large feather hat, fur boa, pearls, and toting a walking cane). Write and illustrate your own alphabet book with words containing **ant** or another common syllable. Separate long words into syllables using syllable strategies described in Part III (e.g., find word stems and apply the rules of 3's, 2's; syllabication generalizations). Use words such as *tantrum, unpleasant, quarantine*.

By the Same Author: *Bug Off!: A Swarm of Insect Words.*

Title: *Cedric Ceballos* by Mark Stewart (1996, Grolier All-Pro Biographies). New York: Children's Press, a division of Grolier Publications.

Genre: biography; picture book

Reading Level: 7

Interest Level: primary–junior high

Synopsis: The 45 page biography of NBA basketball player Cedric Ceballos is portrayed in photographs, illustrations, and short text organized under 14 different headings ranging from growing up through 1995. A Table of Contents provides the organizational structure and a Glossary reinforces 12 vocabulary terms (e.g., dyslexia, tuition, veteran). In the book, the sports star describes his struggles with reading (p. 8). Long sentences boost the reading level; however, large, bold-face headings, time lines, tables and graphs of sport information, short text, and numerous photographs provide opportunities for learning.

Learning Opportunities: What do you know about Ceballos? Look at the headings and illustrations and predict what information will be included in the passage. Turn the bold-face headings into questions and read or listen to the short text to find the answers to your questions. Look at the two graphs on page 15, *Rebounds Per Game* and *Points Per Game*. Describe the information that is represented in each graph. Interpret the time line graph on pages 20–21. What obstacles did the basketball player have to overcome? Why did the biographer write about this player?

By the Same Author: *Barry Sanders (Grolier All-Pro Biographies); Bernie Williams: The Quiet Leader (Sports Stars).*

Title: *Dance* by Bill T. Jones and Susan Kuklin; photographs by Susan Kuklin (1998). New York: Hyperion Books for Children.

Genre: picture book; modern dance

Reading Level: 1

Interest Level: primary–junior high

Synopsis: Full page color photographs of dancer and choreographer Bill T. Jones are accompanied by twelve simple sentences that describe the graceful dancer as he glides through the air, makes lines and curves with his body, and thinks and feels about his dance. There are only 113 words in this beautiful picture book. Many are repeated and all are ones with which students are familiar.

Learning Opportunities: Read and reread the story. Look at the photographs. How do they make you feel? Why do the writers describe dancing as thinking? As feeling? What did you learn about dance? Describe how you feel when participating in your favorite sport. Compare your favorite sport to dancing. Use a Venn Diagram and list similarities and differences.

By the Same Author: *Reaching for Dreams: A Ballet from Rehearsal to Opening Night* by Susan Kuklin (an ALA Best Book for Young Adults).

Title: *Diego* by Jeanette Winter (1991). New York: Alfred A. Knopf.

Genre: picture book; biography

Reading Level: 3

Interest Level: primary–intermediate

Synopsis: A short text and colorful, miniature paintings tell the life of the famous Mexican artist, Diego Rivera. The short text, usually one to three sentences per page, is written in English and Spanish. The rich paintings are outlined in patterned borders and depict Rivera's young life in Guanajuato, Mexico, his travels to Paris and Italy to learn more about painting, and his murals that represent experiences of the Mexican people. More information about the famous artist is written in English and Spanish at the end of the picture book.

Learning Opportunities: Look at the cover illustration and the title. What do you think the story will be about? Where is the setting? Locate Rivera's home, Guanajuato, on a map. Read or listen to the short text. Keep a list of unfamiliar words to write on index cards, review, and illustrate after reading (e.g., medicinal). Enjoy the paintings and discuss the colors and folklike art style. Discuss information in the pictures that add to the story text. Look up Diego Rivera and compare his paintings to the ones in the picture book. Are there similarities? Differences? Make a timeline of the artist's life. Why is the artist so famous? Share (discuss, write, or illustrate) what you learned about the artist. Read about another famous artist and compare him/her to Diego Rivera. Use a Venn Diagram and compare color, line, style, and subject matter.

By the Same Author: *My Name is Georgia: A Portrait; Follow the Drinking Gourd.*

Title: *Dinosaur Dinners* (Eyewitness Readers, Level 2) by Lee Davis (1998). New York: DK Publishing.

Genre: picture book; dinosaurs

Reading Level: 2

Interest Level: primary

Synopsis: Large print, limited text, and fascinating full-page photographs provide information about the eating and hunting habits of 12 meat-eating and plant-eating dinosaurs. Additional interesting facts appear in small information boxes that contain miniature photographs illustrating a fact or concept. The intriguing short picture book includes 32 pages and a glossary that gives names, pronunciation, and characteristics of each dinosaur. *Eyewitness Readers* come on four different levels: level 1—beginning to read, preschool through grade 1; level 2—beginning to read alone, grades 2 and 3; level 3—reading alone, grades 2 and 3; level 4—proficient readers, grades 2 through 4.

Learning Opportunities: Make a time line that reflects the dates that the 12 dinosaurs lived. Include eating habits. Use a Venn Diagram and compare and contrast the meat-eating and plant-eating dinosaurs. Practice syllabication skills: divide the dinosaur names into syllables and sound out each syllable. Use the pronunciation guide as a reference. Look at the photographs and use adjectives to describe the texture and shape of each dinosaur. Pick your favorite dinosaur and write a cinquain poem or acrostic poem (see Part III, Writing Poetry).

By the Same Author: *Dinosaur Dinners.*

Title: *Dinosaur Time* by Peggy Parish, illustrated by Arnold Lobel (1974, an I-Can-Read Book–1). New York: HarperTrophy, a division of HarperCollins.

Genre: easy reading book; dinosaurs

Reading Level: 1

Interest Level: kindergarten–primary

Synopsis: A brief introduction followed by 23 pages of easy text and colorful illustrations introduce the reader to 11 different dinosaurs varying in size, speed, and eating habits. The only words that contain more than three syllables are the names of the dinosaurs, and a dictionary spelling is provided after each name. Caldecott Award wining artist Arnold Lobel illustrates the dinosaurs in fascinating pastel drawings.

Learning Opportunities: Read and reread each page to develop fluency. Compare and contrast dinosaurs by making a Semantic Feature Analysis: make a grid and vertically list dinosaur names. On the horizontal axis list features such as size (big, small), speed (fast, slow), and eating habits (plant, animal). Sound out each name by reading syllable clues. Select your favorite dinosaur and write a short story or summary about it.

By the Same Author: *Amelia Bedelia; Thank You, Amelia Bedelia; Come back, Amelia Bedelia.*

Title: *Each Orange Had 8 Slices* by Paul Giganti, Jr. (1992). New York: Greenwillow Books, a division of William Morrow & Company, Inc.

Genre: picture book; math

Reading Level: 1

Interest Level: primary

Synopsis: Short sentences and colorful illustrations present simple addition and multiplication concepts. For example, the reader must count (or multiply) the legs on two fat cows and four calves (each cow had two calves) to answer the author's question of how many legs he saw on his way to grandma's house. Donald Crew's bold, bright pictures illustrate each clever counting story.

Learning Opportunities: Read the counting story and represent it by number symbols. How many ways can you solve the story problem? Write it (in numbers) several different ways. Make up, illustrate, and write your own counting problem.

By the Same Author: *How Many Snails? A Counting Book; Notorious Numbers Big Book.*

Title: *Eating the Alphabet: Fruits & Vegetables From A to Z* by Louis Ehlert (1989). New York: A Voyager book, Harcourt Brace & Company.

Genre: picture book; alphabet book

Reading Level: NA

Interest Level: primary–intermediate

Synopsis: Colorful collage illustrations of fruits and vegetables from around the world depict letters of the alphabet. Bright lemon-colored apricots, artichokes with layers of different shades of green, green stalks and purple heads of asparagus, light and dark green avocados, and red, yellow, and orange apples represent the letter **A**. Each fruit is labeled in capital and small letters. Unusual fruits and vegetables include **E**—endive, **M**—mango, **O**—okra, and **R**—rutabaga. All fruits and vegetables are described in an informative index at the end of the picture book.

Learning Opportunities: Keep a list of long words and separate into syllables using syllabication strategies. Find unfamiliar fruits and vegetables to sample. Develop a Semantic Feature Analysis (SFA) to compare and contrast four or more fruits and vegetables. Use features of color, texture, taste (sour, sweet, tart) and size (see Part IV, Vocabulary Concepts). Research, write, and illustrate your own alphabet book of fish, mammals, birds, or subject of choice.

By the Same Author: *Mole's Hill; Nuts to you! Moon Rope/Un lazo a la luna; Feathers for Lunch; Fish Eyes: A Book You Can Count On.*

Title: *Eating Fractions* by Bruce McMillan (1991). New York: Scholastic.

Genre: picture book; math concepts—fractions

Reading Level: NA

Interest Level: kindergarten–primary

Synopsis: Colorful photographs of children eating bananas, cloverleaf rolls, pizza, corn on the cob, pear salad, and strawberry pie represent *wholes, halves, thirds,* and *fourths.* Detailed directions and recipes for the author's cloverleaf rabbit rolls, pepper pizza pie, wiggle pear salad, and strawberry pie are included at the end of the book. The purpose of the book is to reinforce fraction concepts by presenting familiar photographs of food divided into fractional parts.

Learning Opportunities: Read and discuss how the photographs relate to corresponding fractions. Write math vocabulary such as *whole, one half, one third, two thirds, one fourth, two fourths, three fourths,* and fraction symbols (e.g., 1, 1/4, 2/3) on index cards. Illustrate two pizza pies and cut one up into four pieces and the other into three pieces. Match fraction words and symbols to pizza pie illustrations. Explain your rationale for doing so. Write and illustrate your own book of fractions. Practice sequencing skills: Follow the author's recipe to make a recipe of your choice.

By the Same Author: *Mary Had a Little Lamb; One, Two, One Pair!; Counting Wildflowers; Apples, How They Grow.*

Title: *Ed Emberley's Drawing Book of Animals* by Ed Emberley (reissue 1994). New York: Little Brown & Company.

Genre: picture book; drawing

Reading Level: NA

Interest Level: kindergarten – primary

Synopsis: There are few words in this step by step book of how to draw animals. Seven or eight drawings show how to draw over 40 animals, birds, reptiles, and a dragon! Animals are also depicted in different positions such as a sitting pig and a standing pig, a sitting and a running cat, and a monkey front view and side view. Emberley begins his book with basic diagrams of shapes, numbers (1,2,3) and letters (y,j,l,c,d,s,v,w,m,u) that he uses in his drawings. If readers can make these, they can make all of the animals in the book!

Learning Opportunities: Practice making the shapes, numbers, and letters at the beginning of the book. Then select a favorite animal and follow the drawing patterns to create the animal. Verbally describe and then write directions for classmate that describe how to draw an animal. The book illustrations are also good to practice sequencing. Photo copy the illustrations, cut apart and jumble, and ask students to arrange the drawings in the correct order.

By the Same Author: *Ed Emberley's Great Thumbprint Drawing Book; Ed Emberley's Drawing Book: Make a World.*

Title: *Get Up and Go!* by Stuart J. Murphy (1996). New York: HarperTrophy.
Genre: picture book; math (time lines).
Reading Level: 1
Interest Level: primary and up
Synopsis: Rhyming verse and colorful water colors describe how a pet (dog) helps his mistress get ready for school. Time lines measure the minutes the little girl takes as she washes her face, eats breakfast, gives her dog a treat, dresses for school, and finds her home work. The easy to read rhymes are in bold print and bright illustrations splash over two pages. Minutes add up and time lines expand as the morning progresses.

Learning Opportunities: The author presents extension activities such as reading the story and describing illustrations, parents asking questions throughout the story, retelling the story using math vocabulary, and drawing pictures of your own morning routine, timing the minutes, and creating a personal time line out of string, yarn, or strips of paper (p. 33).

By the Same Author: *Every Buddy Counts* (counting); *Just Enough Carrots* (comparing amounts); *Give Me Half!* (understanding halves); *Lemonade for Sale* (bar graphs); *Too Many Kangaroo Things to Do!* (multiplying).

Title: *Home Run* by Robert Burleigh, paintings by Mike Wimmer (1998). San Diego: Harcourt Brace & Company.
Genre: biography; picture book; story of Babe Ruth
Reading Level: 1
Interest Level: primary–intermediate
Synopsis: Short, easy-to-read sentences and full-page realistic paintings portray the magic of Babe Ruth and his amazing hitting power. Old baseball cards (from packages of bubble gum) appear below the text (two to four short sentences per page) and contain facts about his life in the ballpark.

Learning Opportunities: Read and reread. Look at the illustrations (e.g., style of clothes, baseball uniforms) and predict the time that the book takes place. Compare the illustrations to today's ballparks, players, and fans. What is similar and what is different? What do you think about the illustrations? Look at the caption on the baseball cards and predict what facts you will read about on the cards. Why is Babe Ruth considered such a great player?

Make a Venn Diagram and compare him to your favorite ball player. What did you think about the book?

By the Same Author: *Flight, the Story of Charles Lindbergh; Hoops.*

Title: *Finding Providence* by Avi (1997, an I-Can-Read Chapter Book). New York: HarperTrophy, a Division of HarperCollins.

Genre: biography; chapter book; story of Roger Williams

Reading Level: high 3, low 4

Interest Level: primary–intermediate

Synopsis: It is 1635 in the Massachusetts Bay Colony and Roger Williams is on trial for preaching new ideas about religious freedom and supporting the right of Indians to retain their land. Williams is found guilty and escapes into the winter forest on foot. He is rescued by the Narragansett Indians, and, with his wife and daughter, establishes a new settlement named Providence. The story is written in first person from the perspective of his young daughter Mary. Realistic chalk drawings accompany the interesting and readable text. The story has 5 chapters and 46 pages.

Learning Opportunities: Read and retell each chapter. Make a chapter map and list the main events, important characters, and time and place. Discuss detail and inference questions: Where and when did the story take place? Why was Williams arrested and convicted of treason? Who helped him to escape? How did he escape? Why did the Narragansett Indians come to his rescue? Why did he call the settlement Providence? How would you describe Roger Williams to someone who knew nothing about him? What information did you learn from the illustrations? Read Chapter 1 and use chapter information to act out the trial: include court members, spectators, John Cotton, and Roger Williams. Use word recognition strategies to sound out long words (e.g., familiar word chunks, syllabication generalizations, detect word stems and apply rules of 2's and 3's—see Part IV, Word Identification).

By the Same Author: *The True Confessions of Charlotte Doyle; Nothing But the Truth; Sometimes I Think I Hear My Name; Poppy* (ALA Notable Book).

Title: *Football Stars* (All Aboard Reading) by S.A. Kramer, illustrated by Jim Campbell (1997). New York: Grosset & Dunlap, Inc.

Genre: biography; short chapter book; football

Reading Level: 3

Interest Level: primary

Synopsis: The 48-page book contains four interesting biographies of football stars Deion Sanders, Jerry Rice, Troy Aikman, and Barry Sanders. Color photographs and illustrations depict the athletes growing up and playing football. Each biography is about 12 pages, including photographs and illustrations. The *All Aboard Reading* Series contains four different levels: Picture Readers (ages 3–6); Level 1 (Preschool–grade 1); Level 2 (Grades 1–3); Level 3 (Grades 2–3). The series also includes fantasy and fiction stories.

Learning Opportunities: What do you know about each player? Look at the illustrations and predict what information will be in the biography. Make a time line of your favorite athlete. Compare and contrast the four players, using a Semantic Feature Analysis grid. For example, list the names of the players on the vertical side of the grid and list features on the horizontal side such as team, position, important game, home town. Select two favorite stars and compare and contrast them using a Venn Diagram. Evaluate the stories. Were they informative? Were the facts accurate? How do you know?

By the Same Author: *Baseball's Greatest Players (Step Into Reading); Baseball's Greatest Hitters (Step Into Reading); Baseball's Greatest Pitchers (Step Into Reading).*

Title: *Hello, Fish! Visiting the Coral Reef* by Silvia A. Earle with photographs by Wolcott Henry (1999). Washington, D.C: National Geographic Society.

Genre: picture book; fish

Reading Level: low fourth

Interest Level: primary–intermediate

Synopsis: Silvia Earle, marine biologist, clearly and succinctly describes 12 colorful fish that live in the coral reef. Her simple, easy to read text is accompanied by fascinating, full-page color photographs by underwater photographer, Wolcott Henry. Each single-page description contains short phrases and from five to six sentences (the long sentences contribute to the higher reading level). The exotic fish include the brown goby, stargazer, spotted stingray, clownfish, and silvertip shark.

Learning Opportunities: Look at the map on the first page and find and describe where the coral reef is located. Compare and contrast two or more fish using a Venn Diagram or Semantic Feature Analysis. Features can include size, color, eating habits, and unusual characteristics. Use a descriptive map to name and describe two or three important characteristics of each fish. Include the author's descriptive words such as *slimy goo, soft, sensitive, toothy.* Use this information to write a short paragraph about fish that live in the coral reef. Make a list of compound words (*stargazers, starfish, silvertip, rainbow, damselfish, seahorse*) and describe why they are used to refer to fish.

By the Same Author: *Dive! Exploring the Deep Frontier.*

Title: *I Have a Dream: The Story of Martin Luther King* by Margaret Davidson (1986). New York: Scholastic.

Genre: biography

Reading Level: 3

Interest Level: primary–intermediate

Synopsis: This fascinating and powerful biography contains 24 photographs ranging from Dr. King's boyhood in Atlanta to his tragic death. The author's readable and interesting text provides dates and background about important events in the life of Dr. Martin Luther King. These include Dr. King's first experience with racism when he was starting school, his first sermon at 17, the bus boycott on December 5, 1955, the Birmingham demonstration, Dr. King's famous letter from Birmingham jail, and winning the Nobel Peace Prize when he was 35 years old. There are 127 pages, 14 short chapters, and full-page photographs that provide additional information about the life of this extraordinary man.

Learning Opportunities: Share what you already know about Martin Luther King. Look at the chapter titles and illustrations to get an overview about the book contents. Read the bold-face type at the beginning of each chapter and predict what the chapter will be about. After reading each chapter summarize the information in your head. Go back and reread if necessary. Make a time line of important dates in Dr. King's life. Write a bio-poem of Dr. King.

By the Same Author: *Dolphins (Step Into Reading, Step 2 Book); Five True Dog Stories; Five True Horse Stories.*

Title: *I Can't Accept Not Trying: Michael Jordan on the Pursuit of Excellence* by Michael Jordan, photographs by Sandro Miller (1994). New York: HarperCollins.

Genre: autobiography; short chapter book

Reading Level: 4

Interest Level: primary–high school

Synopsis: This inspiring, little book describes Michael Jordan's thoughts about goals, fears, commitment, teamwork, fundamentals, and leadership. There are six short chapters, each beginning with a full-page photograph of Michael Jordan and a quote that introduces the reader to the main idea of the chapter. The sentences vary in length, but the short book is not intimidating. Don't miss this book!

Learning Opportunities: What do you know about Michael Jordan? What do you think the book will be about? Read each short chapter and describe the main idea. Provide supporting details. For example, in Chapter 1, why does Michael Jordan set short-term goals? In Chapter 2, he describes fear as an illusion. Why? Select a chapter to illustrate. Evaluate the book. Did you like it? Did the book relate to any of your experiences or feelings? Did you learn anything? Why did the photographer use only facial photographs?

By the Same Author: *For the Love of the Game.*

Title: *Isadora Dances* by Rachel Isadora (1998). New York: Viking, Penguin Group.

Genre: biography; picture book

Reading Level: 5

Interest Level: primary–intermediate

Synopsis: This beautifully written and illustrated picture book biography describes the life of Isadora Duncan, an innovative dancer in the early 20th century, who changed the world of dance. Soft, watercolor illustrations capture the fluid motion of this creative dancer who refused to wear ballet slippers and danced barefoot in flowing tunics. Book events include her love for dance as a child in San Francisco, her recitals, her rebuke in the United States for her innovating dancing, her success in Europe, and the tragedy of the deaths of her two young children that impacted her career. The long sentences boost the reading level to 6th grade. The author/illustrator is a distinguished artist and won the Caldecott Honor Medal for *Ben's Trumpet.*

Learning Opportunities: Use this book as a listening and writing activity for readers that are interested in dance but are reading below the 5th grade reading level. Look at the book cover and predict what the story will be about. Look at the illustrations. Write your own story to go with the expressive watercolors. Then listen to the story and compare your version to the author's story. How did Isadora use her strength to overcome obstacles? Would her style of dance be laughed at today? Support your answer from information in the story. Discuss how the illustrations (color, style) capture the mood of the biography.

By the Same Author: *Ben's Trumpet; The Little Match Girl; Golden Bear.*

Title: *Lou Gehrig: The Luckiest Man* by David Adler, illustrated by Terry Widener (1997). San Diego: Harcourt Brace & Company.

Genre: biography; picture book

Reading Level: 4

Interest Level: primary–junior high

Synopsis: The inspiring story of baseball legend Lou Gehrig is related through facts (he never missed a day in school or a baseball game), quotes *(I consider myself the luckiest man on the face of the earth)*, a moving text, and colorful, bold illustrations. There are some long sentences and words, yet baseball enthusiasts will bring background experiences with which they can predict many words.

Learning Opportunities: What do you know about Lou Gehrig? Look at the book cover for additional information (e.g., on what team did he play?) Look at the illustrations and predict what will happen in the story. Read the picture book. Use word identification strategies (context, letter-sound associations, syllabication) to recognize unfamiliar words. Make a list of compound words and describe the meaning of each: *shortstop, baseman, nickname, baseball, clubhouse, lineup, teammate, everyone.* Make a time line of Lou Gehrig's life. Make a character map and list qualities that the author includes in the book. Write an acrostic poem using the letters in Lou Gehrig's first or last name. Write a short paragraph that describes how you feel about the story.

By the Same Author: *Amazing Magnets; The Babe & I; The Cam Jansen series.*

Title: *Measuring Penny* by Loreen Leedy (1997). New York: Henry Holt and Company.

Genre: picture book; math

Reading Level: 3

Interest Level: primary-intermediate

Synopsis: Lisa measures her dog Penny for a math assignment in which she must use standard and nonstandard measurements. She uses inches and centimeters and dog biscuits and cotton swabs to measure head, nose, ears, and body. She compares Penny's measurements to neighborhood dogs, uses volume units to measure Penny's water bowl, a scale to measure weight, and follows Penny on Saturday to measure the time spent in caring for her dog. Colorful pictures and Penny's notes appear below the easy to read text.

Learning Opportunities: Measure your own pet or household object using standard and nonstandard measurements. Measure and compare another item. Write and illustrate your story.

By the Same Author: *Postcards from Pluto: A Tour of the Solar System; Messages in the Mailbox: How to Write a Letter.*

Title: *NBA Action from A to Z* by James Preller (1997). New York: Scholastic.

Genre: alphabet book; basketball

Reading Level: NA

Interest Level: kindergarten-intermediate

Synopsis: Colorful, action photographs illustrate NBA basketball scenes that begin with large, bright, capital letters. For example, the capital letter **L** appears next to a three-fourths page photograph of Grant Hill preparing to make a pay-up (p. 16). On the opposite page, Mitch Richmond holds his MVP All-Star Game trophy, alongside a dazzling orange **M** that stands for **M**ost valuable player. Short sentences contain facts about players, basketball plays, mascots, and teams. The exciting photographs bring the 26 letters to life!

Learning Opportunities: Before looking at the photographs, predict NBA events that begin with alphabet letters. Look at the photographs and read the corresponding sentence. Describe what is going on in the photographs in your own words. Write the 26 action words (e.g., *action, basketball, coach, dribble*) on index cards. Jumble and arrange in correct alphabetical order. Make up your own action alphabet book using a sport or a particular athlete. Illustrate your book with drawings or photographs.

By the Same Author: *The Case of the Christmas Snowman (A Jigsaw Jones Mystery); the NBA Book of Big and Little; The Case of Hermie the Missing Hamster (A Jigsaw Jones Mystery, No. 1).*

Title: *NBA Game Day: From morning until night, behind the scenes of the NBA* by Joe Layden and James Preller (1997). New York: Scholastic.

Genre: picture book; basketball

Reading Level: 4

Interest Level: primary–junior high

Synopsis: Colorful, full-page action photographs describe a day in the life of the NBA. Twenty-six talented sport photographers have contributed to this action-packed book. Fascinating photographs appear on every page, such as the two-page spread of Dennis Rodman, flying through the air in a prone position—horizontal to the floor with the ball in both hands. Most of the book consists of photographs, with little text. Readers are introduced to game vocabulary such as *shootaround, warmups, huddle, pregame, opponent.*

Learning Opportunities: Look at the photographs and describe the action in your own words. Make a time line map consisting of a day in the life of the NBA. Make index cards of sports vocabulary and illustrate each word (e.g., *shootaround, warmup, huddle, pregame, opponent).*

By the Same Author: *Kobe: The Story of the NBA's Rising Young Star; Home Run Heroes: Mark McGuire and Sammy Sosa.*

Title: *Reach Higher* by Scottie Pippen with Greg Brown, illustrated by Doug Keith (1996). Dallas, Texas: Taylor Publishing.

Genre: biography; picture book

Reading Level: 6

Interest Level: intermediate–high school

Synopsis: Scottie Pippen tells about growing up in Hamburg, Arkansas, his close relationship with his family, events that shaped his life and career throughout school, and finally, playing with the Chicago Bulls and Michael Jordan. In addition to describing triumphs and victories, Pippen talks about his fear of flying and his mistakes, like the time he refused to leave the bench and play because he was angry with the coach. Each page is filled with interesting and exciting photographs and detailed illustrations. The text has short paragraphs, but long sentences raise the reading level.

Learning Opportunities: Make a time line map of the important events in Scottie Pippen's life (see example in Part II, Autobiographies and Biographies). Write a bio-poem including important relationships, feelings, fears, and accomplishments. Write an acrostic poem using Scottie Pippen's first or last name (see Part III, Writing Poetry). Evaluate the book. What did you like? Would you suggest any changes (e.g., organization, format)?

By the Same Author: Greg Brown co-author of *Dan Marinl: First and Goal; Kerri Strug: Heart of Gold; Mo Vaughn: Follow your Dreams; Kirby Puckett: Be the Best You Can Be.*

Title: *Sadako and the Thousand Paper Cranes* by Eleanor Coerr (1977). New York: G.P. Putnam's Sons.

Genre: biography; short chapter book

Reading Level: 5

Interest Level: intermediate–junior high

Synopsis: Nine short chapters tell the moving story of Sadako, who lived in Hiroshima, Japan, from 1943–1955. The atom bomb fell on Hiroshima when she was two years old and she died ten years later from leukemia, known as "the atom bomb disease." Eleanor Coerr's sensitive story describes a loving family, loyal friends, and a brave twelve-year-old girl who wants to be a runner. According to the saying, "if you fold one thousand paper cranes the gods will grant your wish." Sadako folds 644 cranes. Her classmates finish the rest in a loving tribute to their friend. The small book has 64 pages including the Epilogue and soft, black and white chalk drawings.

Learning Opportunities: Share what you know about Hiroshima and the atom bomb. Read the chapter headings and predict what you think will happen. Revise and modify predictions as you read subsequent chapters. Discuss the importance of time and place to the characters and theme. Use a description map (or web) to describe Sadako. Make a time line and sequence events (see story example in Part III, Text Structure). What did Sadako do that was so important? Why is there a statue of her in Hiroshima Peace Park? How do you feel about the story?

By the Same Author: *Sadako (reprint, 1997); The Big Balloon Race; Mieko and the Fifth Treasure.*

Title: *Sadako* by Eleanor Coerr, illustrations by Ed Young (1993). New York: Putnam & Grosset Group.

Genre: biography; picture book

Reading Level: 4

Interest Level: primary–junior high

Synopsis: This is the same moving story but told in picture book form. Ed Young's soft, impressionistic chalk drawings create feelings of sadness, vulnerability, beauty, and strength.

Learning Opportunities: Study each illustration as you read the story. What added information is depicted in the illustrations? Why does the artist use chalk and soft colors? Compare and contrast Sadako and Kenji. How are they alike? How are they different? (Use story information and illustrations.) How are Sadako and Chizuko alike? How are they different? What is Peace Day? Why are paper cranes important? How did you feel about the story? Use chalk and draw an illustration for the book cover. Compare and contrast the picture storybook and the short chapter book. Which did you prefer? Why?

By the Same Author: *Sadako and the Thousand Paper Cranes; Mieko and the Fifth Treasure; The Big Balloon Race.*

Title: *Ten Black Dots* by Donald Crews (1968, 1986). New York: Mulberry Books, an imprint of William Morrow & Co.

Genre: picture book; math

Reading Level: 1

Interest Level: primary

Synopsis: Bold illustrations and rhyming verse tell readers what they can do with one to ten black dots. For example, one dot can make a sun or a moon, two dots can make fox eyes or the eyes on two keys. Large, colorful illustrations and big, black type emphasize counting and circular shapes.

Learning Opportunities: Count the dots and read the rhyming verse. Write rhyming words on a word wall or index cards and sort according to rhyming patterns. Make your own dot book using different shapes or continue the book where the author left off, drawing objects that contain 10 to 20 dots. Make up simple addition problems, illustrate them, and write them in number form.

By the Same Author: *Truck; Freight Train* (both Caldecott Honor Awards).

Title: *The Way Things Work* by David Macaulay (1988). New York: Houghton Mifflin.

Genre: picture book; information; machines

Reading Level: 7-8

Interest Level: all ages

Synopsis: Detailed drawings of machines cover over 300 pages of this fascinating book. The big picture book is organized into four parts: The Mechanics of Movement; Harnessing the Elements; Working with Waves; and Electricity and Automation. A few examples of machines include watches, cranes, propellers, movie cameras, cars, and pulleys. Detailed pen and ink drawings demonstrate how machines work—down to the smallest detail. This informative picture book contains technical vocabulary and long sentences. However, for students that are interested in a particular machine, this is the book for them!

Learning Opportunities: Find a machine that you know something about or want to know something about. Look at the illustrations and describe what is happening. Read or listen to the text. Describe the machine in your own words. Use as a Language Experience Approach (LEA) and write about how the machine works or your experience with the machine. Illustrate your story.

By the Same Author: *Cathedral; Castle; City; Mill.*

Title: *This is Baseball* by Margaret Blackstone, illustrations by John O'Brien (1993). New York: Henry Holt and Company.

Genre: picture book; baseball

Reading Level: 1

Interest Level: primary

Synopsis: Full page color illustrations and 17 easy, short sentences describe baseball: the infield and outfield, the catcher, pitcher, player, umpire, fans, bat and ball, high fly ball, and home run!

Learning Opportunities: Read each page and enjoy the illustrations. What added information do you find in the illustrations? Reread the book. Keep a list of unfamiliar sight words to write on index cards. Illustrate the cards. Use the words to play Bingo or Concentration. Make a cross word puzzle of the words to share with your classmates. Use the same patterned format and write and illustrate your own *This is _____* book (e.g., football, soccer, dancing, swimming).

By the Same Author: *This is Figure Skating; This is Soccer.*

Title: *Truck Trouble* (Eyewitness Readers, Level 1) by Angela Royston (1998). New York: A DK Publishing Book.

Genre: picture book; trucks

Reading Level: 1

Interest Level: kindergarten–primary

Synopsis: Simple vocabulary, short sentences, and colorful full-page pho-tographs tell about a busy, problem-filled day in the life of a truck driver who is delivering packages to a new children's hospital.

Learning Opportunities: Read and reread the short book. Use the illus-trations to describe the truck driver's day. Use phonics patterns and con-text to recognize unfamiliar words. Write unfamiliar words on a Word Wall or index cards. Look for familiar phonics patterns or word chunks (e.g., prefixes, suffixes, words in compound words such as *thunderstorm, freeway, windshield*). Use multisensory instruction to learn and remem-ber difficult sight words (see Part III, Word Recognition). Use a Language Experience Approach (LEA) to describe and write about your day.

By the Same Author: *The Senses (A Life-The-Flap-Body Book); Cars (Eye Openers); The A-To-Z Book of Cars; Trucks (Inside and Out).*

Part V
Working With Parents

Tips

- Model the value of reading; share and read aloud passages from books, magazines, or articles that you are reading.

- Read to your child. Listen to his or her comments or questions and share your own. Compare the story to real life events. Reread favorite books. As you read, point out words that rhyme and that have similar word patterns. Encourage your child to join in when words rhyme or are repeated.

- Take your child to the library or to a bookstore to browse. Let your child select books or magazines that interest him/her.

- Establish a regular time when everyone reads, e.g., after dinner, before bed.

- Listen to your child read aloud. Discuss the story and talk about the characters, problem, main events, and the ending.

- Buy audio-taped books. Tape books for your children to read. Have your children help you; they will enjoy listening to their own voices.

- Provide on-going literacy opportunities. Encourage your child to draw pictures, illustrate, or write stories about his/her experiences. Have crayons, colored markers, pencils, and paper available in places where the family gathers for relaxation such as the family room, living room, and kitchen.

- Subscribe to children's magazines. Bernice Cullinan provides a list of children's magazines in her book *Read to me: raising kids who love to read* (1992, pp. 139-141). For example, *Cricket, the Magazine for Children* (ages 2-12), contains articles on nature, science, history, astronomy, art, music, literature, sports, cartoons, and crafts, (P.O. Box 52961, Boulder, CO 80322-2961); *Highlights for Children* (ages 2-12), includes original stories, articles, hidden pictures, activities, and puzzles, (2300 West Fifth Avenue, Columbus, OH 43272-0002); *National Geographic World* (ages 7-12), includes articles about outdoor adventure, natural history, science, astronomy, sports, games, and crafts, (National Geographic Society, 17th and M Streets NW, Washington, DC 20036); *Ranger Rick* (ages 7-12), a natural history magazine that includes articles about animals, nature, science, astronomy, plus activities, (National Wildlife Federation, 1400 16th Street NW, Washington, DC 20036-2266; *Sports Illustrated for Kids* (ages 7-12), includes articles on professional, amateur, and youth sports, (Time Inc., Time & Life Building, Rockefeller Center, New York, NY 10020-1393).

- Watch television programs that focus on reading such as *The Reading Rainbow* (where authors and celebrities read picture books aloud to children) and *The Magic School* Bus (an animated version of the science based picture storybooks by Joanna Cole). Visit the *Reading Rainbow* website: gpn.unl.edu/rainbow.

Frequently Asked Questions

What books should I choose?

Select books that your child likes, is interested in, and that he or she can comfortably read. Find books that pertain to your child's hobbies, e.g., sports, dancing, art. Try mysteries, biographies, and humorous realistic fiction. There are many easy-to-read, short chapter books written by good writers such as the witty and clever chapter books by Louis Sachar (*Marvin Redpost*) and Jon Scieszka (*The Time Warp Trio*), Cynthia Rylant's humorous chapter books (*Poppleton and Friends*; *Mr. Putter and Tabby*), the easy mystery books by Margorie Weinman Sharmat and Craig Sharmat (*Nate the Great*), and Betsy Byars' three halarious short chapter books about *The Golly Sisters*. Betsy Byars also writes *The Herculeah Jones Mysteries,* fiction novels that have exciting plots, colorful characters, and a second/third grade reading level. Sports writer Matt Christopher writes easy to read fiction and biographies. Look for appropriate reading and interest levels on the back of the book and for award winning books and authors, noted on the front jacket or back cover.

What are award books?

The American Library Association presents two prestigious awards: the Caldecott Award for the most outstanding picture book and the Newbery

Award for the best literature. Look for a large gold or silver medal on the book cover. Silver medals indicate the books are honored as runner-up selections. Other prestigious awards include the Coretta Scott King Award that celebrates contributions to children's literature by African American authors and illustrators and the International Reading Association (IRA) Children's Book Award given to new authors of promise.

Does it matter what my child reads?

It is not so important what your child reads but that he or she is read-ing and enjoying books. Many children love series books, such as *Goosebumps* by R.L. Stine. When you know about a good story that you think your child will like, try reading it to her (him). You may snag her interest in a good author! For example, the suspenseful *Herculeah Jones* Mystery Series by Betsy Byars; Avi's exciting adventures and fantasies such as *Who Stole the Wizard of Oz* and *Poppy*; Jerry Spinelli's *Crash, Maniac Magee,* and *Fourth Grade Rats*; and Louis Sachar's *Wayside School* books all have colorful characters and good stories that promote reading com-prehension.

How do I know if a book is too difficult for my child?

Ask your child to read a page or two out loud. If he (she) misses five or more words and has difficulty telling you what he has just read try an easier book. Look for the reading level on the back of the book, lower right- or left-hand corner. The reading level (RL) refers to grade. For ex-ample, a RL 5.8 means that the average student in the fifth grade, eighth month of school can read and understand the book. That level may or may not be appropriate for your child. Look for audio taped books if your child is interested in a book that is too difficult for him to read independently.

What can I do to help my child read?

Read to your child and with your child. Talk about the story and illustra-tions. Make connections between the illustrations and the story. As you read, predict what will happen next, why you think so, and ask your child to do the same. Share your predictions. Make connections to real life expe-riences. Listen to your child read. Help your child use illustrations, letter sounds, and the surrounding context to identify unfamiliar words.

Point our familiar spelling patterns, e.g., *ing* words. Poetry books by Shel Silverstein (*Where the Sidewalk Ends, A Light in the Attic, Falling Up*) and Jack Prelutsky (*A Pizza the Size of the Sun* and *For Laughing Out Loud*) contain short, humorous poems with rhyming patterns and are fun to read aloud. Make letters out of clay or dough and spell easy words with rhyming patterns, e.g., *hat, fat, cat,* with magnetic letters on the refrigerator.

What if I am not a reader?

Take your child to the library or bookstore and select books that are audio-taped. Ask your child to bring home books from school that are taped and ones that he or she wants to read. Listen to the book with your child and discuss the story, talk about the characters (e.g., why you think characters act the way they do), and your feelings about the book. When you stop at the end of a chapter, predict what you think will happen next and why you think so. Compare your predictions. If you read the newspaper, share a section in which you are interested. Encourage your child to read at the same time (e.g., newspaper, magazine, or book) and share his or her favorite parts with you. There are a number of good magazines for children and young adults such as *Cricket, National Geographic World, Ranger Rick, Highlights for Children, Sports Illustrated for Kids.* In some newspapers you'll find book serials for children (Breakfast Serials) such as Avi's book series about *Amanda* the raccoon.

What is dyslexia? How do we fix it? Will it go away?

Dyslexia is a developmental language disorder in which phonological processing problems hinder an individual's ability to decode printed words (Catts and Kamhi, 1999, pp. 63–64). Many successful individuals have experienced severe reading disabilities such as Nelson Rockefeller (politician), Hans Christian Anderson (children's author), Cher (singer/actress), and Robin Williams (actor/comedian). See *Outstanding Dyslexics: Inspirations for Success,* a color-calendar developed by the International Dyslexia Association (LA Branch) that features photographs and quotes from individuals with dyslexia and related learning disabilities who have achieved success in their chosen field. Dale Jordan (1996) provides the following definition and explanation of dyslexia from 40 years of experience in working with this population.

> Dyslexia is the inability of an intelligent person to become fluent in the basic skills of reading, spelling, and handwriting in spite of prolonged teaching and tutoring. Math computation may also remain at a level of struggle. Dyslexia means that the person will always struggle to some degree with reading printed passages, writing with a pen or pencil, spelling accurately from memory, and developing sentences and paragraphs with correct grammar and punctuation. Dyslexia may also include difficulty telling information orally as well as listening to oral information accurately. No matter how hard the person tries, certain types of errors continue

to appear in reading, writing, and spelling. Dyslexia is a brain-based dysfunction that is often genetic. It tends to run in families. Through certain kinds of remedial training, dyslexic patterns can be partly overcome or reduced, but dyslexia cannot be completely eliminated. It is a life-long, brain-based condition for which individuals with dyslexia can learn successfully to compensate (p. 43).

Resources

Web Sites

www.amazon.com: Provides information about books and authors and is a source for ordering books.

www.acs.ucalgary.ca/~dkbrown/lists.html: Children's Literature—Best Books Lists. The year's best books; recommended book lists; subject bibliographies.

www.ala.org/alsc/parents.links.html: For Parents and Caregivers: born to read; how to raise a reader; the children's literature web guide; helping your child learn to read; the keeping kids reading page.

www.ed.gov/pubs/parents/Reading/ImportantThings.html: Helping your child learn to read—important things to know.

www.ed.gov/pubs/parents/Reading/ReadAlong.html: Read along: reading with your child.

www.ed.gov/pubs/parents/Reading/WriteAndTalk.,html: Provides activities that encourage your child to speak, read, write, and listen.

www.ed.gov/pubs/parents/Reading/Resources.html: Provides resources for children that relate to real-life events; poems; magazines.

www.ed.gov/pubs/parents/Reading/Postscript.html: Provides suggestions for helping older children become enthusiastic and fluent readers.

www.candlelightstories.com: Includes Audio Stories performed with voice, music, and sound effects. In order to listen to Story Theatre you need Windows Media Player. Stories include *Jack in the Beanstalk* (Brothers Grimm), *The Nightingale* (Hans Christian Andersen), *The Boy in the Paper Boat* (Alexander Cima), and *How the Whale got His Throat* (Rudyard Kipling).

www.npac.syr.edu/textbook/kidsweb: Kids Web is a Digital Library for K–12 children that includes information on the Arts, Sciences, and Social Studies. Look under Arts and find *Literature—Children's Books* that contains articles, reviews, book lists, and information about children's authors.

http://trelease-on-reading.com: Jim Trelease provides information and tips on reading books to children.

Children's Literature—CD Roms

The Living Books Series features read-alongs by Dr. Seuss (*Green Eggs and Ham, The Cat in the Hat*), Mercer Mayer, Kevin Henkes, and others.

The Way Things Work is based on the picture book by David Macaulay.

The Polar Express is based on the Caldecott Award picture book by Chris Van Allsburg.

The Magic School Bus Explores the Solar System is based on the *Magic School Bus* books written by Joanna Cole and illustrated by Bruce Degen.

Children's Literature—Books on Tape

Days with Frog and Toad by Arnold Lobel (I-Can-Read Book), Harper Children's Audio (book and cassette).

No More Monsters for Me! by Peggy Parish (I-Can-Read Book), Harper Children's Audio (book and cassette).

Thank You, Amelia Bedelia by Peggy Parish (I-Can-Read Book), Harper Children's Audio (book and cassette).

I Like Me by Nancy Carlson, Puffin Storytape (book and cassette).

Where the Wild Things Are and Other Stories by Maurice Sendak, Harper Children's Audio (book and cassette).

Alexander and the Terrible, Horrible, No Good, Very Bad Day by Judith Viorst, Harper Children's Audio (book and cassette).

Madeline and Other Bemelmans by Ludwig Bemelmans, Harper Children's Audio.

Beezus and Ramona by Beverly Cleary, Listening Libray, Inc.

Ramona the Brave by Beverly Cleary, Listening Library, Inc.

Matilda by Roald Dahl, Harper Children's Audio.

The Boxcar Children by Gertrude Chandler Warner, Listening Library, Inc.

Sideways Stories from Wayside School by Louis Sachar, Listening Library, Inc.

Sarah Plain and Tall by Patricia MacLahan, Harper Children's Audio.

The Mighty by Rodman Philbrick, Listening Library, Informational Books.

Professional Literature

Children's Choices. Newark, DE: International Reading Association.

Calkins, L. (1997). *Raising Life Long Learners: A Parent's Guide.* Reading, MA: Perseus Book Group.

Cullinan, B. (1992). *Read to Me: Raising Kids Who Love to Read.* New York: Scholastic.

Liqqett, T. and Benfield, C. (1996). *Reading Rainbow Guide to Children's Books: The 101 Best Titles.* New York: Citadel Press Book, Carol Publishing.

Reid, B. (1999) *Family Storytime.* 50 East Huron Street, Chicago, IL: American Library Association.

Teacher's Choices. Newark, DE: International Reading Association.

Trelease, J. (1995). *The Read-Aloud Handbook.* New York: Penguin Group.

Stoll, D. (1997). *Magazines for Kids and Teens.* Newark, DE: International Reading Association (IRA).

Young Adult's Choices. Newark, DE: IRA.

Bridges to Reading: What To Do When You Suspect Your Child Has a Reading Problem: A Kit of First-Step Strategies (1995). San Mateo, CA: Parent's Educational Resource Center, 1660 S. Amphlett Blvd.

Informational Videos

Read to Me—13 minute video that introduces parents to reading. Newark, DE: International Reading Association (IRA).

Becoming a Family of Readers—parents and child model book sharing. Newark, DE: International Reading Association (IRA).

How Difficult Can This Be? The F.A.T. City Workshop—Richard Lavoie (1989) helps parents and professionals understand the nature of learning disabilities and discusses strategies for more effective instruction. PBS Video with WETA, Washington, DC., Eagle Hill Foundation, Inc.

Educational Services and Organizations

• Parents' Educational Resource Center (PERC). 1660 South Amphlett Boulevard, Suite 200, San Mateo, CA. Provides information and guidance to parents seeking resources to help students with learnng differences.

• Children and Adults with Attention Deficit Disorder (C.H.A.D.D.). 499 N.W. 70th Avenue, Suite 308, Plantation, FL 38817. Provides family support and advocacy, public and professional education, and encourages scientific research.

• Orton Dyslexia Society. Chester Building Suite 382, Baltimore, MD 21204. The Orton Dyslexia Society has branches over the country that offer informational meetings and support groups. (See additional resources in *Bridges to Reading: A Kit of First-Step Strategies,* 1995).

References

Bridges to reading: What to do when you suspect your child has a reading problem: A kit of first-step strategies (1996). San Mateo, CA: Parents' Educational Resource Center.

Catts, H. and Kamhi, A. (Eds.) (1999). *Language and reading disabilities.* Needham Heights, MA: Allyn and Bacon.

Jordan, D. (1996). *Overcoming dyslexia in children, adolescents and adults (2nd ed.).* Austin, Texas: Pro-Ed.

Cullinan, B. (1992). *Read to me: Raising kids who love to read.* New York: Scholastic.

Outstanding dyslexics: Inspirations for success (1999) (calendar). Studio City, CA: International Dyslexia Association LA Branch, 439 Tujunga Avenue.

Appendix A
Related References
for Teachers

Journals

Language Arts. Urbana, IL: National Council of Teachers of English. Publishes original contributions on all facets of language arts learning and teaching, focusing on preschool through middle school ages.

Learning Disabilities Research & Practice. A publication of the Division for Learning Disabilities, the Council for Exceptional Children. Mahwah, NJ: Lawrence Erlbaum Associates. Presents current research and information important to practitioners in the field of learning disabilities.

Teaching Exceptional Children. A publication of the Council for Exceptional Children, Baltimore, MD. Features articles that deal with practical methods and classroom materials for teachers who work with students with disabilities and children who are gifted.

Riverbank Review of books for young readers. Published quarterly at the University of St. Thomas, Minneapolis, MN. The *Riverbank Review* presents essays, reviews (picture books, fiction, and nonfiction), and features such as books for summer (Summer, 1999 issue), interviews, profiles, and creative works by authors and illustrators.

Professional Literature

Bamford, R. and Kristo, J. (Eds.). (1999). *Making facts come alive: choosing quality nonfiction literature K-8.* Norwood, MA: Christopher-Gordon.

Burke, E. and Glazer, S. (1994). *Using nonfiction in the classroom.* New York: Scholastic.

Fox, M. (1993). *Radical reflections: Passionate opinions on teaching, learning, and living.* Orlando, FL: Harcourt Brace & Company.

Gunning, T. (1998). *Best books for beginning readers.* Needham Heights, MA: Allyn & Bacon.

Hickman, J., Hepler, S., and Cullinan, B. (Eds.). (1989). *Children's literature in the classroom: Weaving Charlotte's Web.* Norwood, MA: Christopher-Gordon.

Hickman, J., Hepler, S., Cullinan, B. (1996). *Children's literature in the classroom: Extending Charlotte's Web.* Norwood, MA: Christopher-Gordon.

Harvey, S. (1998). *Nonfiction matters: Reading, writing, and research in grades 3-8.* York, ME: Stenhouse.

Hart-Hewins, L., and Wells, J. (1999). *Better books! Better readers! How to choose, use, and level books for children in the primary grades.* York, ME: Stenhouse.

Raphael, T. and Au, K. (1999). *Literature-based instruction: Reshaping the curriculum.* Norwood, MA: Christopher-Gordon.

Trelease, J. (1995). *Read aloud handbook (4th ed.).* New York: Penguin Books.

Additional Resources

Web Sites

www.amazon.com: Provides information about books and authors and is a source for ordering books.

www.acs.ucalgary.ca/~dkbrown/lists.html: Children's Literature—Best Books Lists. The year's best books; recommended book lists; subject bibliographies.

www.cec-sped.org: The Council for Exceptional Children.

www.ed.golv/pubs/parents/Reading/ImportantThings.html: Suggestions for parents to help children learn to read.

Project Gutenberg (www.promo.net/pg): Offers full text of quality literature for which copyright restrictions do not apply, e.g., *Alice in Wonderland.*

Calendar

Outstanding Dyslexics: Inspirations for Success. A motivating color calendar that boosts self-concepts. It features photographs and quotes from individuals with dyslexia and related learning disabilities who have achieved success in their chosen field. For example, the 1999 calendar includes an award winning scientist, a dancer, choreographer, actor and singer, professor and researcher, and US Olympic Team Captain. Order from the International Dyslexia Association LA Branch, 4379 Tujunga Avenue, Studio City, CA 91604. Phone: (818) 506-8866.

Appendix B
Book Lists of Selected Subjects

Biography

Grandfather's Journey (Allen Say, 1993) (picture book).

Cedric Ceballas: All Pro Biographies (Mark Stewart, 1996) (picture book).

Cool Melons—Turn to Frogs! The Life and Poems of Issa (translated by Matthew Gollub, 1998) (picture book).

Diego (Jeanette Winter, 1991) (picture book).

Finding Providence: The Story of Roger Williams (Avi, 1997) (an I-Can-Read Chapter Book).

Football Stars (S.A. Kramer, 1997) (picture book).

Home Run (Robert Burleigh, 1998).

I Have A Dream: The Story of Martin Luther King (Margaret Davidson, 1996).

I Can't Accept Not Trying: Michael Jordan on the Pursuit of Excellence (Michael Jordan, 1994).

Isadora Dances (Rachael Isadora, 1998) (picture book).

Lou Gehrig: The Luckiest Man (David Adler, 1997) (picture book).

Reach Higher (Scotttie Pippen with Greg Brown, 1996) (picture book).

Sadako and the One Thousand Paper Cranes (Eleanor Coerr, 1977).

Sadako (Eleanor Coerr and Ed Young, 1993) (picture book).

Diversity

Picture Books
Abuela (Arthur Dorros, 1991).
Chicken Sunday (Patricia Polacco, 1992).
Diego (Jeanette Winter, 1991).
Grandfather's Journey (Allen Say, 1993).
Goggles (Ezra Jack Keats, 1969).
Koala Lou (Mem Fox, 1988).
My House, Mi Casa (Rebecca Emberley, 1990).
Pink and Say (Patricia Polacco, 1994).
Sadako (Eleanor Coerr and Ed Young, 1993).
Smoky Night (Eve Bunting, 1994).
The Encounter (Jane Yolen, 1992).
The Girl Who Loved Wild Horses (1978).
The Snowy Day (Ezra Jack Keats, 1962).
To Every Thing There Is A Season (Leo and Diane Dillon, 1998).
Tree of Cranes (Allen Say, 1991).
Yo! Yes! (Chris Raschka, 1993).

Short Chapter Books/Easy Reading Books
It's a Fiesta, Benjamin (Patricia Reilly Giff, 1996).
Molly's Pilgrim (Barbara Cohen, 1983).
Summer Wheels (Eve Bunting, 1992).

Novels
An Island Like You: Stories from the Barrio (Judith Ortiz Cofer, 1995).
Egg-Drop Blues (Jacqueline Turner Banks, 1995).
From the Notebooks of Melanin Sun (Jacqueline Woodson, 1995).
I Hadn't Meant to Tell You This (Jacqueline Woodson, 1994).
Maniac Magee (Jerry Spinelli, 1990).
Nightjohn (Gary Paulsen, 1993).
Scorpions (Walter Dean Myers, 1988).
Slam (Walter Dean Myers, 1996).
Song of the Trees (Mildred Taylor, 1975).
The Hundred Dresses (Eleanor Estes, 1944).
The Skirt (Gary Soto, 1992).
Tunes For Bears To Dance To (Robert Cormier, 1992).

Nonfiction
I Have A Dream: The Story of Martin Luther King (Margaret Davidson,
   1996).

Poetry
Cool Melons—Turn to Frogs! The Life and Poems of Issa (translated by Matthew Gollub, 1998).
Reach for the Moon (Samantha Abeel, 1994).
The Dream Keeper and Other Poems (Langston Hughes, 1932, 1994)

Family Relations

Picture Books/Short Chapter Books
Abuela (Arthur Dorros, 1991).
Fly Away Home (Eve Bunting, 1991).
Grandfather's Journey (Allen Say, 1993).
Grandpa (John Burningham, 1984).
Tree of Cranes (Allen Say, 1991).
The Wall (Eve Bunting, 1990).

Easy Reading Books/Short Chapter Books
Ant Plays Bear (Betsy Byars, 1997).
It's a Fiesta, Benjamin (Paticia Reilly Giff, 1996).
Sarah, Plain and Tall (Patricia MacLachlan, 1985).

Novels
A Fine White Dust (Cynthia Rylant, 1986).
Adam Zigzag (Barbara Barrie, 1994).
Dear Mr. Henshaw (Beverly Cleary, 1983).
Don't you dare read this, Mrs. Dunphrey (Margaret Peterson Haddix, 1996).
From the Notebooks of Melanin Sun (Jacqueline Woodson, 1995).
Freaky Friday (Mary Rodgers, 1972).
Henry and Ribsy (Beverly Cleary, 1954).
Scorpions (Walter Dean Myers, 1988).
Song of the Trees (Mildred Taylor, 1975).
Stone Fox (John Reynolds Gardiner, 1980).
That Was Then, This Is Now (S.E. Hinton, 1971).
The Puppy Sister (S.E. Hinton, 1995).
The Skirt (Gary Soto, 1992).

Poetry
Evertt Anderson's Goodbye (Lucille Clifton, 1983).

Humor

Picture Books
A Chocolate Moose for Dinner (Fred Gwynne, 1976).
Alexander and the Terrible, Horrible, No Good, Very Bad Day (Judith Viorst, 1972).

Bears in the Night (Stan and Jan Berenstain, 1971).
Green Eggs and Ham (Dr. Seuss, 1960).
Horton Hatches the Egg (Dr. Seuss, 1940;1968)
King Bidgood's in the Bathtub (Audrey and Don Wood, 1985).
Miss Nelson is Missing (Henry Allard, 1977).
The Cat in the Hat (Dr. Seuss, 1957).
The Napping House (Audrey and Don Wood, 1984).
There's a Nightmare in My Closet (Mercer Mayer, 1968).
Tuesday (David Wiesner, 1991).
The True Story of the Three Little Pigs (Jon Sciezka, 1989).

Short Chapter Books/ Easy Reading Books
Aliens for Dinner (Stephanie Spinner, 1994).
Amelia Bedelia (Peggy Parish, 1963).
Annie Bananie Moves to Barry Avenue (Leah Komaiko, 1996).
Bravo Amelia Bedelia (Henry Parish, 1997).
Commander Toad and the Voyage Home (Jane Yolen, 1998).
Freckle Juice (Judy Blume, 1971).
Frog and Toad Are Friends (Arnold Lobel, 1971).
Keep Your Eye on Amanda (Avi, 1996, 1997).
Marvin Redpost: Is He a Girl? (Louis Sachar, 1993).
Mine's the Best (Crosby Bonsall, 1973, 1996).
Mr. Putter and Tabby Walk the Dog (Cynthia Rylant, 1994).
Muggie Maggie (Beverly Cleary, 1990).
Owl At Home (Arnold Lobel, 1975).
Poppleton and Friends (Cynthia Rylant, 1997).
Rats on the Range and Other Stories (James Marshall, 1993).
The Cut-Ups Crack Up (James Marshall, 1992).
The Golly Sisters Go West (Betsy Byars, 1985).
The Seven Treasure Hunts (Betsy Byars, 1991).
The Time Warp Trio: The Not-So-Jolly Roger (Jon Scieszka, 1991).

Novels
Bunnicula: A Rabbit Tale of Mystery (Deborah and James Howe, 1979).
Freaky Friday (Mary Rogers, 1972).
Henry and Ribsy (Beverly Cleary, 1954).
How to Eat Fried Worms (Norman Rockwell, 1973).
James and the Giant Peach (Roald Dahl, 1961).
Matilda (Roald Dahl, 1988).
Ramona Quimbly, Age 8 (Beverly Cleary, 1981).
The Puppy Sister (S.E. Hinton, 1995).
Wayside School Gets a Little Stranger (Louis Sachar, 1995).

Poetry
A pizza the size of the sun (Jack Prelutsky, 1997).
beast feast (Douglas Florian, 1998).
For Laughing Out Loud: Poems to Tickle Your Funnybone (Jack Prelutsky, 1991).
If I Were In Charge of the World (Judith Viorst, 1984).
Insect Soup: Bug Poems (Barry Louis Polisar, 1999).
Lunch Money and Other Poems About School (Carol Diggory Shields, 1995).
The Way I Feel Sometimes (Beatrice Schenk de Regniers, 1988).
Where the Sidewalk Ends (Shel Silverstein, 1974).
A Light in the Attic (Shel Silverstein, 1981).
Falling Up (Shel Silverstein, 1996).

Identity/Overcoming Difficulties
Picture Books/Short Chapter Books
Emma's Magic Winter (Jean Little, 1998).
Fly Away Home (Eve Bunting, 1991).
I Like Me (Nancy Carlson, 1988).
Lou Gehrig: The Luckiest Man (David Adler, 1997).
Thank You, Mr. Falker (Patricia Polacco, 1998).

Novels
A Fine White Dust (Cynthia Rylant, 1986).
Adam Zigzag (Barbara Barrie, 1994).
An Island Like You: Stories of the Barrio (Judith Cortez Cofer, 1995).
Brian's Return (Gary Paulsen, 1999).
Bridge to Terabithia (Katherine Patterson, 1977).
Crash (Jerry Spinelli, 1996).
Dear Mr. Henshaw (Beverly Cleary, 1983).
Don't you dare read this, Mrs. Dunphrey (Margaret Peterson Haddix, 1996).
Egg-Drop Blues (Jacqueline Turner Banks, 1995).
Freak the Mighty (Rodman Philbrick, 1993).
From the Notebooks of Melanin Sun (Jacqueline Woodson, 1995).
Hatchet (Gary Paulsen, 1987).
Holes (Louis Sachar, 1998).
I Hadn't Meant To Tell You This (Jacqueline Woodson, 1995).
Maniac Magee (Jerry Spinelli, 1990).
Scorpions (Walter Dean Myers, 1988).
Slam (Walter Dean Myers, 1996).
Stone Fox (John Reynolds Gardiner, 1980).
That Was Then, This Is Now (S.E. Hinton, 1971).

Tunes for Bears to Dance to (Robert Cormier, 1992).
Wringer (Jerry Spinelli, 1998).

Poetry
Everett Anderson's Goodbye (Lucille Clifton, 1983).
Life Doesn't Frighten Me (Maya Angelou, Jean-Michel Basquiat, 1993).
Reach for the Moon (Samantha Abeel, 1994).
The Dream Keeper and Other Poems (Lanston Hughes, 1932,1994).

Mystery/Suspense
Short Chapter Books/Easy Reading Books
A to Z Mysteries:The Absent Author (Ron Roy, 1997).
Cam Jansen and the Scary Snake Mystery (David Adler, 1997).
Hour of the Olympics (Mary Pope Osborne, 1998).
In a Dark, Dark, Room and Other Scary Stories (Alvin Schwartz, 1984).
Nate the Great and the Tardy Tortoise (Marjorie Weinman Sharmat and Craig Sharmat, 1995).

Novels
Bunnicula:A Rabbit Tale of Mystery (Deborah and James Howe, 1979).
Disappearing Acts (Betsy Byars, 1998).
Dead Letter (Betsy Byars, 1996).
Encyclopedia Brown and the Case of the Mysterious Handprints (Donald J. Sobol, 1985).
Holes (Louis Sachar, 1998).
More Scary Stories to Tell in the Dark (Alvin Schwartz, 1984).
Poppy (Avi, 1996).
Running Out Of Time (Margaret Peterson Haddix, 1995).
The Box Car Children:The Panther Mystery (Gertrude Chandler Warner, 1998).
The Giver (Louis Lowry, 1993).
The Purloined Corn Popper:A Felicity Snell Mystery (E.W. Hildick, 1997).
What Do Fish Have To Do With Anything? (Avi, 1997, Short Stories).
Who Stole the Wizard of Oz? (Avi, 1981).

Math/Science
A Fair Bear Share (Stuart J. Murphy, 1998) (regrouping).
Anno's Math Games III (Mitsumasa Anno, 1982).
Each Orange Had 8 Slices (Paul Giganti, Jr., 1992).
Eating Fractions (Bruce McMillan, 1991).
Hello, Fish! Visiting the Coral Reef (Silvia A. Earle, 1999).
Dinosaur Dinners (Lee Davies, 1998).

Dinosaur Time (Peggy Parish, 1974).
Get Up and Go! (Stuart J. Murphy, 1996) (time lines).
Measuring Penny (Loreen Leedy, 1997).
Ten Black Dots (Donald Crews, 1968, 1986).
The Magic School Bus in the Time of Dinosaurs (Joanna Cole, 1994).

Siblings

Easy Reading Books/Short Chapter Books
Ant Plays Bear (Betsy Byars, 1971).
Keep Your Eye on Amanda! (Avi, 1996,1997).
The Golly Sisters Go West (Betsy Byars, 1985).

Novels
Adam ZigZag (Barbara Barrie, 1994).
Don't you dare read this, Mrs. Dumphrey (Margaret P. Hadix, 1996).
Egg-Drop Blues (Jacqueline Turner Banks, 1995).
Freaky Friday (Mary Rodgers, 1972).
Romana Quimbly, Age 8 (Beverly Cleary, 1981).
The Box Car Children (Gertrude Chandler Warner) (series).
Who Stole the Wizard of Oz? (Avi, 1981).

Sports/Dance

Fiction
Baseball Pals (Matt Christopher, 1956,1984).
Crash (Jerry Spinelli (1996).
Slam (Walter Dean Myers, 1996).
Rosies Big City Ballet (Patricia Reilly Giff, 1998).

Nonfiction
All-Time Great World Series (Andrew Gutelle, 1994).
Cedric Ceballos: Grollier All-Pro Biographies (Mark Stewert, 1996).
Dance (Bill T. Jones and Susan Kuklin, 1998) (picture book).
Football Stars: Sanders; Rice; Aikman; Sanders (S.A. Kramer, 1997).
Home Run (Robert Burleigh, 1998).
I Can't Accept Not Trying: Michael Jordan on the Pursuit of Excellence (Michael Jordan, 1994).
Isadora Dances (Rachael Isadora, 1998).
Lou Gehrig: The Luckiest Man (David Adler, 1997).
NBA Action from A to Z (James Preller, 1997).
NBA Game Day: From morning until night, behind the scenes of the NBA (Joe Layden and James Preller, 1997).

Reach Higher (Scottie Pippen with Greg Brown, 1996).
This is Baseball (Margaret Blackstone, 1993).

Poetry
Extra Innings: Baseball Poems (Lee Bennett Hopkins, 1993).
For The Love Of The Game: Michael Jordan and Me (Eloise Greenfield, 1997).
Sports! Sports! Sports! (Lee Bennett Hopkins, 1999).

Writing

Easy Reading Books/Short Chapter Books
Muggie Maggie (Beverly Cleary, 1983).

Novels
Dear Mr. Henshaw (Beverly Cleary, 1983).
Don't you dare read this, Mrs. Dunphrey (Margaret P. Haddix, 1996).
From the Notebooks of Melanin Sun (Jacqueline Woodson, 1995).
Ramona Quimbly, Age 8 (Beverly Clearly, 1981).

Appendix C
Children's Literature
Book Titles

Picture Books

**Books with Rhyming Words, Repeated Phrases,
and Cumulative Stories**

Alexander and the Terrible, Horrible, No Good, Very Bad Day (Judith
Viorst, 1972)

Are You My Mother? (P.D. Eastman, 1960).

Bears in the Night (Stan and Jan Berenstain, 1987).

Brown Bear, Brown Bear, What Do You See? (Bill Martin Jr, 1992).

Clifford: The Big Red Dog (Norman Bridwell, 1963).

Go, Dog, Go! (P.H. Eastman, 1961).

Green Eggs and Ham (Dr. Seuss, 1960).

Horton Hatches the Egg (Dr. Seuss, 1940; 1968).

King Bidgood's in the Bathtub (Audrey and Don Wood, 1985).

Koala Lou (Mem Fox, 1988).

Madeline (Ludwig Bemelmans, 1939).

My Many Colored Days (Dr. Seuss, 1996).

The Cat in the Hat (Dr. Seuss, 1957).

The Gingerbread Boy (illustrated by Scott Cook, 1987).

The Napping House (Audrey and Don Wood, 1984).

The Very Hungry Caterpillar (Eric Carle, 1969).

**Picture Books, Picture Storybooks, and
Wordless Picture Books**

A Chocolate Moose for Dinner (Fred Gwynne, 1976).

Abuela (Arthur Dorros, 1991).

Chicken Sunday (Patricia Polacco, 1992).

Encounter (Jane Yolen, 1992).

Fly Away Home (Eve Bunting, 1991).

Free Fall (David Wiesner, 1988).

Grandfather's Journey (Allen Say, 1993).

Granpa (John Burningham, 1984).

Goggles (Ezra Jack Keats, 1969).

I Like Me! (Nancy Carlson, 1988).

Jumanji (Chris Van Allsburg, 1981).

Miss Nelson Is Missing (Henry Allard, 1977).

My House Mi Casa (Rebecca Emberley, 1990).

Pink and Say (Patricia Polacco, 1994).

Smoky Night (Eve Bunting, 1994).

Thank You, Mr. Falker (Patricia Polacco, 1998).

The Giving Tree (Shel Silverstein, 1964).

The Girl Who Loved Wild Horses (Paul Goble, 1978).

The Magic School Bus in the Time of the Dinosaurs (Joanna Cole, 1994).

The Mysteries of Harris Burdick (Chris Van Allsburg, 1984).

The Paper Princess (Elisa Kleven, 1994).

The Snowy Day (Ezra Jack Keats, 1962).

The Steadfast Tin Soldier (Hans Christian Andersen, retold by Katie Campbell, 1990).

There's a Nightmare in My Closet (Mercer Mayer, 1968).

To Every Thing There Is A Season (Leo and Diane Dillon, 1998).

Tree of Cranes (Allen Say, 1991).

The True Story of the Three Little Pigs (Jon Scieszka, 1989).

The Wall (Eve Bunting, 1990).

Tuesday (David Wiesner, 1991).

Yo! Yes! (Chris Raschka, 1993).

Where the Wild Things Are (Maurice Sendak, 1964).

Easy Reading Books and Short Chapter Books

A to Z Mysteries: The Absent Author (Ron Roy, 1997).

Aliens for Dinner (Stephanie Spinner, 1994).

Amelia Bedelia (Peggy Parish, 1963).

Annie Bananie Moves to Barry Avenue (Leah Komaiko, 1996).

Ant Plays Bear (Betsy Byars, 1997).

Bravo Amelia Bedelia (Henry Parish, 1997).

Cam Jansen and the Scary Snake Mystery (David Adler, 1997).

Commander Toad and the Voyage Home (Jan Yolen, 1998).

Emma's Magic Winter (Jean Little, 1998).

Freckle Juice (Judy Blume, 1971).

Frog and Toad Are Friends (Arnold Lobel, 1971).

Henry and Mudge and the Long Weekend (Cynthia Rylant, 1992).
Hour of the Olylmpics (Mary Pope Osborne, 1998).
In a Dark, Dark, Room and Other Scary Stories (Alvin Schwartz, 1984).
It's a Fiesta, Benjamin (Patricia Reilly Giff, 1996).
Keep Your Eye on Amanda (Avi, 1996, 1997).
Marvin Redpost: Is He a Girl? (Louis Sachar, 1993).
Mine's the Best (Crosby Bonsall, 1973, 1996).
Molly's Pilgrim (Barbara Cohen, 1983).
Mr. Putter and Tabby Walk the Dog (Cynthia Rylant, 1994).
Muggie Maggie (Beverly Cleary, 1990).
Nate the Great and the Tardy Tortoise (Margorie Weinman Sharmat and Craig Sharmat, 1995).
Owl At Home (Arnold Lobel, 1975).
Poppleton and Friends (Cynthia Rylant, 1997).
Rats on the Range and Other Stories (James Marshall, 1993).
Rosie's Big City Ballet (Patricia Reilly Giff, 1998).
Sarah, Plain and Tall (Patricia MacLachlan, 1985).
Summer Wheels (Eve Bunting, 1992).
The Cut-Ups Crack Up (James Marshall, 1992).
The Golly Sisters Go West (Betsy Byars, 1985).
The King's Equal (Katherine Paterson, 1992).
The Seven Treasure Hunts (Betsy Byars, 1991).
The Time Warp Trio: The Not-So-Jolly Rodger (Jon Scieszka, 1991).
Tornado (Betsy Byars, 1996).

Novels

A Fine White Dust (Cynthia Rylant, 1986).
Adam Zigzag (Barbara Barrie, 1994).
An Island Like You: Stories of the Barrio (Judith Ortiz Coffer, 1995).
Baseball Pals (Matt Christopher, 1956, 1984).
Brian's Return (Gary Paulsen, 1999).
Bridge to Terabithia (Katherine Paterson, 1977).
Bunnicula: A Rabbit Tale of Mystery (Deborah and James Howe, 1979).
Crash (Jerry Spinelli, 1996).
Dead Letter (Betsy Byars, 1996).
Dear Mr. Henshaw (Beverly Cleary, 1983).
Disappearing Acts (Betsy Byars, 1998).
Don't you dare read this, Mrs. Dunphrey (Margaret Peterson Haddix, 1996).
Egg-Drop Blues (Jacqueline Turner Banks, 1995).
Encyclopedia Brown and the Case of the Mysterious Handprints (Donald J. Sobol, 1985).
Freak the Mighty (Rodman Philbrick, 1993).
Freaky Friday (Mary Rodgers, 1972).

Fourth Grade Rats (Jerry Spinelli, 1991).
From the Notebooks of Melanin Sun (Jacqueline Woodson, 1995).
Hatchet (Gary Paulsen, 1987).
Henry and Ribsy (Beverly Cleary, 1954).
Holes (Louis Sachar, 1998).
How To Eat Fried Worms (Norman Rockwell, 1973).
I Hadn't Meant to Tell You This (Jacqueline Woodson, 1994).
James and the Giant Peach (Roald Dahl, 1961).
Maniac Magee (Jerry Spinelli, 1990).
Matilda (Roald Dahl, 1988).
More Scary Stories to Tell in the Dark (Alvin Schwartz, 1984).
Nightjohn (Gary Paulsen, 1993).
Poppy (Avi, 1996).
Ramona Quimbly, Age 8 (Beverly Cleary, 1981).
Running Out of Time (Margaret Peterson Haaddix, 1995).
Scorpions (Walter Dean Myers, 1988).
Slam (Walter Dean Myers, 1996).
Song of the Trees (Mildred Taylor, 1975).
Stone Fox (John Reynolds Gardiner, 1980).
That Was Then, This Is Now (S.E. Hinton, 1971).
The Box Car Children: The Panther Mystery (Gertrude Chandler Warner, 1998).
The Giver (Lois Lowry, 1993).
The Hundred Dresses (Eleanor Estes, 1944).
The Puppy Sister (S.E. Hinton, 1995).
The Purloined Corn Popper: A Felicity Snell Mystery (E.W. Hildick, 1997).
The Skirt (Gary Soto, 1992).
Tunes For Bears To Dance To (Robert Cormier, 1992).
Wayside School Gets a Little Stranger (Louis Sachar, 1995).
What Do Fish Have To Do With Anything (Avi, 1997, Short Stories).
Who Stole the Wizard of Oz? (Avi, 1981).
Wringer (Jerry Spinelli, 1998).

Poetry

a Pizza the size of the Sun (Jack Prelutsky, 1994, 1996).
beast feast (Douglas Florian, 1994).
Cool Melons—Turn to Frogs! The Life and Poems of Issa (Matthew Gollub, 1998).
Evertt Anderson's Goodbye (Lucille Clifton, 1983).
Extra Innings: Baseball Poems (Lee Bennett Hopkins, 1993).
For Laughing Out Loud—Poems to Tickle Your Funnybone (Jack Prelutsky, 1991).

For the Love of the Game—Michael Jordan and Me (Eloise Greenfield, 1997).

Honey I Love and Other Love Poems (Eloise Greenfield, 1972).

If I Were In Charge Of The World (Judith Viorst, 1984).

Insect Soup: Bug Poems (Barry Louis Polisar, 1999).

Life Doesn't Frighten Me (Maya Angelou, paintings by Jean-Michel Basquiat (1993).

Lunch Money and Other Poems About School (Carol Diggory Schields, 1995).

Mine, All Mine: A Book About Pronouns (Ruth Heller, 1997).

Reach for the Moon (Samantha Abeel, 1994).

Sports! Sports! Sports! (Lee Bennett Hopkins, 1999).

The Dream Keeper and Other Poems (Langston Hughes, 1932, 1994).

The Owl and the Pussycat (Edward Lear [1812-1888] 1991, 1996).

The Way I Feel Sometimes (Beatrice Schenk de Regniers, 1988).

Where the Sidewalk Ends (Shel Silverstein, 1974).

Nonfiction

A Fair Share (Stuart J. Murphy, 1998).

All-Time Great World Series (All Aboard Series) (Andrew Gutelle, 1994).

Anno's Math Games III (Mitsumasa Anno, 1982).

Antics! An Alphabetical Anthology (Cathi Hepworth, 1992).

Cedric Ceballos: Grolier All-Pro Biographies (Mark Stewart, 1996).

Dance (Bill T. Jones and Susan Kuklin, 1998).

Diego (Jeanette Winter, 1991).

Dinosaur Dinners (Eyewitness Readers) (Lee Davies, 1998).

Dinosaur Time (Peggy Parish, illustrations by Arnold Lobel, 1974) (an I-Can-Read Book –1)

Each Orange Had 8 Slices (Paul Giganti, Jr. 1992).

Eating the Alphabet: Fruits & Vegetables from A to Z (Louis Ehlert, 1989).

Eating Fractions (Bruce McMillan, 1991).

Ed Emberley's Drawing Book of Animals (Ed Emberley, reissue 1994).

Get Up and Go! (Stuart J. Murphy, 1996).

Home Run (Robert Burleigh, 1998).

Finding Providence: The Story of Roger Williams (Avi, 1997) (an I-Can-Read Chapter Book).

Football Stars (All Aboard Reading) (S.A. Kramer, 1997).

Hello, Fish! Visiting the Coral Reef (Silvia A. Earle, 1999).

I Have A Dream: The Story of Martin Luther King (Margaret Davidson, 1986).

I Can't Accept Not Trying: Michael Jordan on the Pursuit of Excellence (Michael Jordan, 1994).

Isadora Dances (Rachel Isadora, 1998).

Lou Gehrig: The Luckiest Man (David Adler, 1997).

Measuring Penny (Loren Leedy, 1997).

NBA Action from A to Z (James Preller, 1997).

NBA Game Day: From Morning Until Night, Behind the Scenes of the NBA (Joe Layden and James Preller, 1997).

Reach Higher (Scottie Pippen with Greg Brown, 1996).

Sadako and the Thousand Paper Cranes (Eleanor Coerr, 1977).

Sadako (Eleanor Coerr, 1993).

Ten Black Dots (Donald Crews, 1968, 1986).

The Way Things Work (David Macaulay, 1988).

The Z Was Zapped (Chris Van Allsburg, 1987).

This is Baseball (Margaret Blackstone, 1993).

Truck Trouble (Eyewitness Readers) (Angela Royston, 1998).

Index

Author Biography

Nancy Williams is an Associate Professor in the School of Education at DePaul University. Presently she is Associate Dean in the School of Education. She has taught courses in reading, children's literature, supervised remediation practica in reading and learning disabilities, and served as program coordinator in a collaborative university/school partnership program preparing career change individuals as teachers. She received her Ph.D. from Northwestern University in the field of learning disabilities, her M.A. from Southern Methodist University as a reading specialist, and a B.A.E. from the University of Kansas in art education. She was an art instructor, reading specialist, learning disabilities resource room teacher, and learning strategist in public elementary and secondary schools and has worked as a learning specialist and cognitive rehabilitation therapist in a hospital setting. She has published articles about university/school partnerships, literacy, and co-authored a book that helps teachers use trade books to develop literacy in clinical and classroom settings. Her current research concerns the selection and use of quality children's literature with children and young adults for whom reading is difficult.